LIFE IN THREE DIMENSIONS

LIFE IN THREE DIMENSIONS

How Curiosity, Exploration, and
Experience Make a Fuller, Better Life

SHIGEHIRO OISHI, PHD

Doubleday  New York

www.doubleday.com

DOUBLEDAY and the portrayal of an anchor with a dolphin are
registered trademarks of Penguin Random House LLC.

Book design by Michael Collica
Jacket photograph (flower petal) © SENEZ/Moment/Getty Images
Jacket design by Oliver Munday

Library of Congress Cataloging-in-Publication Data
Names: Oishi, Shigehiro, author.
Title: Life in three dimensions : how curiosity, exploration, and
experience make a fuller, better life / Shigehiro Oishi, PhD.
Description: First edition. | New York : Doubleday, [2025] |
Includes bibliographical references and index.
Identifiers: LCCN 2024023455 (print) | LCCN 2024023456 (ebook) |
ISBN 9780385550390 (hardcover) | ISBN 9780385550406 (ebook) |
ISBN 9780385551700 (open-market)
Subjects: LCSH: Happiness. | Meaning (Psychology) | Quality of life.
Classification: LCC BF575.H27 O35 2025 (print) | LCC BF575.
H27 (ebook) | DDC 152.4/2—dc23/eng/20240716
LC record available at https://lccn.loc.gov/2024023455
LC ebook record available at https://lccn.loc.gov/2024023456

MANUFACTURED IN THE UNITED STATES OF AMERICA

1 3 5 7 9 10 8 6 4 2

First Edition

For Ed Diener,
who lived a happy, meaningful,
and psychologically rich life

CONTENTS

1 **Should I Stay or Should I Go?**   1

2 **The Happiness Trap**   12

3 **The Meaning Trap**   24

4 **A Life of Exploration**   33

5 **Ingredients of Psychological Richness**   43

6 **Who Is Rich, Psychologically Rich?**   53

7 **Playfulness**   69

8 **The Beauty of DIY**   81

9 **Do Aesthetic Experiences Count?**   92

10 **The Point of Exploration**   108

11 **Turn Adversity into a Psychologically Rich Experience**   130

12 **A Story We Tell**   142

13 **Two Remaining Questions: Too Much Richness?**
    Is It Possible to Find Richness in the Familiar?   154

14 **A Good Life Without Regrets**   172

Acknowledgments   185

Notes   189

Appendix 1: Psychologically Rich Life Questionnaire (PRLQ)   221

Appendix 2: Meta-Analytic Correlations Between a
Good Life and Big Five Personality   225

Appendix 3: An Alternative Summary of the Book   227

Index   231

LIFE IN THREE DIMENSIONS

CHAPTER ONE

SHOULD I STAY OR SHOULD I GO?

If I go there will be trouble
And if I stay it will be double.

—The Clash

1. A Cozy Life

Yoshi was born in a small mountain town on the island of Kyushu, Japan, known for its green tea and clementines. Like his father, grandfather, and every male ancestor before him, Yoshi has lived his entire life there, cultivating rice and tea. He chose this path after just a year of agricultural high school, when he dropped out to become a farmer. At the age of twenty-seven, Yoshi married a woman from a neighboring town and had three children. He played in a neighborhood softball league into his fifties and enjoyed annual neighborhood association trips to various hot springs. He still lives in the same town; he still has the same wife; and he still has the same close friends he has known since elementary school. In making these choices, Yoshi followed the path laid out by his ancestors, connecting with them through common threads of not just blood, but occupation, place, expectations, and way of life.

Yoshi is my father, and I am his son a world away. After my eighteenth birthday, it took me exactly eighteen days to leave our small town for college in Tokyo. In my fourth year of college, I got a scholarship from Rotary International to study abroad in Maine. Before I started the program in Maine, I attended a summer English program on Staten Island in New York City. I had just broken up with my girlfriend in Tokyo and was tired of being in a relationship. I simply wanted to improve my English. Yet, I met a student from Korea and fell in love. She was about to start graduate school in Boston. I was about to start a year in Lewiston, Maine. During the 1991–1992 academic year, I took a Greyhound bus to Boston to see her every weekend. In May, I had to go back to Tokyo. Though my career plan before studying abroad was to work for the Ministry of Education in Japan, and I hadn't had any intention of attending graduate school in the U.S., by then I was determined to come back. In June 1993, after graduation, I left Japan for good. Next were stops of varying lengths in New York City; Champaign, Illinois; Minneapolis, Minnesota; and Charlottesville, Virginia, before moving onward to Chicago. Along the way, I married the Korean woman I met on Staten Island and we had two children, born in two different cities. I have not seen any of my elementary school friends in years.

Three decades after leaving my hometown, as I get older and try to maintain what remains of our family connection, I often find myself wondering how my life could have diverged from my father's to such an extraordinary extent. I wonder why he didn't move away when he had the chance, and why, in contrast, I have moved so many times.

My father's life has been stable, familiar, and comfortable. An annual cherry blossom party in spring, the Obon dance festival in summer, a foliage tour in fall, and hot springs in winter. It's a cozy life, a good life. My life, on the other hand, has been far less stable, far less familiar, and far more stressful with constant deadlines for lecturing, grading, and writing mixed with countless rejections (e.g., grants, papers, book proposals, job applications). Though I love my job most days, I do envy my father's simple, convivial life sometimes; I wish I could spend an evening drinking sake with my old friends every week, reminiscing about our school days and talking about life on the farm. But in my most honest moments, I know that I could not have lived like this: I had an intense yearning to see the outside world, too intense to follow the well-trodden life path of my ancestors.

2. Happiness, Meaning, and Something Else

I think back to when I was graduating high school, when I was faced with the question framed in the immortal words of The Clash: "Should I stay or should I go?" It was easy, then. Just go. As I get older, though, it has become more and more difficult. This question has been at the center of both my personal life and my academic research for decades. I imagine most of you have also asked yourselves that very same question, not just once or twice, but many times over. Some of you might be like my father: loyal, prudent, and nostalgic, prioritizing a stable life. Others may be more like me: impressionable, whimsical, and risk-taking, embracing an adventurous life. There are, of course, trade-offs between a stable life and a mobile life, a simple life and a dramatic life, a comfortable life and a challenging life, a conventional life and an unconventional life. But which one gets us closer to a *good* life?

To answer this question, I will draw from decades of research in psychological science, supplementing the available data with examples from literature, film, and philosophy. But first we need to start with the question: What *is* a good life?

When author Donna Tartt was asked what questions she was grappling with in her novel *The Goldfinch*, she said, "What is a good life? . . . To be happy oneself? Is it personal happiness? Or is it to make other people happy even at the expense of one's own happiness?" Tartt's question is profound. Should we strive to be happy? Or should we work for others' happiness before thinking of our own?

First, what is personal happiness? What makes you happy? Freedom to do whatever you want to do? Pursuing and accomplishing your career goals? A trip to the beach or the spa? I have made many selfish decisions in life, including moving to New York City to take a job at a prestigious university while my sons were still in middle and high school. Though my sons did not want to move away from their friends and their hometown, I chose to maximize my own personal happiness. In the end, I did not find myself any happier. My father, on the other hand, decided to stay in his hometown, perhaps to make my mother and others happy at the expense of his own happiness. He could have made far more money if he had moved to a booming city in the same prefecture. Ironically, years later, he seems to be happier with his decision than I. This may sound like the makings of a Chinese proverb, but it illustrates a larger truth: psychological research shows that trying to make others happy will make you happy, while trying to make yourself happy sometimes fails to do so. Indeed, psychologists have found that prosocial spending, writing gratitude letters, and having a satisficer (i.e., happy with good enough) mindset all promote happiness. It is possible that the main reason my father has been so happy is that he adjusted his expectations so that he came to cherish everyday life on the farm, enjoying smaller pleasures alongside his longtime spouse.

Perhaps the key to my father's good life has been his decision to put the needs of others—my mother and family tradition—above his own. But is a life of self-sacrifice and virtue—which we might call a "meaningful life"—a life without regrets? In the short term, people regret action, like saying or doing something stupid. In the long run, however, people regret inaction, like not saying "I love you" or not going back to school. Some people may lead a life of self-sacrifice and virtue but forgo opportunities that ultimately lead to more regrets and "what ifs." Self-sacrifice is admirable, to be sure, but prioritizing it can lead people to lose sight of their own desires and ideals until their lives no longer feel authentic. French philosopher Jean-Paul Sartre would have called this a life of "bad faith." An example is found in Toni Morrison's novel *Sula*, where Nel Wright puts aside her childhood dreams of adventure to seek perfection in her role as a wife and mother, just as her family expects of her.

At the opposite end of the spectrum is the neurologist and writer Oliver Sacks, who was an enthusiastic Hells Angels motorcyclist, bodybuilder, and LSD user before launching his writing career. He struggled with depression in his college days; his own mother told him that she wished he had never been born when she learned that he was gay; and he spent thirty-five years of his adult life celibate. Yet, even though he had some tough years, his life was full of adventure and curiosity, challenged professional boundaries, and was deeply experientially and emotionally rich—it was an authentic life, the kind that Sartre would have approved of.

3. What Is a Psychologically Rich Life?

Oliver Sacks's story presents a quandary. He had depression and a long period of inner struggle, yet he kept exploring new frontiers. His 2015 autobiography was fittingly entitled *On the Move: A Life*. Neither personal happiness and contentment nor self-sacrifice and virtue fully capture what was so admirable about Sacks's life. We need a new term, one my students and I have decided to call *a psychologically rich life*. A psychologically rich life is a life filled with diverse, unusual, interesting experiences that change your perspective; a life with twists and turns; a dramatic, eventful life instead of a simple and straightforward one; a life with multiplicity and complexity; a life with lots of stops, detours, and turning points; a life that feels like a long, winding hike rather than many laps of the same racing circuit.

A good analogy is dark vs. sweet chocolate. When you eat a fine, dark chocolate, you immediately notice that it is different from a typical, sugary chocolate. It is sweet but also bitter, or even salty. It keeps you surprised, and it has heightened intensity, complexity, and depth. In other words, it's rich. Likewise, a psychologically rich experience is different from a typical experience; there is something unexpected and powerful. It has a variety of qualities, not just good or bad. Over time, the accumulation of psychologically rich experiences makes for a psychologically rich life, one with a distinct multitude of flavors. A psychologically rich life is, well, rich in terms of life experiences.

But why do we need this new term? To explain why, let's take a slight detour into the history of psychological research on the good life, which I think of as having three phases.

Phase 1: The Rise of Happiness Research

Ed Diener, my graduate school advisor, was one of the first researchers to study happiness. He published a paper entitled "Subjective Well-Being" in 1984. Ed and his students, such as Randy Larsen and Bob Emmons, went on to publish a series of papers on subjective well-being throughout the 1980s, legitimizing the scientific study of happiness within psychology. Martin Seligman and Mihaly Csikszentmihalyi then built and popularized positive psychology based on the study of happiness as well as other related topics like hope, optimism, and flow.

Phase 2: The Eudaimonic Challenge

Then, in 1989, Carol Ryff published a paper entitled "Happiness Is Everything, or Is It?," presenting an alternative model of a good life that focused on autonomy, self-acceptance, purpose, positive relations, environmental mastery, and personal growth. Along with Ed Deci and Richard Ryan's self-determination theory, Ryff's approach to the good life has come to be called the "eudaimonic approach"—a meaningful life, in short—in contrast to Ed Diener, Daniel Kahneman, Dan Gilbert, Sonja Lyubomirsky, and others' approach to the good life, which has come to be called the "hedonic approach"—a happy life.

Phase 3: Battles

Over the last two decades, well-being researchers have debated the relative importance of hedonic vs. eudaimonic well-being. For example, people who say their lives are easy tend also to say they are happy, but don't necessarily say their lives are meaningful. Workers are happier during a break than during work. However, they feel more engaged during the work than during the break. Some researchers even claimed to have found different epigenetic patterns between hedonic and eudaimonic well-being, suggesting that our very genes are expressed differently. However, other researchers found that almost all people who say they are happy tend to also say that their lives are meaningful, and vice versa. The overlap between hedonic and eudaimonic well-being is so great that some researchers argue that they are virtually the same thing. Others argue that both happiness and meaning in life are so important that there is no point debating which is more important.

4. The Utility of a Third Dimension

Well-being researchers have debated the relative importance of happiness vs. meaning, arguing that one is more important than the other. My own take is that happiness and meaning are both important. But they do not capture an adventurous, unconventional, and dramatic life like Sacks's. So psychologists have never had the adequate vocabulary to describe such a life. In a way, the happiness vs. meaning debates parallel debates in psychology over the most important factor in predicting intelligence: nature (genetics) or nurture (environment). In the end, both nature and nurture are important. Then Carol Dweck proposed and popularized a third idea: the growth mindset. How we think about our intelligence—specifically, whether we believe that intelligence can be improved—is also important in predicting intelligence and human performance, she showed.

Over dinner one day, my wife asked me if I could fix the broken window sash cords in our living room (our late-nineteenth-century Victorian house had original double-hung windows that still operated with sash cords). I answered, "We should just hire someone. I'm not handy." Our second son, who was in middle school, immediately responded, "Dad, that's a fixed mindset! You can get better!" It turned out he had just learned about Dweck's growth mindset in school. My son's suggestion motivated me to fix the window and become a better handyman, a small example of how concepts like growth mindsets broaden the way we think about the self, others, and the world. Just as the growth mindset revealed a new dimension of human intelligence and ability, I hope that psychological richness can reveal a new dimension of a good life.

How, then, is psychological richness different from happiness and meaning? The main body of my book answers this question in detail (see Table 1 for a brief summary). But, very briefly, happiness is a subjective feeling that rises and falls to indicate where one's life stands. It is a bit like a balloon. With the right wind and air pressure, it floats high. Smooth sailing. Life is going well. But when the weather is bad, it deflates. Grounded and stuck. Life is not going well. In another sense, happiness is like your batting average in baseball. It goes up and down, but what matters most is the frequency of your hits. An infield hit is as worthy as a huge home run when it comes to the batting average. You should aim for as many hits as possible. In other words, frequent small, pleasant social interactions add up to long-term happiness more quickly than occasional big promotions.

The snag is that happiness—like the batting average—changes over time; one season you hit well; another season not so well. In *The Varieties of Religious Experience,* William James declared, "To begin with, how *can* things so insecure as the successful experiences of this world afford a stable anchorage? A chain is no stronger than its weakest link, and life is after all a chain. In the healthiest and most prosperous existence, how many links of illness, danger, and disaster are always interposed?" So it goes. The fragility of happiness.

Meaning in life, on the other hand, boils down to whether your life has a "point." When you're devoted to making a difference in the world, your life certainly has a point. You see the fruits of your labor, your legacy. There is a reason for your existence. But when your efforts are not making a clear difference, it is harder to see the point of your life. The Scottish singer-songwriter Lewis Capaldi sang in the song "Pointless": "Of all the dreams I'm chasing . . . Everything is pointless without you." Imagine that he broke up with this woman. His dedication would be wasted, and his life would feel pointless.

Tolstoy was happy and productive. Yet, without any obvious loss, he had a sudden existential crisis at about the age of fifty (years after the publication of *War and Peace*): "I had a good wife who loved me and whom I loved; good children and a large property which was increasing with no pains taken on my part. I was more respected by my kinsfolk and acquaintance than I had ever been; I was loaded with praise by strangers; and without exaggeration I could believe my name already famous. . . . And yet I could give no reasonable meaning to any actions of my life." So it goes. The precariousness of meaning.

5. This Book Is About . . .

Psychological richness is different from happiness and meaning in the sense that it is not about an overall feeling of where life is going or what the point of your life is, but about an experience, or more precisely the *accumulation* of experiences over time. In the same way that material richness can be quantified by money—the more money you have, the richer you are materially—psychological richness can be quantified by experiences. The more interesting experiences and stories you have, the more psychologically rich you are. Just as you can accumulate wealth and become materially rich, you can accumulate experiences and become psychologically rich. If happiness is like the batting average that changes with every game, psychological richness is more like the total number of career home runs: it adds up.

Table 1: Core Features and Metaphors of Happiness, Meaning, and Psychological Richness

	Core Features	Metaphors
Happiness	Joy, Comfort, Stability	Balloon, Batting Average, Sweet Chocolate
Meaning	Point, Impact, Coherence	Angel, Activist, Monk
Richness	Novelty, Play, Perspective Change	Treasure Box, Home Runs, Dark Chocolate

A psychologically rich life is not for everyone. It suits the curious more than the content. The comfort and security of a happy or meaningful life provide a safety net that a psychologically rich life, with all its unknowns, often lacks. Yet the paradox of happiness and meaning is that the complacency they foster *can* make for an incomplete life with major regrets, doubts, and unanswered questions. Thankfully, our lives are not zero-sum games in which we must choose a single path to a good life; some people lead happy, meaningful, *and* psychologically rich lives. Therefore, anyone can benefit from the lessons of psychological richness research. By reminding ourselves that what counts is not just the destination but also the journey, we learn to find value in seeking new experiences and new knowledge, hopefully leading to a life without regrets, or at least fewer regrets.

So, should you stay or should you go? For those who stay, psychological richness will add a new dimension of interest and resilience to life. And those who go are already on the path toward psychological richness.

What are the other ingredients of a psychologically rich life? Who else has led a psychologically rich life? How is a psychologically rich life different from a happy life or a meaningful one? Do you need to accumulate experiences firsthand, or do vicarious experiences count as well? What are the benefits of a psychologically rich life? How can we enrich our lives psychologically? This book will venture deeply into these questions.

CHAPTER TWO

THE HAPPINESS TRAP

Despite whatever's going on—if you're stressed, a bit depressed, if you're overwhelmed—you want to put up this positive front.

—Kahaari Kenyatta, a UPenn senior, on the culture of "Penn Face," the practice of acting happy and self-assured even when sad or stressed, *The New York Times*, July 27, 2015

1. Life's Chief Concern

Happiness is the ultimate goal of goals, according to Aristotle. When William James asked himself, "What is human life's chief concern?" his answer was: "It is happiness. How to gain, how to keep, how to recover happiness, is in fact for most men at all times the secret motive of all they do, and of all they are willing to endure." It is a goal shared by many across the globe; in a large international study conducted by Ed Diener, 69 percent of respondents rated happiness as extremely important (a perfect 7 on a 1 to 7 point scale), ahead of money, love, and health. It is a worthy goal, as research shows that happy people are healthier and more prosocial. They're also better workers, and they live longer than unhappy people.

The irony is that our blind pursuit of happiness sometimes leads to unhappiness. We put undue pressure and stress on ourselves to always be happy, preventing ourselves from reaping the benefits. Take Madison Holleran, a "popular, attractive, and talented" first-year student at the University of Pennsylvania. According to *The New York Times,* she "posted images that show her smiling, dappled in sunshine or kicking back at a party." Her social media epitomized happiness. Yet her reality was more tenuous. To her sister, she revealed feeling that her social life was inferior to that of her friends. On January 17, 2014, Madison jumped off the top of a parking garage and took her own life.

Suicide is an extremely complex behavior. Madison's suicide must have been driven not just from feeling inferior to her friends' social lives, but also from many other things. What is shocking is how good she was at pretending to be happy in public, and that a person who appeared so well adjusted and happy also had profound inner struggles leading to a tragic fate. Was she an exception or a rule?

According to vital statistics from the Centers for Disease Control (CDC), suicide among Americans increased 38 percent between 2000 to 2018. Suicide is still somewhat rare. In the peak year of 2018, the rate of Americans dying by suicide reached 14 out of 100,000, a figure that might make Madison's case seem like the exception. However, suicidal ideation is not. According to the CDC, in 2020 there were 1.2 million suicide attempts and 12.2 million American adults who "seriously" thought about suicide. That means roughly 1 in 20 American adults seriously thought about dying by suicide that year. That is a lot. If you look at the frequency of suicidal thoughts, then, Madison's case doesn't seem so rare. So, the next question is: Why did she feel so much pressure to put on a happy face, despite having suicidal thoughts?

At the core of the pressure to be happy is the American cultural construction of happiness as something achievable. In one study, American college students were asked to write about anything that came to mind when they thought about "happiness." Many wrote something like, "Happiness is a reward for all the hard work you employ" and "Happiness is the feeling of succeeding." One student wrote simply that happiness is a "victory"! That is, there is a strong association between happiness and success. Another study asked college students to write about "different aspects, features, or effects of either happiness or unhappiness." The earlier findings were replicated: American college students tend to equate happiness with personal achievement.

If happiness is a victory, the pursuit of happiness is equated with the pursuit of a victory. Success brings happiness. Failure begets unhappiness. To many, if you are not happy, you are not successful. If you are unhappy, you are a loser. The pressure to be happy might come from this cultural narrative of happiness as a sign of success. In Saul Steinberg's iconic 1959 *New Yorker* cover, Prosperity wins the contest of the Pursuit of Happiness, suggesting that it takes success and prosperity to be happy.

2. So What Does Increase Happiness?

What happiness researchers found was quite different from the achievement-oriented concept of happiness; a victory rarely results in everlasting (or even long-lasting) happiness. The effect of a major accomplishment like a promotion on happiness seems to disappear within six months. Decades of research on the "affective forecasting error" suggest that we tend to overestimate the happiness that our success will bring about, while also overestimating the unhappiness that our failure will generate. In one study, Dan Gilbert and colleagues asked untenured assistant professors how happy they would feel if they got tenure, as well as how unhappy they would feel if they were denied tenure. It sounds like an obvious question. Indeed, the assistant professors all said they would be delighted if they got tenure and would be devastated if they were denied tenure. Next, the researchers interviewed former assistant professors who did get tenure and others who did not get tenure. Well, the bad news is that those who got tenure were not as happy as the current assistant professors imagined. The good news is that those who were denied tenure were far happier than the current assistant professors imagined.

The first insight from the science of happiness is that people overestimate the role of success in their own happiness. The joy of a big promotion, marriage, or a first child is relatively short-lived. It is not a big win that brings happiness. Rather, it's the small things in life, like having a coffee with your best friend every day, that build long-term happiness. Happiness is the frequency, not the intensity, of positive events. Relatedly, studies show that happiness is the product of close relationships rather than personal accomplishments. That is, happiness is not personal success, but *interpersonal* success.

3. The Pressure to Be Happy

So why do people fake happiness? There is, of course, the saying "Fake it till you make it." Many people take to heart the belief that if you continue to pretend you are successful, you will eventually succeed. Quentin Tarantino, who went on to write and direct the iconic film *Pulp Fiction* among others, was working as a clerk at a video store in Manhattan Beach, California, when, in order to get his first Hollywood job as a production assistant, he lied, saying that he had worked in the movie industry. Steve Jobs faked it till he made it, too. The first iPhone had a memory problem. It could not run multiple programs simultaneously. At the product launch of the first iPhone, Steve Jobs used multiple iPhones, switching to a new one as soon as the old one crashed during the demonstration. It also had a bandwidth problem. So, when the iPhone onstage had a poor connection, they faked it and consistently showed five bars of signal. Eventually, Apple fixed the memory problem. Likewise, might many Americans assume that, if they pretend to be happy, they will eventually become happy?

We don't know definitively whether most Americans assume pretending to be happy will make them happy. Even so, there is a famous experiment in which participants held a pen in their mouth so as to mimic either smiling or not smiling. They then saw several cartoons and rated how funny they were. What the researchers found was quite striking. Those in the "smile" condition rated the same cartoons as funnier than those in the non-smile condition! Just moving their facial muscles to look like a smiley face made them enjoy the cartoons more. Some failed to replicate the original findings, though others were able to replicate them. Nonetheless, the original experiment has been mentioned in major news outlets. As a result, many believe that when you are sad, you should put on a happy face.

There have also been many experiments in which participants were asked to behave like extraverts. Afterward, they reported more happiness than those who were asked to behave normally. Surprisingly, the intervention worked even for natural introverts. Similarly, when people were asked to talk to a stranger (i.e., acting like an extravert), people felt far happier than they had anticipated. These findings have been replicated. So, acting like an extravert does tend to make people happier, even if fake smiling does not.

The key takeaway here is that it is only natural that we feel sad, angry, and anxious in some situations. Too much emphasis on happiness has led to a dangerous misconception that unhappiness is a sign of failure. In one experiment, participants were asked to solve anagrams with or without the pressure to be happy. The anagrams were impossible to solve, and everyone failed. The participants who were pressured to be happy ruminated about the failure more than the participants in the control condition, where there was no pressure to be happy. The same failure feels worse when you believe that you are supposed to be happy.

A large international study found that Americans on average feel far more pressure to be happy than Japanese, Ukrainians, and Germans. Interestingly, in the countries where happiness is more strongly associated with good luck and fortune than personal accomplishments (e.g., Japan and Germany), there appears to be less pressure to be happy. Furthermore, these researchers found that individuals who feel pressure to feel happy also feel pressure not to feel sadness and anger. In short, many Americans are stuck in a happiness trap.

4. But Negative Emotions Are Normal

The happiness trap has two faces. First, there is the pressure to be happy, which makes feeling sadness, anger, and anguish seem undesirable and alienating. And yet it is not possible to avoid negative emotions. When you miss a train, when someone criticizes you, when your child shows no sign of gratitude for what you do, you feel bad. It is only natural.

For example, take an experience I had multiple times when I lived in New York City. I lived in a building without a door attendant. One day, when I came back to my building with some takeout food from the local Chinese restaurant, a young woman opened the door for me. So I said, "Thank you!" When she replied, "Thank YOU!" I was completely thrown off. Then I realized: she assumed I was the Chinese deliveryman bringing her food. It happened when I was a graduate student and it happened when I was a full professor as well. I felt insulted. But stuff happens, right?

Speaking of graduate school, when I was a fifth-year PhD student, my advisor told me the following story. Daniel Kahneman, a famous psychologist at Princeton, called my advisor, Ed Diener, up and asked him about me. At that time, there was an assistant professor job at Princeton that I had applied for. After they talked for a while, Kahneman asked my advisor, "Is Shige cocky?" My advisor said, "No, he's not." Kahneman said, "Well, in order to survive at Princeton, you have to be cocky." Then my advisor did what a good advisor does, I suppose. "There is another student of mine who is cocky." A week later, I found out that I did not get the job interview at Princeton, while my "cocky" lab mate did! The world is not always fair, is it?

When events such as these happen, you will feel bad. And when you feel bad, what do you do?

People who feel pressure to feel happy will try almost anything to repair their moods. Some people do very healthy things, like exercise and hiking, while others do very unhealthy things, like over-drinking or impulsive shopping. In *Brave New World*, Aldous Huxley writes, "What you need is a gramme of *soma*," a pill that has "all the advantages of Christianity and alcohol; none of their defects." Personally, when I feel down, I listen to my favorite songs. Sometimes I even sing along. Other times, I talk to my wife. If she's not around, I just take a nap.

There are more sophisticated methods for dealing with a persistent, negative mood. Emotion regulation researchers classify them into a few major categories. For instance, people can try to positively reinterpret the event. A divorced father of two young children might reinterpret the divorce as a God-sent opportunity to spend more time on his hobbies while his ex-wife has custody of the children. Other people might try to distance themselves from the divorce and start seeing the same event from the other person's perspective, which could dampen their negative reaction to the trigger event. Others try to see themselves from the perspective of their future self. Five years later, will I be suffering in the same way? In the future, this event might feel like a tiny bump in the road.

In contrast, those who don't feel pressure to feel happy would not do as much to repair a negative mood, as they think it is only natural to feel bad once in a while. Here there is more emotional acceptance. These people believe that time heals everything. And they are right. Although active emotion regulation strategies such as reappraisal and self-distancing are effective, humans do have a natural ability to heal and recover from negative mood states. This is what Dan Gilbert, Tim Wilson, and their colleagues call the "psychological immune system." Just as the biological immune system kicks in when a virus enters the body, the psychological immune system automatically kicks in when an undesirable event happens.

What is surprising is how much people underestimate the power of their psychological immune system and instead rely heavily on their homemade remedies for mood repair, from alcohol to sweets to shopping. If we didn't feel as much pressure to feel happy and simply let our negative moods linger a bit, our own psychological immune system would kick in, attack the "psychological virus" of unhappiness, and remove it. This element of the happiness trap leads us down a potentially destructive path of unhealthy coping.

5. How to Transcend the Happiness Trap

The second element of the happiness trap is that happiness is actually easier to attain if you don't want too much of it. The social psychologist Barry Schwartz found the power of "good enough." If you are the type of person who often accepts "good enough," also known as a "satisficer"—one who sacrifices the best choice for a satisfactory choice—you are much more likely to be happy with your decisions. Let's say you are a high school senior. You have an almost perfect GPA. You have high SAT scores. You did a bunch of extracurricular activities. Which college do you want to go to? You might want to go to the best possible college you could get into. So you apply to ten schools. If this is you, you are a maximizer. Now, let's say you're a satisficer. You could probably get into one of the Ivies or other super elite schools like Duke. But instead you say, "I think the University of Virginia has everything I want. Plus, I get in-state tuition." You apply only to UVA and get in.

Let's assume one of the maximizers got into Cornell while the satisficer went to UVA. At the end of the first year, which one is likely to be happier? A study featuring a similar scenario found that the person who went to UVA was likely to be happier than the person who went to Cornell. It has nothing to do with UVA vs. Cornell, but rather with the notion of alternative options. The Cornell student applied to ten schools, which means they had nine counterfactuals. *If I had scored 20 points higher on the SAT, I might have gotten into Yale. If I had one more extracurricular activity, I might have gotten into Princeton.* In contrast, the satisficer UVA student had zero counterfactuals, as this person found a school that met all their requirements and they did not apply to any other. No alternative, no counterfactual, no regret. There is a strong belief among some Americans that going to an elite school is the path to a happy life, when in reality having a good-enough mindset is the more reliable route. If you did not get into your top school, stop thinking about it and start looking for what is good about your current school. Easier said than done, but that will make you happier.

Closely related to the maximizer mindset, upward social comparison is another source of unhappiness. Jim Clark, who cofounded Netscape, had a series of successes as a Silicon Valley entrepreneur. He recounted to journalist Michael Lewis how he had initially thought he would be happy if he made $10 million early on. But then Netscape was a smashing success. He now thought he would be happy if he made $100 million. But then there was another smashing success, and he now thought he would be really happy if he made $1 billion. Then he did make $1 billion. Now he said, "I want . . . more money than Larry Ellison. Then I will stop." According to *Forbes*, in 2023 Clark's net worth was $3.8 billion, while Larry Ellison's net worth was $158 billion. I wonder if Jim Clark has ever gotten his satisfaction, despite his enormous success. On this point, research findings are very clear. Sonja Lyubomirsky and Lee Ross found that individuals who do not engage in upward social comparison are happier than those who are obsessed with social comparison.

With social media, we are bombarded with carefully curated images of others. Everyone else seems to be having the best time of their lives! It is difficult to avoid upward social comparison. But it *is* possible. I remember a story told to us parents and students by Mr. Johnson, the principal of Buford Middle School in Charlottesville, about when he was a college student at UVA. On move-in day, Johnson, an African American from Tennessee, was carrying his stuff in a bunch of black trash bags. He noticed other UVA kids were carrying their stuff in suitcases. So he asked his dad, who was a house painter, "Why don't we have suitcases?" What was his dad's answer? "Son, it is OK to be different." When you feel inferior to others who are showing off on social media, remember Mr. Johnson's dad. It is OK to be different.

Since Denmark often ranks as one of the happiest countries in the world, the BBC went to the Danes in search of the key to happiness. The secret? Many Danes said they don't expect much in life. *Lower your expectations. Be content with what you have*, Danish wisdom advised. Like my father, many Danes cherish *hygge*, the coziness and small joys of life, along with the idea of a life of contentment.

Does this mean that we should promote the satisficer mindset over the maximizer mindset? I don't think so. There is an important place in life for the satisficer mindset. I actively use it when I am buying something, planning something, or making everyday decisions. But this mindset can have a dark side as well.

For instance, it makes you content with the status quo, which in turn discourages you from embracing necessary challenges and personal growth. This is the second part of the happiness trap: settling for less than you can achieve. Heed the warning of John, the "Savage" in *Brave New World,* who said, "Well, I'd rather be unhappy than have the sort of false, lying happiness you were having here."

Friedrich Nietzsche would have approved of John's proclamation. He believed that most people are deceived to be happy and virtuous. In *Thus Spoke Zarathustra* he describes the temptation to lead a happy and virtuous life as follows: "They would laud and lure me into a small virtue; they would persuade my foot to the ticktock of a small happiness. I walk among this people and I keep my eyes open: they have become smaller, and they are becoming smaller and smaller; *but this is due to their doctrine of happiness and virtue.* For they are modest in virtue, too—because they want contentment. But only a modest virtue gets along with contentment. . . . Modestly to embrace a small happiness—that they call 'resignation'—and modestly they squint the whole for another small happiness. At bottom, these simpletons want a single thing most of all: that nobody should hurt them. Thus they try to please and gratify everybody. This, however, is cowardice, even if it be called virtue."

Instead of a conventional, simple, and comfortable life, Nietzsche advocated for the life of a wanderer. Zarathustra said to himself: "I am a wanderer and a mountain climber. . . . Only now are you going your way to greatness! Peak and abyss—they are now joined together. You are going your way to greatness: now that which has hitherto been your ultimate danger has become your ultimate refuge." Zarathustra was a "friend of all who travel far and do not like to live without danger. . . . To you, the bold searchers, researchers, and whoever embarks with cunning sails on terrible seas—to you, drunk with riddles, glad of the twilight, whose soul flutes lure astray to every whirlpool, because you do not want to grope along a threat with cowardly hand; and where you can *guess,* you hate to *deduce*—to you alone I tell the riddle that I *saw,* the vision of the loneliest." Small happiness and meaning are dangerous because they are so seductive. Almost unconsciously, most people are drawn to convention, so that they can live a harmonious, conflict-free life. For Zarathustra, it was not a life worth living.

If you feel pressure to feel happy all the time, remember that it is OK to be sad, angry, or fearful every now and then. These emotions add complexity and richness to your inner life. And if you're already happy with your life, you're doing great. But take a moment to reflect on your satisficer mindset. Perhaps there could be more to life than coziness and small joys, at least once in a while. Happiness is not the only way to lead a good life, as we shall see.

CHAPTER THREE

THE MEANING TRAP

You've got to find what you love. And that is as true for your work as it is for your lovers. Your work is going to fill a large part of your life, and the only way to be truly satisfied is to do what you believe is great work. And the only way to do great work is to love what you do. If you haven't found it yet, keep looking. Don't settle. As with all matters of the heart, you'll know when you find it.

—Steve Jobs, Stanford University commencement speech in 2005

1. Happiness Is a Bore?

Happiness has many fans. But, there are also many doubters, ranging from the Stoics to Gustave Flaubert. Flaubert wrote to Louise Colet, "To be stupid, selfish, and have good health are three requirements for happiness, though if stupidity is lacking, all is lost." In a similar spirit, Tony Schwartz wrote an article entitled "Happiness Is Overrated" in the *Harvard Business Review,* saying, "'Happy' people are some of the dullest people I know." Shel Silverstein's poem "The Land of Happy" might be the most poignant critique of happiness. He describes the land of happy as a place where everyone is happy and everything is jolly. He ends his poem with: "What a bore."

Why so down on happiness? One common critique is that a happy life might be a selfish one. In reality, there is lots of evidence that suggests otherwise. For example, spending money on others as opposed to on oneself increases happiness. Happy people volunteer more than unhappy people. But, for now, let's assume the critique of happiness-as-selfishness and proceed with a question: What makes for a good life, if not happiness?

The novelist Donna Tartt suggested that it is "to make other people happy even at the expense of one's own happiness"—in other words, what many scholars call a "meaningful life." Meaning in life is typically defined by significance, purpose, and coherence. First, a meaningful life is a life that matters. It matters not just to one's family members and friends, but also to strangers. A meaningful life is a life that makes a difference in the world. Second, a meaningful life has a clear purpose. A person who leads a meaningful life knows where they're going. There is a clear sense of direction and a guiding principle. Third, a meaningful life is well organized. All of a person's divergent experiences fit together under their own guiding principles.

In contrast, a meaningless life is a life that does not make any difference in the world. Anthropologist David Graeber, in his book *Bullshit Jobs: A Theory,* argues that there are millions of people around the world who are toiling away their lives in meaningless jobs. He defines a bullshit job as a job that the person who is doing it can't really justify the existence of that job. Meaningless jobs, according to Graeber, are not just repetitive factory or clerical jobs, but also include corporate lawyers, public relations consultants, telemarketers, and brand managers. For instance, he claims that most corporate lawyers secretly believe that the world would probably be a better place if they did not exist. Of course, people can make a difference in the world outside of their jobs. So this doesn't mean corporate lawyers and public relations consultants lead meaningless lives. But if you are not making any positive difference in the world, your life may feel pointless. Likewise, a meaningless life has no clear purpose. People without a clear purpose tend to go through their lives aimlessly. Finally, a meaningless life feels torn and highly fragmented. The different roles one plays do not add up to a coherent whole.

2. Be Great?

Needless to say, a meaningful life sounds a lot more appealing than a meaningless one. Thus, people say you should find a reason for living—whether via career, religion, social roles (e.g., parenthood), scientific discovery, or social change. Many commencement speakers preach along these lines, including Michelle Obama in her speech to CUNY's class of 2016: "Be great. Build great lives for yourselves. . . . And please, please, always, always do your part to help others do the same."

Dr. Donna Adams-Pickett did exactly what Michele Obama promoted. As a child, she learned that her paternal grandmother, who lived on a tobacco farm, died while giving birth. The baby died as well, and her father was left motherless at age twelve. After hearing this story, she was determined to become an ob-gyn doctor. As she shared with *PBS NewsHour,* Dr. Adams-Pickett delivered over 6,000 babies over the last twenty years in Augusta, Georgia, an area located in a maternity care desert. Her life is certainly meaningful, as she has a clear purpose (provide good maternal care to the people of Georgia, especially Black women, who have a much higher rate of maternal mortality before and after delivery than other women) and significance (some mothers and babies might have died without her care). Her family tragedy also gives a convincing narrative and coherence to the course of her life.

When we think of people who live meaningful lives, we might think of those who have done great things, like Dr. Donna

Adams-Pickett, Michelle Obama, or Barack Obama—the kind of people who give graduation speeches! These are extraordinary achievements. These people are heroes. However, these accomplishments are so rare that it's hard to imagine ever achieving such feats. Like the happiness trap, there is also a meaning trap. The first element of the meaning trap is that the type of accomplishment associated with a meaningful life is so grand that aiming for it will set us up for a failure.

3. Life Is Pretty Meaningful

The second element of the meaning trap is that people tend to misunderstand what is required. These images of heroes with supersized ambitions do not necessarily fit with the research findings. Although many people think that the number of people who lead a meaningful life is small, survey data show that, in fact, most people say they do have a meaningful life. In the cleverly entitled paper "Life Is Pretty Meaningful," Samantha Heintzelman and Laura King report that 90 percent of Americans said they have meaning in life, according to the Gallup World Polls.

How is it possible that we think the meaningful life is for over-achieving heroes, yet most people say their lives are meaning-ful? One answer might lie in how the question about meaning in life was asked. The Gallup survey phrased it like this: "Do you feel your life has an important purpose or meaning?" with a yes-or-no answer format. To say, "No, my life has no purpose nor meaning," is almost to say one's life is pointless. Those who did not feel like their lives were utterly pointless were likely to say yes to this question. This means that even if someone did not feel their life was particularly meaningful, they might have said yes.

Another Gallup survey that focused on purpose ("My life has a real purpose") found that 28.5 percent of Americans "strongly" agreed (a 5 on a 1 to 5 point scale), while 1.1 percent "strongly" disagreed (a 1 on the same 1 to 5 point scale), and 9.1 percent disagreed (a 2 on the 1 to 5 point scale). The percentage of people who strongly disagreed or who disagreed with the statement "My life has a real purpose" matches up quite well with the original Gallup data (10 percent said no vs. 10.2 percent disagreed).

4. But Why?

Still, the fact that 28.5 percent of Americans report having a real purpose in life and another 54.9 percent report having a more or less real purpose is impressive. Are there so many heroic individuals making a difference in the U.S.? Or is this some kind of overly positive illusion? It turns out that this is not simply a self-reporting bias. Psychologist Michael Steger and colleagues asked participants to report how meaningful they feel their lives are. In addition, he asked their friends and family members to report the participant's meaning in life. If the high percentage of self-reported meaning in life is only an illusion, informant reports would not correlate with self-reports. What he found was different: self-reported meaning in life is correlated with informant-reported meaning in life. The self-informant correlation on meaning in life was similar to that in studies testing more familiar personality traits such as extraversion and neuroticism (a tendency to worry excessively). Scientifically, then, self-reports of meaning in life are quite valid.

So who are these 28.5 percent of Americans who say their lives are meaningful? For one, they tend to be religious. Religious people follow certain principles of faith, which help them interpret difficult life situations accordingly and give them clarity. When Hurricane Katrina swept away some neighborhoods of New Orleans in 2005, many residents struggled to understand why it happened. Religious people were better able to psychologically deal with this catastrophe than non-religious people. So you don't have to be a maverick inventor like Steve Jobs to feel like your life is meaningful. One way to find meaning is by following a traditional religion.

Steger's research also finds that people who say they have a meaningful life tend to be optimistic about the future, extraverted, non-neurotic, agreeable, conscientious, and have high self-esteem. Meaning in life is by nature very subjective. Some well-respected, well-liked, award-winning scientists nonetheless see their lives to be meaningless and die by suicide. In contrast, some ordinary people see their lives as linked to a significant mission. In a famous folk legend, when John F. Kennedy once visited NASA he said to a janitor, "Hi, I'm Jack Kennedy. What are you doing?" The janitor replied: "Well, Mr. President, I'm helping put a man on the moon!"

Second, people with high self-esteem are more likely to say that their lives matter than those who do not like themselves. Non-neurotic people (those who don't worry too much or are not too stress prone) are more likely to say that their lives have a clear purpose and direction than neurotic people. Conscientious people achieve more of their goals than unconscientious people. Therefore, they are also more likely to feel that they are moving toward a larger goal in life than unconscientious people. They are likely to feel that their lives have a sense of direction, purpose, and meaning. To the extent that the majority of Americans have high self-esteem, are optimistic about their futures, and say they are extraverted, non-neurotic, agreeable, and conscientious, it makes sense that a lot of people say their lives have meaning.

These personality traits and attitudes express themselves in predictable ways. People tend to choose one or two causes they care about dearly (e.g., a soup kitchen, a church), volunteer in the same location for an extended period of time, and achieve meaning by trying to make a difference in a well-defined area. Others derive meaning in life from their work, family, and community, again a narrowly defined realm of life. Research on meaning in life shows that successfully achieving a meaningful life often comes with focus and narrowness. In most cases, this is not a problem.

5. Troubles with Meaning

There are some troubling implications, however. Think of a hypothetical military prison guard, Mason. He cares about U.S. national security dearly. Mason wants to devote his life to the protection of the American people. He gets assigned to a prison housing mostly those suspected of terrorism. He abuses these suspected terrorists, as in the infamous prison abuse case at Abu Ghraib. Mason thinks he is leading a meaningful life because he is making a difference in the world by protecting the American people. But is this a good life? In this case, it may be subjectively meaningful, but objectively not so good.

So far, the case of Mason, the military prison officer, is merely hypothetical. Is there any scientific evidence for this phenomenon of misplaced meaning in life? Recent studies have found that meaning in life is associated with right-wing authoritarianism, a belief system defined as uncritical submission to authority, feelings of aggression toward those who violate social norms, and strict adherence to conventional values. That is, right-wing authoritarians reported higher levels of meaning in life than non-authoritarians. They do plenty of civic work, in their way. But their cause might be very narrow, and potentially antagonistic toward those they consider outsiders. Likewise, multiple studies have found that political conservatives (who are known to draw a sharp line between ingroups and outgroups) report higher levels of meaning in life as well as happiness than political liberals.

Or consider the ultimate antisocial behavior, terrorism. The criminologist Simon Cottee argues that one of the main reasons people join terrorist organizations is the desire for ultimate meaning: "Terrorist groups provide an important source of identity and purpose for their members, and . . . this may well be part of what motivates people to join them. Not only does the terrorist organization furnish its recruits with an all-embracing narrative for understanding the world and how it works . . . it also supplies them with a narrative for understanding their own place in this wider world. From within this narrative, the fundamental existential questions in life are given a bracingly decisive answer." These recent findings, then, suggest that many people's meaningful lives *could* be built on a narrow sense of ingroup favoritism and tradition at the cost of outgroup members.

6. How to Avoid the Meaning Trap

Like the happiness trap, the meaning trap has two parts. First, for the majority of us who have not invented anything or participated in the Peace Corps, it is easy to feel like a failure in the face of the call to be great. Pressure to make a difference in the world can be emotionally taxing, just like the pressure to be happy. Most of us feel that way once in a while. If you feel like you haven't made any meaningful difference in the world, consider that you could achieve meaning through devotion to a certain cause, starting out small in your neighborhood. Take your time, and you will make a difference in the long run. The second part of the meaning trap is that the pursuit of a meaningful life can promote a narrow viewpoint. As research shows, meaning in life is sometimes attained through prosocial behaviors toward a small ingroup, and antisocial behaviors or apathy toward outgroups. If you lead a meaningful life in a narrow sense, you might want to consider expanding your perspective.

Decades of psychological research, including some of my own studies, have undoubtedly established happiness and meaning as paths to a good life with countless benefits. Yet by limiting ourselves to these two paths, we have put a good life out of reach for too many. There is another way to achieve a good life. It may not be stable or comfortable, but it is exhilarating. It may not be filled with contentment, but it is dramatic. It has ups and downs, twists and turns, and by the end of the ride it offers a life with fewer regrets; a life of adventure, playfulness, spontaneity, serendipity, and learning; a life of going with the flow, trotting the path less traveled—in other words, a life rich in experiences. This third way to a good life is the psychologically rich life, and it is a way to transcend the happiness and meaning traps.

A LIFE OF EXPLORATION

The world is a great book, of which they that never stir from home read only one page.

—Attributed to St. Augustine

1. Narcissus or Goldmund?

So far, I have told you some secrets to happiness and meaning in life. It isn't big wins that bring happiness, but rather the small joys in life, like having tea with your best friend. It is not career success but rather *interpersonal* success that typically leads to long-term happiness. Similarly, meaning in life comes from dedication to a particular cause you care about dearly and making a difference in that chosen realm. Overall, a life of stability, rather than a life of exploration and change, gets you closer to happiness and meaning in life. If the benefits of a stable life are happiness and meaning, what might be the benefits of a life of exploration?

Hermann Hesse, one of the most influential German novelists of the twentieth century and the 1946 Nobel laureate, depicted memorable characters struggling to find a path to the good life in several novels. *Narcissus and Goldmund* is one of the most popular Hesse novels, which also became a feature film in 2020. Narcissus, one of the title characters, is one of those people who chooses a life of stability. He is smart and popular. He is happy with his cloistered life and finds his simple, religious life very meaningful. Narcissus becomes a well-respected Aristotelian scholar and the head of his monastery. On the surface, Narcissus is the epitome of success.

Meanwhile, his childhood friend Goldmund yearns for a life outside the cloister and decides to lead the life of a vagabond artist, lacking food, shelter, and stable companions. In the course of his journeying, he witnesses innumerable deaths due to a pandemic. At some point, he questions his decisions: "Did all this make sense? Was it worth experiencing?" Unlike Narcissus, Goldmund often feels guilty, unhappy, and as if his life is meaningless. Eventually, he is inspired by a wooden statue of the Madonna: finding the statue "inexpressibly beautiful," he decides to become a sculptor's apprentice and start carving his own statues.

At the end of the novel, it is Narcissus who wonders if his happy and meaningful life was lacking something. Narcissus knows that those who remained in the cloister view his life as far "better, righter, steadier, more orderly, and more exemplary" than Goldmund's life of exploration and moral digression. Yet Narcissus can't help but wonder, "Was this exemplary life of order and discipline . . . any better than Goldmund's life?" Narcissus wishes he had had more interesting life experiences. His life is happy and meaningful but utterly missing experiential richness. By contrast, Goldmund's life is hard, but spontaneous, creative, and unpredictable: a psychologically rich life. According to Hesse, a life of exploration is a good life, even at the cost of much happiness or meaning. Which life would you choose?

2. Aesthetics or Virtue?

Hesse is not the only author to suggest the importance of exploration. As with *Narcissus and Goldmund,* at the core of Søren

Kierkegaard's *Either/Or* is this dilemma: Should we pursue an aesthetic life or a virtuous life? The book is written in the form of correspondence between Author A, presumably a young man, and Author B, presumably a retired judge. A promotes an aesthetic life, or the life of beauty and adventure. He argues that spontaneity and acceptance of arbitrariness are the keys to this life. One should always look out for the accidental: "The so-called social pleasures, for which one prepares eight or fourteen days in advance, have no great interest. Through accident, on the other hand, even the least significant thing can become a rich source of amusement." Unsurprisingly, A is against marriage, characterizing it as fearful monotony, perpetual sameness, and dreadful stillness. In contrast, B promotes a virtuous life, defending marriage as "a school for character; one marries in order to elevate and improve one's character." Like Goldmund, A chooses the life of the aesthetic, accidental, and *expeditus* (Latin for "ready to march"), embracing possibilities more than responsibilities.

Again and again, what these novels focus on is a fascination with and admiration of a life of exploration. Stephen Dedalus in James Joyce's *A Portrait of the Artist as a Young Man* also chooses the life of aesthetics over virtue. His boyhood motto of "A life of grace and virtue and happiness!" evolves into his adult motto: *Per aspera ad astra*—through hardship to the stars. There are characters like Stephen Dedalus in numerous works of literature, ranging from Homer's *Odyssey* and Cervantes's *Don Quixote* to Voltaire's *Candide* and Melville's *Moby-Dick* to Lewis Carroll's *Alice's Adventures in Wonderland* and Toni Morrison's *Sula*. At key moments, the main characters in these novels embrace uncertainty over certainty, freedom over security, and self-expression over duty, ultimately choosing to go rather than to stay. The popularity of these novels tells us that this life of exploration is admired by many. Even so, these are fictional characters. Are there real people like Goldmund and Sula?

3. The Adventure of Alison in Wonderland

In a 2015 *Atlantic* essay, Alison Gopnik, a world-famous professor of psychology at UC Berkeley, wrote, "In 2006, I was 50—I was falling apart." When her children left for college, her long marriage to her husband unraveled. She moved out of her "big, professorial home" and into "a room in a crumbling old house" to live alone. It was then that she discovered she liked women. When her love affair with a woman ended, however, depression set in: "Everything that had defined me was gone. I was no longer a scientist or a philosopher or a wife or a mother or a lover." Her doctors prescribed Prozac, yoga, and meditation. She hated the first two, but the last one stuck.

Gopnik's newfound interest in Buddhism provoked a question, one that would lead her down an *Alice in Wonderland*–esque intellectual rabbit hole. As she read more about Buddhist philosophy, she noticed a similarity in its ideas to David Hume's *Treatise of Human Nature,* and she began to wonder if there were Eastern roots in the Western Enlightenment. So began her quest to link Ippolito Desideri, a Jesuit missionary to Tibet who wrote about Buddhism in 1728, with David Hume, who completed his *Treatise* in 1738. Though her research prowess and clever experimental designs had made her a renowned developmental psychologist, this historical project represented a completely new type of scholarship.

Gopnik consulted Ernest Mossner's biography of Hume and found that Hume lived in La Flèche, France, while working on his *Treatise.* She also learned that La Flèche was home to the Jesuit Royal College. Had Ippolito Desideri lived at the Jesuit Royal College around that time? By the time she started grappling with this question, she found herself looking forward to tomorrow for the first time since her depressive episode.

The life of Ippolito Desideri proved to be mysterious, and

Gopnik's questions about Desideri were far more difficult to answer than those about Hume. She went on sabbatical in 2007 and spent it at Caltech, where she met an expert in the history of seventeenth- and eighteenth-century Jesuits. The expert told her that the Jesuits documented everything. Based on this tip, Gopnik went to the Jesuit archives in Rome. On her last day in Rome, she learned that Desideri had visited the Royal College again when David Hume was there. Moreover, Gopnik uncovered another link: Dolu, a French ambassador to Buddhist Siam in the 1680s, retired to La Flèche in 1723. Her question was answered: David Hume must have read about Buddhism in La Flèche. She had connected Eastern philosophy to the Western Enlightenment.

Gopnik ends her *Atlantic* article by saying: "Once again, I was an exceptionally fortunate and happy woman, full of irrational exuberance and everyday joy. But that's not all I was. I'd discovered that I could love women as well as men, history as well as science, and that I could make my way through sadness and solitude, not just happiness. . . . I had found my salvation in the sheer endless curiosity of the human mind—and the sheer endless variety of human experience."

Gopnik faced a loss of happiness and meaning in her time of crisis. But all was not lost. Dramatic life changes brought ups and downs that continually shifted her perspective. The result was that, at midlife, she discovered new passion, fresh intellectual horizons, and wisdom. Today she lives a psychologically rich life she values for its "sheer endless variety."

4. Steve's India

Steve Jobs is another example of someone who chose a life of exploration. Born to Abdulfattah Jandali and Joanne Schieble, he was adopted by Paul and Clara Jobs. He was smart but hated school. He liked to spend time with his father in their garage, fixing and making stuff. In high school, he played pranks and threw parties with elaborate electronic light shows.

After dropping out of college, Jobs worked in an apple orchard and became deeply interested in Eastern spirituality and LSD. When he was nineteen, he went to India, spending seven months in search of a guru and spiritual enlightenment. He was unable to find enlightenment in India. Instead, he got dysentery and lost forty pounds in a week. But, he did gain a new perspective during his trip. Decades later he reflected, "Coming back to America was, for me, much more of a cultural shock than going to India. The people in the Indian countryside don't use their intellect like we do, they use their intuition instead, and their intuition is far more developed than in the rest of the world. . . . In the villages of India . . . they learned something else, which is in some ways just as valuable but in other ways is not. That's the power of intuition and experiential wisdom."

Jobs eventually mastered how to use both his intellect and his intuition. Of course, his career was not always smooth sailing. By age thirty, he had a smashing success with the launch of the Macintosh computer. But in 1985, he got fired from the company he had established. So, he started his own computer company, NeXT, but sales were disappointing. Meanwhile, he bought Lucasfilm's computer graphics division in January 1986. Its first feature film, *Toy Story* (1995), was a huge success, but it took him nearly ten years to get there. In 1997, Jobs returned to Apple, and had a legendary run with the release of the iPod in 2001, the iMac in 2002, the iPhone in 2007, and the iPad in 2010. In 2003, when he was forty-eight, his doctor found a tumor in his pancreas.

Near the end of his life, Steve Jobs invited Ann Bower, who was Apple's human resources director in the early 1980s, to his bedside. He asked her, "Tell me, what was I like when I was young?" Bowers replied, "You were very impetuous and very difficult. But your vision was compelling. You told us, 'The journey is the reward.' That turned out to be true." Jobs responded, "I did learn some things along the way . . . I did learn some things. I really did." Jobs told Walter Isaacson, his biographer, "I've had a very lucky career, a very lucky life. I've done all that I can do."

On his deathbed, Steve Jobs seemed to have no regrets. That is a defining characteristic of a psychologically rich life.

5. The Joy of National Parks

Those are the stories of outwardly extraordinary, accomplished people. What about the story of the type of person we all encounter every day?

For the past sixty-seven years, Joy Ryan has lived in the same house in the two-stoplight town of Duncan Falls, Ohio. She married in 1949 and raised three children there. Her simple life was marked by tragedies; her husband died of cancer in 1994, and a decade later she lost two of her adult children. As she toiled away at her grocery store job into her mid-80s, she drifted apart from her family and her health declined. But then a phone call from an estranged grandson interrupted her monotonous life.

Brad Ryan was thirty-four at the time. As a veterinary school student struggling with his mental health, he had been shaken by the recent suicide of a classmate. So one day, in the middle of making banana bread, he phoned his grandma for some advice. He had only recently started talking to her after a ten-year stretch of estrangement.

The phone call led Brad to a stunning revelation: in her eighty-five years, Joy had never seen a mountain or the ocean, much less a glacier or a desert, a bison or a whale. It inspired them to take a trip to the mountains, and what started as twenty-eight days of camping in the Smoky Mountains became a journey of reconciliation through every national park in the U.S. It wasn't always a pleasant journey; an ugly divorce between Brad's parents had started the rift between Brad and Joy. But as they spent hours on the road together resolving past conflicts, they shared remarkable experiences: getting trapped in a herd of bison in Yellowstone, watching a humpback whale leap right in front of their boat in the Channel Islands off the coast of California, helicoptering over glaciers in Alaska. Joy became the oldest person to ever zipline in New River Gorge National Park in West Virginia.

Watching Brad and Joy in an interview with *PBS NewsHour,* one can't help but notice the sparkle of wonder in their eyes as they describe their expedition. Just nine years ago Joy was living a plain life, distanced from Brad and battling depression. Joy's life had been far from a psychologically rich one. In her own words:

> It's just hard to imagine all the beautiful, wonderful things that you find outside . . . it's just been miraculous. And I've enjoyed every minute of it. . . . It gave me something when I get older, I can sit and talk about.

Now ninety-four years old, Joy has many stories to tell about her incredibly rich—psychologically rich—life.

6. The Taxi Driver

On March 11, 2022, I was taking a taxi from my hotel in Riverside, California, to the airport. The driver—I'll call her Linda—told me her life story, and what a story that was. She had worked for a county government and retired years before. She was driving part-time to keep herself busy and make extra money. She asked me why I was in Riverside (answer: visiting UC Riverside) and what my job was (answer: professor at the University of Virginia at the time). That led her to talk about her youngest daughter, who had just moved to Riverside, and then about her other children, one of whom lived in Washington D.C. She asked me if I had a family (answer: yes, two kids) and shared that she had four kids and seven grandchildren, two of whom she had given birth to. Wait, she had carried her grandkids? I couldn't believe what I was hearing. So she went on to explain: she became a surrogate mother (gestational carrier) for her daughter and son-in-law, meaning she was impregnated through the use of in vitro fertilization (IVF) with her son-in-law's sperm and daughter's eggs when she was fifty-two and fifty-five! She did so because her daughter had medical conditions that made pregnancy and delivery life-threatening.

Linda was almost crying as she told me the story. She had a C-section for each grandchild's birth and breastfed each one. When I asked if she felt like they were her own children, she confessed that, while all seven grandkids are special, she shared a special bond with the two she carried.

Her story only got more interesting from there. She mentioned that she had donated one of her kidneys to her ex-husband. I remarked that she must be extremely altruistic, and she responded that, no, it was simply the right thing to do. Her answer reminded me of Abigail Marsh's research on extraordinary altruists, who, she found, tend to downplay their good deeds. Linda explained that she could never have raised four kids who all turned out to be very successful without having the stability that her (now ex) husband had provided. She had had two of the four (twins!) at age eighteen before they met. Giving a kidney to him was the right thing to do.

She went on to sing the praises of California, with its mountains, desert, and ocean, and said she loves being retired and able to travel two to three months a year. She had just returned from three months in France, and had spent two months the previous year in Vietnam, Cambodia, and Thailand. She retired early because she didn't live to work; she worked to live. Once she had enough, she wanted to just enjoy her life: work here and there, and structure her life in the way she wanted. She talked to all four adult children daily, and they visited each other regularly.

What an interesting life, I thought. Linda might not be financially rich, but she is psychologically and experientially rich. I think it's also fair to say that she is happy, and that she has led a meaningful life as well. Despite her difficulties as a single mother early on, she now seems to live her life in all three dimensions.

INGREDIENTS OF PSYCHOLOGICAL RICHNESS

Read, every day, something no one else is reading. Think, every day, something no one else is thinking. Do, every day, something no one else would be silly enough to do. It is bad for the mind to continually be part of unanimity.

—Christopher Morley

1. Grace and Rachel's Rich Weekend

If a life of exploration tends to lead to a psychologically rich life, what exactly are the ingredients of psychological richness? What kinds of experiences contribute to psychological richness? What kinds of experiences are psychologically impoverished?

To find out, I held two focus group meetings in September 2015. One group consisted of my undergraduate research assistants, and the other consisted of my graduate students and postdocs at UVA. First, I asked them to reflect on their weekend and think about what they did. Then I asked what the happiest event was. The majority answered that going out with friends or family was their happiest event. Then I asked what the most meaningful event was. The majority of answers involved helping someone, attending a religious service, or volunteering. Finally, I asked what the most psychologically rich event was. I explained it as an event that was unusual and interesting, not just happy or meaningful per se.

Grace and Rachel gave the most memorable answers. Grace was a sophomore from a suburb of Washington D.C. She went to her first professional wrestling event with friends over the weekend. She went in expecting stereotypical fake violence and cheesy drama. To her surprise, she left with the discovery that professional wrestlers can be inspiring role models for children, as World Wrestling Entertainment (WWE) is heavily devoted to children's charities. She laughed, cheered, felt outraged and pained, and ultimately found herself deeply moved by the experience. In addition to the novelty of attending a wrestling match for the first time, her unexpected change in perspective made this experience much richer than a typical outing.

Rachel was another sophomore at UVA, from central Virginia. That same weekend, she went to a lounge of her apartment building and encountered something unusual. A young man (most likely another UVA student) was writing something on his laptop. What was strange was that he was shirtless. It was not warm in the lounge. He didn't seem to be showing off his upper body, either, as he was not particularly well built. This puzzled Rachel. She could not quite figure out why he was working shirtless in a common area.

In your opinion, which experience is psychologically richer, Grace's WWE outing or Rachel's shirtless guy? Both Grace's and Rachel's experiences have an element of novelty and unexpectedness. Grace had never been to a pro wrestling match before, and Rachel had never seen an ordinary guy typing shirtless in a common area of her apartment building. Both are certainly interesting experiences. But were they rich? First, whereas Grace experienced a lot of different, intense emotions, such as excitement, joy, fear, anger, and surprise, Rachel experienced only mild surprise and apprehension. So Grace's WWE experience was far more emotionally complex than Rachel's. Second, Grace went into her experience with some preconceptions of what a WWE match would be like, but came back with a different perspective, learning, for instance, that WWE supports an anti-bullying campaign and that many kids admire wrestlers. That is, Grace's perspective changed after the event. In contrast, Rachel's experience was novel and unusual, but it did not change her perspective in any way. Overall, the two focus group sessions revealed that psychologically rich experiences involve not only novelty but also intensity, complexity, and a change in perspective.

2. A Psychologically Rich Day via Poetry

Now that we have figured out what makes a weekend outing psychologically rich, what about a psychologically rich day? What makes a day psychologically rich or not rich? Relatedly, what makes a day happy or meaningful?

In his poem "Happiness," Raymond Carver describes his morning routines. He is sitting by the window with a cup of coffee and looking out. He sees the newspaper boy with his friend walking up to his driveway, just smiling: "Happiness. It comes on unexpectedly. And goes beyond, really, any early morning talk about it." Carver finds happiness in this mundane scene. This is a predictable, repeatable scene. Yet it is also sudden and ephemeral. If you don't pay attention, you might miss it. A happy day comes from noticing something heartwarming, having a good laugh with friends, and, according to Carver, not thinking about death, ambition, love, or anything too deep.

What is a meaningful day? This question is a bit more difficult to answer. When you flip the question to ask what a meaning*less* day is, all of sudden it becomes much easier to answer. A meaningless day is a day wasted, an utterly pointless day. Like listening to a lecture on material you already know well, a meaningless day does not add much to your life. A meaningful day is the opposite. There is a point to that day. You've accomplished something. Maybe you wrote a letter, for instance. You helped someone. You did laundry or exercised. You got something done, and the day was not totally wasted. Even if you didn't get much done, maybe you got some much-needed rest to prepare you for another day of hard work. There are many ways to make a day meaningful.

Like Raymond Carver, Jane Kenyon writes about her routines in her poem "Otherwise." She gets out of bed, eats breakfast, has lunch, takes a nap, eats dinner, and sleeps. Nothing special, except that she might have been unable to get out of bed, unable to do all the routines. There are many counterfactuals in "Otherwise." It could have been a lot worse, which makes this typical day precious. It's clear that she cherishes her mundane life. A meaningful day is not just a day with explicit gains. It is also a day you appreciate because "one day, I know, it will be otherwise."

What about a psychologically rich day? Mary Oliver in her poem "Wild Geese" tells us that we don't have to be extraordinarily good or virtuous, that despair is a part of life, and that insignificance is a part of existence. Even so, she encourages us to be like wild geese: "the world offers itself to your imagination." The world has so much to offer and explore: "harsh and exciting." A psychologically rich day is a day when you experience something unfamiliar, feel a wide range of emotions, and gain a new perspective on life.

3. A Psychologically Rich Day: Data

I wondered whether the key factors of a happy day, a meaningful day, and a psychologically rich day that I identified based on the poems above actually make ordinary college students' days happy, meaningful, or psychologically rich, respectively. Hyewon Choi and I asked more than two hundred college students to keep daily records of what they did and how they felt for fourteen days, resulting in over 2,600 daily reports. In addition to asking about happiness, meaning, and psychological richness, we asked them how typical or atypical each day was, how many routine activities they participated in, how much free time they had, and whether they did something new, met someone new, or ate something new. We also presented them with an activity checklist that asked them whether they volunteered, went to a concert, hiked, played a video game, and so on. These daily reports gave us a nice picture of how the students spent their days.

First, we found some common factors associated with all three aspects of well-being. It turned out that doing something new, eating something new, or meeting someone new enhanced not only psychological richness but also happiness and meaning. That is, most students reported that their day was happier, more meaningful, and richer on a day when they did something new, ate something new, or met someone new.

Second, we found some unique predictors of a psychologically rich day. For instance, an atypical day was psychologically richer than a typical day, but an atypical day was not happier than a typical day. A day with more free time was psychologically richer than a day with less free time. In contrast, a free day was no more meaningful than a less free day. Finally, a day with more required work was happier and more meaningful than a day with less required work. That is, getting things done made the day happier and more meaningful, whereas doing something unusual made the day psychologically richer. Whether you're taking a short trip to a vineyard, walking in an unfamiliar part of town, going to a baseball game, or calling an old friend from elementary school, doing something that you don't usually do is more interesting and psychologically rich than doing things you do every day.

Subsequent analyses also showed that a happy day was one in which participants experienced a lot of positive emotions and did not feel many negative emotions. In contrast, a psychologically rich day was one in which they felt more emotions—both positive and negative—than on a typical day. For example, if you are a liberal, watching Fox News might make you upset, but it would be more interesting than watching CNN or another network that more closely reflects your views.

4. Study Abroad!

If novelty, complexity, and perspective change are the key ingredients to psychological richness, studying abroad must rank near the top of the ranking of psychologically rich events. After all, study abroad involves putting yourself in an unfamiliar culture with different landscapes, customs, and norms—a totally new way of life. It's exciting but also challenging at many levels.

According to the Institute of International Education, 344,099 Americans studied abroad during the 2018–2019 academic year. Due to the global pandemic, during the 2020–2021 academic year the total number of Americans who studied abroad decreased by nearly 96 percent, to 14,549, demonstrating how many college students during the COVID era were deprived of opportunities for exploration.

Studying abroad is expensive. Airplane tickets. Room and board. New clothes. Consequently, it is harder for students from a lower socioeconomic status to participate. I couldn't have done it myself if I hadn't gotten the Rotary International scholarship (which paid for full tuition, room and board, textbooks, round-trip airfare, and even a one-month summer English class!). When I got this scholarship, I asked my undergraduate advisor, Professor Hara, where I should go. He was a big fan of liberal arts colleges and recommended three in Maine. His assumption was that I would not see other Japanese students and would learn English best there. In July 1991, I left Tokyo for New York City. I spent one month at Wagner College on Staten Island studying

English. Then I flew to Portland, Maine, in August. Dean James Reese picked me up at the airport and drove us up to Bates College in Lewiston. Thirty-plus years later, I still remember our conversation in the car on that warm afternoon. "What is your favorite music?" Dean Reese asked. "Jazz," I said. Dean Reese, who is Black, replied, "I love jazz, too!" He then asked, "Who's your favorite musician?" Somehow the most well-known names, like Charlie Parker and Miles Davis, escaped me at that moment. After a long pause, I said, "Bill Evans." Dean Reese immediately said, "Get out of here!" I was scared. I thought he meant that I should get out of the car right that moment. Then he explained that another former Japanese student's favorite musician was also Bill Evans!

I don't remember many conversations I had in Tokyo with professors, deans, or even friends around that time. Yet many things that happened during my study abroad are still vivid in my memory. For instance, I shared my dorm room with a student named Mike. I'd often pick up the phone and hear, "Is Mike there?" and I'd say, "No." Then the voice on the other end usually said, "Could you tell him so-and-so called?" Since I was still learning English, I was never able to make out who this was, so I needed to ask, "Could you please spell it out?" so I could write it down.

One day, I got a call and followed the same routine. When I asked the speaker's name, he spelled out, "H-I-S-F-A-T-H-E-R."

I repeated, "H-I-S-F-A-T-H-E-R?"

"Yes."

"Great, thanks."

I hung up. I didn't realize until I put down the phone that it was Mike's father! I of course knew the words "his" and "father." I just could not understand the words on the phone. My listening comprehension of English was very low at that point. It was humiliating. Indeed, I had never been more humiliated. But this incident made me realize that many immigrants in the U.S. experience similar humiliation, as do many less fortunate people in Japan.

Until my "his father" incident, I hadn't thought about how my experience as an exchange student would be similar to immigrants' experiences in the U.S. Until then, I hadn't identified myself with other immigrants at all. Of course, I also had a lot of awesome experiences while studying abroad, like going to Acadia National Park and Martha's Vineyard, where I saw rocky beaches and lighthouses for the first time. This wide range of unexpected experiences and unusual emotions makes studying abroad extremely psychologically rich and rewarding in the long run. Traveling abroad as a tourist is also novel and interesting, but as a tourist you rarely have authentic interactions with locals. Living abroad is much more challenging and evokes a wider range of emotions. In short, psychological richness requires a lot of ingredients, not just novelty but also challenges and perspective change.

With this in mind, Jaime Kurtz and I recruited students studying abroad one semester, as well as students who were interested in studying abroad but had stayed on campus. Every week, participants abroad and on campus completed a brief survey similar to the daily diary survey described earlier in the chapter. At the beginning of the semester, study abroad students and on-campus students had similar levels of happiness, meaning in life, and psychological richness. Thirteen weeks later, however, study abroad students reported more psychological richness than on-campus students, though they didn't differ in terms of happiness or meaning in life.

How come? We looked deeper into the weekly reports and found that study abroad students were far more likely to engage in artistic activities (e.g., going to concerts and museums), shop, party, and take short trips. They were far less likely to engage in club meetings, sporting events, video games, or volunteer activities than on-campus students. Analyses showed that the more artistic activities they engaged in, the richer they reported their lives to be at the end of the semester. The other activities were not ultimately associated with psychological richness. Perhaps artistic activities challenge you to expand your perspective more than shopping, partying, or taking a short trip.

5. Bittersweet

In her popular book *Bittersweet,* Susan Cain contends that "light and dark, birth and death—bitter and sweet—are forever paired" and that negative emotions such as sorrow and longing "make us whole." She argues that negative emotions play a central role in our emotional lives and make us more empathetic and even more creative. Similarly, I think that negative emotions such as sorrow and longing, along with positive emotions, make our lives psychologically richer.

What role does emotional complexity play in psychological richness? In six studies, we explored the role of positive and negative emotions in happiness, meaning, and psychological richness. In all six, those who were leading a happy life experienced a lot of joy, contentment, and pleasantness but infrequently experienced sadness, anger, and fear. Those who were leading a meaningful life were quite similar to those leading a happy life in that they had more positive emotions than negative emotions. Interestingly, those who were leading a psychologically rich life experienced a lot of positive emotions but also experienced negative emotions quite a bit.

In the final experiment, we tested whether we could make people feel like they had a richer week. Some participants wrote about the best event and the worst event they had experienced over the previous seven days, while other participants wrote about their best event and their second-best event. After the writing task, they evaluated their lives over the previous week, reflecting on how much the writing task had made them think differently about themselves and the world (perspective change, in other words). We found that compared to the participants who wrote about two positive events, those who wrote about both the best and the worst events reported a greater degree of perspective change. Writing about the worst event, in short, increased the likelihood of perspective change. Most important, the more perspective changes they reported, the psychologically richer they reported their lives to be. Interestingly, the more perspective change they reported, the less happiness they reported. Just as negative emotions such as fear and jealousy add drama to books and movies, the worst event had induced perspective change and made the participants' lives psychologically richer.

6. To Sum Up

So what are the ingredients of psychological richness? The examples in this chapter, ranging from Grace's WWE outing to an atypical day to a semester abroad, had some common elements. Novelty: there's something different from the same old, same old. Diversity: a wide range of attention and emotion is deployed. Challenge: life is more difficult and complex than usual. Memorable: life is vivid. Above all, you learn something new. You gain some new perspective. Together, our findings paint a clear picture (see also Table 1 in Chapter 1). Simplifying one's life so as to have reliably positive experiences, or contentment, is key to happiness. Dedicating one's life to others with compassion is key to meaning. Experiencing the unusual, challenging oneself, and learning new things—though frustrating and unpleasant at times—are key to psychological richness.

CHAPTER SIX

WHO IS RICH, PSYCHOLOGICALLY RICH?

It is better to live rich than die rich.

—Samuel Johnson

1. Quantifying the Psychologically Rich Life

As interesting as Joy Ryan and Linda's lives are, they also feel exceptional. How common is it for ordinary folks to live a psychologically rich life? Is there any scientific evidence that a sizable number of people are leading psychologically rich lives? Our lab set out to quantify psychological richness in people's lives and determine how common it is.

We realized that we had a valuable tool to evaluate people's lives at the end of them, in their obituaries. Every obituary tells a life story. Perhaps by analyzing their contents, we could figure out how happy, meaningful, and psychologically rich a person's life was. By coding hundreds of obituaries for different life characteristics, we could cover a wide swath of people, from CEOs and politicians to musicians and athletes.

We hired three research assistants and asked them to read and rate *New York Times* obituaries, 101 of them, in June 2016, using twelve different themes. Blind to our hypotheses, they rated the happiness, meaningfulness, and psychological richness of the lives described in each obituary. We started by giving the raters clear definitions of a happy life (a life in which a person is comfortable, satisfied, and joyful), a meaningful life (a life in which a person makes a contribution to society and makes a difference), and a psychologically rich life (a life in which a person encounters many diverse, unusual experiences). We then asked them to rate each life, on a scale of 1 to 5, by answering questions such as, "How happy was this person's life?," "How fulfilling?," and "How interesting?" We checked that ratings were consistent across the three research assistants before analyzing our data.

First, how many of the people profiled led a happy life, a meaningful life, or a psychologically rich life? In order for a person's life to be classified as happy, meaningful, or psychologically rich, the three raters had to assign it an average score of at least 3.67 out of 5 across four items. This is quite a high bar. According to this criterion, fifteen people of the 101 obituaries featured in *The New York Times* that month led a psychologically rich life. In contrast, thirty-two people led a happy life, and another thirty-two people led a meaningful life (see Figure 1). In general, then, there were more people who led a happy or meaningful life than those who led a psychologically rich life.

We also looked at how many of them led a happy, meaningful, AND psychologically rich life. There were two who did it all: Nicholas Clinch (lawyer, mountaineer, and onetime executive director of the Sierra Club) and Simon Ramo (engineer, inventor, and author). As can be seen in the Venn diagram below, ten people led a rich and meaningful life, eight people led a happy and meaningful life, and three led a rich and happy life. Sadly, forty-one of the subjects were rated to have led neither a happy, meaningful, nor psychologically rich life (of course, their obituaries might have failed to describe relevant events).

That said, *New York Times* obituaries tend to feature extraordinary individuals, like Muhammad Ali. Certainly, their lives are not representative of the general population. So, next, we hired three other research assistants to code 116 obituaries found in *The*

The *New York Times* Obituary Study:
Number of People Who Led a Happy, Meaningful, or Psych Rich Life

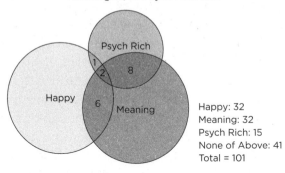

Happy: 32
Meaning: 32
Psych Rich: 15
None of Above: 41
Total = 101

Figure 1. How many people led a happy, meaningful, or psychologically rich life?

Daily Progress, a local newspaper in Charlottesville, Virginia, in June, July, and August 2016. We again made sure that the ratings were reliable before analyzing the data.

How many of these Virginians were perceived to have led a psychologically rich life? Using the same criterion (an average of 3.67 or higher on the 1 to 5 point scale), only five out of 116 (4.3 percent) qualified. Is it true that people featured in *The Daily Progress* are less likely to have led a psychologically rich life? It could be that these folks led less adventurous lives than the cosmopolitans featured in *The New York Times.* An alternative explanation is that the obituaries in *The Daily Progress* are shorter than those in *The New York Times,* leaving out potentially interesting details. On the other hand, it is noteworthy that sixty-six (or 56.9 percent of subjects) were rated to have led a happy life. Likewise, ninety-six (82.8 percent) were rated to have led a meaningful life. There was one person rated to have led a happy, meaningful, AND psychologically rich life: Henry Saint Dahl (Buenos Aires native, onetime secretary-general of the Inter-American Bar Association, and author of Spanish and French legal dictionaries).

As interesting as these findings are, *The New York Times* and *The Daily Progress* mainly feature Americans. We wondered if people lead more psychologically rich lives outside of the U.S. We had two other research assistants code 111 obituaries in *The Straits Times,* a Singaporean newspaper. How many of the *Straits Times* folks were rated to have led a psychologically rich life? Forty! That is, 34.5 percent of the people featured in *Straits Times* obituaries were rated to have led a rich life, far more than in the first two newspapers. Meanwhile, twenty-five (21.6 percent) were rated to have led a happy life, and sixty-five (56.5 percent) were rated to have led a meaningful life. Eight individuals (6.9 percent) were deemed to have it all: happy, meaningful, AND psychologically rich, including I. M. Pei (architect) and Tow Siang Hwa (gynecologist and pastor). Our studies demonstrate that a significant number of people lead a psychologically rich life.

It brings us back to the big question: Is it possible to lead a good life without happiness or meaning? Goldmund's life, for example, was probably rated low in happiness and meaning, but high in psychological richness. The relative independence of the three forms of a good life evident in the obituary studies shows that it is possible to lead a psychologically rich life without happiness or meaning. Indeed, out of the fifteen individuals who were rated to have led a psychologically rich life in the *New York Times* obituaries, we found four who led a psychologically rich life without happiness or meaning.

In addition, we identified eight individuals in the *New York Times* obituaries who were rated to have led a rich and meaningful life. Steve Jobs is a real-life example. He was often angry and alienated many people around him. He might not have led a happy life, but it was an interesting one, full of adventures and learning. His life would have been rated low in happiness but high in meaning and psychological richness.

Equally important is that some people do lead a psychologically rich as well as a happy and meaningful life. Alison Gopnik's post–midlife crisis life is just that. So is the life of Linda, the taxi driver. In sum, our research supports that a life of exploration is a distinct kind of good life, a psychologically rich one. But it also shows that it is possible to have two or three of these dimensions of a good life.

2. The Big Five in Five Minutes

Are there any personality characteristics that differentiate those who lead a psychologically rich life from those who lead a happy or a meaningful life? To answer this question, we need to know the basics of personality psychology. Since I used to teach an intro to personality psychology class, I'm equipped to deliver this five-minute lecture on the Big Five personality traits.

A bit of history first. In 1936, psychologists Gordon W. Allport and Henry S. Odbert set out to identify all the words describing personality or personal behavior in Webster's 1925 *New International Dictionary*. That dictionary contained roughly 400,000 entries, of which they found 17,953 personal descriptors, or 4.5 percent of the English vocabulary recorded there. Personality is often defined as *characteristic* patterns of thinking, feeling, and behavior, so the researchers removed all the words about temporary states, such as "frantic" and "rejoicing." Allport and Odbert also distinguished personality from the moral, evaluative concept of "character." Their idea was that, in order to establish the scientific field of personality psychology, they needed a judgment-free, relatively neutral vocabulary to avoid biases. So they removed all the character-evaluative terms, such as "excellent," "acceptable," and "insignificant." Allport and Odbert ended up with 4,504 "pure" personality trait words in English. In other words, they discovered that there were 4,504 different ways to describe someone's personality, based on the dictionary treatment.

But why rely on words to illuminate an inner quality? Allport and Odbert argued, "If many human beings were not in fact *ego-tistic, aggressive,* or *timid,* the epithets would not have found a permanent place in language. If traits exist at all it is natural and proper to name them." If there is a trait name, there must be some corresponding pattern of behavior, thinking, or feeling.

Some criticized Allport and Odbert's research, claiming there were too many synonyms. For instance, the pure personality traits list included both "adventurous" and "venturous." Are they two separate personality traits? (Not really.) Others argued that many of the words, like "aery" and "breme," were archaic and most people didn't use them. (Indeed, these words are not very useful.) Yet others argued that there were large individual differences in vocabulary and that esoteric terms should be removed. (Probably true.) Despite all the criticisms, Allport and Odbert's early effort to catalog personality trait words has survived as the "lexical approach" to personality.

Later, psychologists had a large pool of participants rate themselves using many of the original Allport-Odbert terms, then applied the statistical technique of factor analysis to sort the terms into larger groups, or "factors." For example, Lew Goldberg had 187 college students rate themselves on 1,710 terms: "How jolly are you in general? How reserved are you in general? How sadistic are you in general?" and so on.

Goldberg's study and others like it found that many personality traits cluster neatly into the following five factors: extraversion (e.g., jolly, talkative, sociable, active), neuroticism (e.g., touchy, fearful, self-critical), conscientiousness (e.g., persistent, tidy, dependable), agreeableness (e.g., generous, kind, trustful), and openness to experience (e.g., literary, insightful, perceptive). In a sense, personality psychologists created a map. Like cities and towns across the world, there are countless words descriptive of personality. By classifying all these words into five factors, personality psychologists essentially organized them into "continents" on the map. These factors, known as the "Big Five," were the most influential discovery in personality psychology in the 1980s and early 1990s.

3. The Personality of Psychological Richness

The type of person who goes to a pro wrestling match on the weekend might be a very different kind of person than someone who avoids those kinds of activities. The type of person who studies abroad could be very different from the type of person who doesn't. Are there distinct personality traits characteristic of the psychologically rich? If so, which of the Big Five factors are associated with a psychologically rich life?

In order to answer these questions, we collected data from over 5,000 respondents in seven separate samples across the U.S., Korea, and India. We asked them a series of questions about a psychologically rich life (e.g., "I have had a lot of interesting experiences," "On my deathbed, I am likely to say, 'I have seen and learned a lot'"; see Appendix 1 for the full list and find out your own psychological richness score), a series of questions about a happy life (e.g., "I am satisfied with my life," "So far I have gotten the important things I want in life"), and a series of questions about a meaningful life (e.g., "I have a good sense of what makes my life meaningful," "My life has a clear sense of purpose"). In addition, we asked about respondents' personality: the degree to which each word described who they are in general: imaginative, organized, talkative, sympathetic, tense, and so on.

Two main personality predictors of a psychologically rich life were openness to experiences and extraversion (see Appendix 2 for all the correlations). The .47 correlation between openness to experience and psychological richness is similar to the correlation between heights of fathers and their sons, which is quite strong, though far from absolute. That is, open people tend to lead a psychologically rich life, just like sons whose fathers are tall tend to be tall themselves. But, just as some sons are very different from their fathers in height, there are also plenty of exceptions: people low in openness who lead psychologically rich lives as well as people who are high in openness who don't lead psychologically rich lives. For now, let's focus on the link between openness and psychological richness.

Why do people who are high in openness to experience tend to lead psychologically rich lives? Open people are imaginative, curious, and interested in intellectual and artistic pursuits. People low in openness are conventional and down-to-earth, preferring routine and less interested in intellectual or artistic pursuits. Students who are open to experience are more likely to study abroad, an activity known to enhance psychological richness, than those low in openness. Interestingly, those who studied abroad became more open to experience over time than those who didn't. Based on this information, we concluded that there is a reciprocal relationship between openness to experience and psychological richness, such that openness to experience increases one's chance of engaging in richness-enhancing activities, which in turn boosts one's openness further. Your personality is not your destiny, though; the later chapters of this book are dedicated to strategies that everyone, no matter what your personality is, can implement to make your life more psychologically rich.

The .47 correlation also means that having an open personality doesn't necessarily guarantee that you will lead a psychologically rich life. Joy Ryan, the ninety-four-year-old national park enthusiast we met in Chapter 4, might have always been open to experience. But, until she turned eighty-five, she hadn't had many opportunities to explore the world. Once she was exposed to Smoky Mountain National Park, she was hooked. She became open to even more new experiences and thereafter wanted to visit all the national parks. In other words, having an open personality plus opportunities and resources opens the door to psychologically rich experiences.

Besides opportunities and resources, intellectual and artistic abilities are also factors. Simon Ramo, whose *New York Times* obituary was rated as particularly psychologically rich, was an aerospace engineer. He earned a PhD in physics and engineering from the California Institute of Technology and later developed intercontinental ballistic missiles, or ICBMs. He published sixty-two books over the course of his life; he had twenty-five patents before he was thirty, and earned his final patent at age one hundred. He died at age 103. Simon started out working for large corporations but got sick of the bureaucracy. So he started his own company in a former barbershop, where he developed an initial prototype of an ICBM. He was also interested in other topics, including tennis strategy—he later wrote a book on that, too. And he had a great sense of humor. When he was asked about his politics, he replied, "I am a registered opportunist." Ramo's fascination with the world could not be codified by a particular belief system. He had diverse interests and an amazing intellect.

Another example of a person who lived a psychologically rich life is novelist Louis Cha (also known as Jin Yong), whose obituary was featured in the *Straits Times.* Cha was born in China and started out as a journalist in Shanghai before transferring to his newspaper's Hong Kong office in the 1950s. He wrote an enormously popular series of novels inspired by martial arts history from 1955 until 1972. Despite his popularity, Cha didn't write any new novels after this period. Instead, he reread his own novels and continued to revise them. He would cry while reading his favorite characters' breakup in his own novel. He was unconventional, even defiant. In the late 1960s he wrote a series of anti-Mao articles, which put Cha on the Chinese Communist Party's assassination list. He escaped to Singapore and stayed there for almost a year to avoid assassination. Cha's tumultuous life can hardly be characterized as happy or worry-free. Yet he had a unique, interesting life.

Personality psychologists have classified openness to experience into two subfactors: openness and intellect. People high in openness tend to have more creative accomplishments in the arts, whereas people high in intellect tend to have more creative accomplishments both in arts and sciences. Simon Ramo must have been high in the intellect dimension of openness to experience, as he explored and found many creative solutions to diverse engineering problems, while Louis Cha must have been high in the openness dimension, as he led an emotionally rich, imaginative life.

4. The Role of Extraversion

While the link between openness to experience and psychological richness seems obvious, the role of extraversion in a psychologically rich life might not be. The easiest way to think about the link is to conceive of extraversion as an interest in exploring the social world. That is, if openness to experience is concerned with the exploration of sensory and abstract information, extraversion is concerned with the exploration of interpersonal information. If open people are curious about ideas, extraverts are curious about other people. Because people are different, the more people you interact with, the more diverse experiences you will have and the richer your life becomes.

At a party, who do you talk to? I am an introvert, so I gravitate toward someone I already know. I usually stick with one or two people and try to have a deeper conversation. An extravert has a very different strategy. They talk to many new people and make more friends. Extraverts become friends with other extraverts, a phenomenon called the "network extraversion bias." Since extraverts have more friends than introverts, making an extraverted friend is likely to expand your social networks more than making an introverted friend. In the long run, then, extraverts are more likely to meet different kinds of people and are more likely to learn new things than an introvert like myself. This is one way that extraversion is linked to a psychologically rich life.

On a basic level, why do extraverts explore the social world more? One factor is their confidence and self-assurance. When you are confident, meeting a new person is not threatening. What is there to lose? You are not worried about being negatively evaluated by this person or making a bad impression. Instead, you are thinking about the benefits: getting to know someone new, learning something new, sharing interesting stories. There is a positive spiral here, too. The more confident you are, the more likely you are to enter a new conversation. The more new conversations you enter, the psychologically richer the party becomes for you. Someone who has a psychologically enriching experience at one party is more likely to go to another party.

Another aspect of extraversion that might be related to psychological richness is energy. Extraverts tend to be more energetic than introverts. The more energy one has, the more activities one can engage in. One study, for instance, found that extraverts were involved with more college activities, such as intramural athletics, campus clubs, and service and volunteer clubs, than introverts. Joy Ryan is again a great example here. Compared to other ninety-somethings, she is full of energy. Thanks to this, she can visit remote national parks and enjoy unusual, psychologically rich experiences.

5. The Personality of Happiness

Is a happy person different from a psychologically rich person? One example of a "happy" person is Mr. Rogers in *Mister Rogers' Neighborhood*. In this show, he is a friendly neighbor with a cheerful smile. The show consists of lots of singing, dancing, and puppet shows. That's a lot of fun! Who wouldn't want to hang out with a guy who sings, "Please, won't you be my neighbor?"

Mr. Rogers demonstrates the essential characteristics of happy people: extraverted, emotionally stable (lacking neuroticism), conscientious, and agreeable. The patterns of correlation for psychological richness are quite different from those for happiness. According to Anglim and colleagues' meta-analysis, a happy life is characterized by emotional stability, extraversion, conscientiousness, and agreeableness, but not by openness to experiences.

The two strongest personality predictors of a happy life are emotional stability and extraversion. Some personality scholars conceptualize extraversion as positive affectivity (good moods) and neuroticism as negative affectivity (bad moods). Since by definition a happy life is the preponderance of positive emotions and relative lack of negative emotions, it makes sense that extraversion and emotional stability are the most characteristic of a happy life.

Overall, the key difference between a happy personality and a psychologically rich personality is that happy people are not necessarily open to experiences, whereas psychologically rich people are quite open. This means that there are almost as many people who, like travel writer Rick Steves, are happy and open to experience as there are people who, like chef and travel documentarian Anthony Bourdain, are less happy but open to experience.

Why are emotional stability, extraversion, conscientiousness, and agreeableness good for a happy life? Primarily because the quality of social relationships is a big predictor of happiness. Who has good social relationships? Well, someone like Mr. Rogers: friendly, stable, reliable, and kind. Someone who is emotionally volatile, introverted, unreliable, and argumentative doesn't win many friends.

Second, financial stability and relationship stability are important for a happy life. In order to achieve these, we must work hard on our finances and our relationships. We need to remember the deadlines of various tasks and the birthdays of children and in-laws. We need to do some things that we don't want to do. So, conscientiousness does help. Agreeableness improves work relationships as well as family relationships. If your boss likes you, you are more likely to receive a raise or a promotion than if they don't like you.

Third, the positivity associated with extraversion is helpful when we face difficult life circumstances. Emotional stability will help us recover from negative news more quickly. Bad things happen to good people. But when they do, extraversion and emotional stability are a boon (and our psychological immune system is there to help either way).

Finally, why is openness to experience uncorrelated to a happy life? One potential reason is the greater motivation to explore among open people. When an exploration (e.g., trying out a new restaurant) results in a positive outcome, it is associated with higher levels of happiness. But when the exploration results in a negative experience, it is not. Exploration is also antithetical to the stability that is the foundation for a happy life.

6. The Personality of Meaningfulness

Now let's think about the type of people who lead a meaningful life. Greta Thunberg, the Swedish environmental activist, comes to mind. At the opposite end of the political spectrum, Mike Huckabee also comes to mind. What do their personalities have in common?

At age fifteen, Greta began protesting in front of the Swedish parliament every Friday with a sign that read, "School Strike for Climate." Her movement, dubbed "Fridays for Future," spread around the world. She catalyzed a host of youth climate activism, and to date continues to advocate for reducing carbon emissions and increasing sustainability. Greta is endlessly committed to her work. In 2019, she even took a sabbatical from school to dedicate all her energy to activism. She prioritizes her environmental activism work over other commitments and works relentlessly. A woman of conviction.

Mike Huckabee was born in Arkansas. He studied religion in college, then became a staffer for televangelist James Robison, then a pastor in Texarkana. As a pastor, he listened to so many personal stories of struggles that were policy-related that he turned to politics and became the governor of Arkansas. He thinks about policy issues from the perspective of his religious beliefs (e.g., he is a believer in forgiveness, therefore supports a generous policy regarding clemencies) and he uses food metaphors frequently (e.g., on whether the U.S. should accept Syrian refugees, he said, "If you bought a 5 lb. bag of peanuts and you knew that in the 5 lb. bag of peanuts there were about 10 peanuts that were deadly poisonous, would you feed them to your kids? The answer is no"). He probably thinks his life is meaningful because he has dedicated his life to religious causes, he has made differences in others' lives, and his life has been guided by clear principles. A man of conviction.

There are numerous paths to achieving a meaningful life, but personality research has shown that people who lead a meaningful life are characterized first by conscientiousness, followed by emotional stability, extraversion, agreeableness, and, as with happy people, least by openness to experience.

Conscientious people are well organized, careful, and thorough. They have clear goals and pursue them diligently. It follows that, in order to pursue your goals successfully, you can't worry too much about various barriers to success or get discouraged too easily when things don't go well. Thus, lower levels of neuroticism (not worrying too much) are helpful. It is interesting to note that Greta Thunberg appears more neurotic than most. She worries intensely about environmental disasters and climate change. However, she seems to leverage her anxiety to fuel her work. So long as one's neuroticism is not overwhelming, a meaningful life is possible.

In contrast, openness is difficult for those who have strong convictions. It's easy to become self-righteous about your causes. Mike Huckabee is unlikely to be open to immigration from Muslim countries because of his conviction that a small minority could be terrorists. Greta Thunberg is unlikely to be open to climate change deniers' opinions, as she is convinced that climate change is driven by human activities.

7. A Lesson from Personality Psychology

So, who is likely to lead a psychologically rich life? In terms of personality traits, people who are open to experience and extraverted are most likely to lead a psychologically rich life. They are more likely to do something new, meet someone new, or learn something new, like Goldmund in *Narcissus and Goldmund.* These relationships are not deterministic, however. There are plenty of introverts who lead a psychologically rich life. The type of intellectual journey that Alison Gopnik had is available to introverts who seek new intellectual knowledge. Likewise, Joy Ryan went to so many national parks with her grandson Brad. Led by someone like Brad, introverted people might do something unusual. It should be noted that conscientiousness, agreeableness, and emotional stability are secondarily predictors of a rich life. That means that you can set a goal to be open to new experiences and conscientiously work on that goal and lead a psychologically rich life. You can be agreeable to your friend's and partner's suggestions for a new adventure and expand your horizons. There really are numerous ways to lead a psychologically rich life.

Who is happy? Extraverts and emotionally stable people tend to lead a happy life perhaps in part because they tend to have good relationships and find something positive in most situations. Conscientious people tend to be happy as well, perhaps because they tend to achieve their goals, whereas agreeable people tend to be happy in part because they have warm, conflict-free relationships with others.

Finally, who leads a meaningful life? Conscientious and emotionally stable people tend to do so in part because they can devote themselves to a few causes for an extended period of time without worrying too much, and in the end make a difference in the world.

In short, openness to experiences represents the most striking difference between the personality correlates of a psychologically rich life and those of a happy and meaningful life. Whereas openness to experience plays a relatively minor role in happiness and meaning, it plays a major role in a psychologically rich life. Personality research on psychological richness reveals that there is a path to a good life via being open to new experiences. A lesson from personality psychology, then, is that it is important to know who you are (you can take a Big Five personality test on my website!). It is also important to know which personality traits are associated with each dimension of a good life. Harness this understanding of our personality and the personality traits associated with psychological richness, happiness, and meaning to develop strategies for achieving the good life. The following chapters give some tips for how we all can incorporate a bit of psychological richness into our everyday lives. Even if you are neurotic, disagreeable, unconscientious, introverted, and closed to new experiences, personality can change with effort. Don't give up. Keep on reading!

CHAPTER SEVEN

PLAYFULNESS

All work and no play makes Jack a dull boy.

—*The Shining* by Stanley Kubrick

1. Serious Business

At the core of a psychologically rich personality are openness to experience and extraversion. One might ask, though: How can those of us who don't have those basic personality traits become more open and extraverted? One answer is to embrace playfulness. In a 1980 study, when Robert McCrae and Paul Costa asked 240 men to complete various sentences such as, "What gets me into trouble is . . ." and "When his wife asked him to do the housework . . . ," open-minded men's responses were far more playful than closed-minded men's responses. For instance, a man high in openness to experience said, "When my wife asked me to do the housework, I invented an urgent excuse." A closed-minded man would have responded, "When my wife asked me to do the housework, I reluctantly did." McCrae and Costa observed, "The final distinguishing characteristic of open men is a playful, sometimes odd, sense of humor. A slight twist may be given to meanings, and obviously playful objections to the test are frequently made." So, playfulness, quirkiness, and lightheartedness may be central to both openness and psychological richness.

But what exactly is being playful? The psychoanalyst Erik Erikson described it best: when you are playful, you are "on vacation from social and economic reality." All of us adults have a lot of social and economic responsibilities. That is the reality. But Erikson encourages us to go somewhere between fantasy and actuality once in a while. Free yourself from duties and responsibilities. Play basketball and imitate Steph Curry. Watch a movie and pretend to be like Roger Ebert. Watch the evening news and impersonate the president. Sing along with Beyoncé.

The importance of playfulness is most noticeable during events when there is a lot at stake. For instance, the Olympics. Michael Phelps won thirteen Olympic gold medals in individual events and is widely considered one of the best swimmers of all time. He was already training at eight years old and breaking all kinds of age group records. Phelps continued to train hard under coach Bob Bowman from age eleven on. His older sister Hilary was an Olympic-level swimmer as well. He grew up soaked in the world of competitive swimming. Phelps swam about six hours a day for six days a week. He also lifted weights and stretched. Michael Phelps is supremely talented and full of grit.

Simone Biles is another extraordinary athlete. She won gold medals in the all-around, vault, and floor events at 2016 Rio Olympics. Overall, she has won more Olympic medals than any other American gymnast. Like Phelps, Biles started training seriously at age eight. She has enormous talent. Simone was home-schooled so that she could train twenty to thirty-two hours per week. She demonstrated unparalleled devotion to gymnastics.

In addition to grueling training, very small details are crucial in both swimming and gymnastics. In swimming, a win or loss is literally a matter of a split second. In gymnastics, any fall or the slightest loss of balance could ruin your performance. In other words, they are extremely high-pressure sports. A tiny mistake could cost you a medal. Moreover, the Olympic Games take place every four years, so the preparation period is extremely long. A moment can rob you of your dream and a decade of dedication. Despite achieving spectacular success, both Michael Phelps and Simone Biles suffered from anxiety and depression. They lost interest in the sports in which they excelled. Single-minded dedication is surely admirable, even virtuous. But, too much single-mindedness could rob you of the simple joy of just being able to jump, run, or swim.

In the world of elite athletes, practice, practice, and more practice is the name of the game. There is not much space for playfulness. Yet play and playfulness are critical for healthy child development. Alison Gopnik argues that humans have an extraordinarily long childhood, during which they can try out many things before they are forced to specialize in one area as adults. This prolonged period of exploration is a time of play, which is crucial for learning social norms and diverse skills in informal settings.

A recent study examined whether higher performance would be achieved through single-minded dedication to one main sport or playing multiple sports before specializing in one sport. This study meta-analyzed fifty-five studies that included 6,096 athletes, including 772 of the world's top performers (defined as top ten performers in an international competition such as the Olympics, World Athletics Championships, or Pan American Games), 3,028 national class performers (members of a national selection team or squad, or placed in the top ten at national championships), 1,706 regional class athletes (minor-league baseball, NCAA Division I), and 590 local or county-level athletes.

The researchers found that elite athletes who played multiple sports until later in life were less likely to burn out and more likely to succeed in national and international competitions in adulthood than elite athletes who started specializing early in their career. For every Michael Phelps and Simone Biles, there are athletes like Michael Jordan and Alex Morgan. Michael Jordan played baseball and football as well as basketball in high school. While he was mourning his father, he took a sabbatical from basketball for two years in his prime and played baseball. Alex Morgan grew up playing multiple sports and didn't play in a club team until age fourteen. She played volleyball and ran track as well as played soccer in high school.

Another key finding from this study is that the success rate at the junior competition level is predicted by the earlier start age (the earlier, the more success), whereas the success rate at the adult competition level is predicted by the later start age. That is, in adult elite competition, the athletes who started the sport later in their lives were more successful than those who started early. Relatedly, world-class athletes reached a major milestone (e.g., first participation in a national championship, first nomination for a selection team/squad) significantly later than did their national-class counterparts.

In the short term, specialization translates to success. In the long term, however, it doesn't always pay off. Indeed, this study found that a higher amount of youth-led play (e.g., pickup games) outside of an athlete's primary sport was associated with higher performance among adult players. Surprisingly, a high number of main-sport practice hours was associated with *lower* performance among the world-class adult athletes. These findings, combined with the findings on youth-led play in other sports, suggest that if you are an elite athlete, it is better to increase playful engagement in other sports and reduce coach-led practice time for your main sport.

Intriguingly, the early specialization effect was replicated in a completely different professional domain: science. Another study compared forty-eight German Nobel laureates in physics, chemistry, economics, and medicine/physiology with the winners of the Leibniz Prize, which is Germany's highest national science award. Forty-two of the forty-eight Nobel laureates had engaged in multidisciplinary study or work experiences, suggesting a later specialization. The Leibniz Prize winners who did not win the Nobel Prize had earlier success than those who went on to be Nobel winners. For instance, Leibniz winners were more likely to have won a scholarship as students than Nobel laureates. My favorite finding: it took significantly longer for the eventual Nobel winners to earn full professorships than the Leibniz winners. So, Nobel laureates explored more diverse areas of study and made slower progress than Leibniz winners, but eventually reached the top without burning out.

In the essay "Human, All Too Human" in his work *Ecce Homo,* Friedrich Nietzsche wrote about German specialization as follows: "I have discovered that a large number of young men experience the same distress: one antinatural step virtually compels the second. In Germany, the *Reich*—to speak unambiguously— all too many are condemned to choose vocations too early, and then to waste away under a burden they can no longer shake off. These people require Wagner as an *opium:* they forget themselves, they are rid of themselves for a moment—what am I saying? For *five or six hours!*"

The story of William James Sidis presents another cautionary tale. He is often considered the smartest man to have ever lived. At age eight, he passed the Harvard Medical School's anatomy exam, as well as the entrance exam to MIT. When Sidis was eleven years old, he gave a lecture on astrophysics at Harvard. An MIT physics professor in attendance remarked that Sidis would be a great astronomical mathematician and a scientific leader. But the professor's prediction was wrong. Sidis burned out. Early specialization might dispel interest in other activities in life and could lead to early burnout. The high prevalence of burnout and depression among elite athletes and academics makes me wonder if a singular grit needs to be paired with playfulness.

2. Jokers

The Major League Baseball season is long and grueling, consisting of 33 spring training games, 162 regular season games, and up to 22 postseason games—a total of 217 games! This schedule is especially demanding for Shohei Ohtani of the Dodgers, as he hits in most games and pitches at least once a week. He has grit and confidence. But he also has playfulness.

Ohtani had a terrible start to the 2022 season as a hitter, going 3 for 24 (.125). A stat like this might make a baseball player feel depressed. But during one game, after he failed to get a hit again and was making his way back to the dugout, Ohtani jokingly gave his bat CPR. His sense of humor in the face of difficulty appears to help Ohtani relax and perform at an elite level consistently. As MLB becomes increasingly dominated by data analytics, the game is becoming more and more logical; it is turning into more of a chess game than a "national pastime." Lightheartedness punctures the monotony and puts fun back into work.

Shaquille O'Neal is another elite athlete who was feared as well as loved as a player. Unlike his teammate Kobe Bryant, who was known for his grueling work ethic, Shaq was known for not working as hard. In an interview with Patrick Bet-David, Shaq said, "Kobe was a beast, nobody works harder than him. . . . See, Kobe was just getting married and getting into his family, I'm already four kids in. So after I put my two to three hours of work, now I have to be Daddy, now I have to be husband, now I have to take care of business." In many ways, Shaq was more relaxed, lighthearted, and whimsical. He continued in the interview, "I think you can find success in many ways." Shohei and Shaq are both plenty successful. Ohtani was the American League Rookie of the Year in 2018 and the MVP in 2021 and 2023. Shaq was the Rookie of the Year in 1993 and the MVP in 2000, and won four NBA championships. If Shaq had Kobe's work ethic, Shaq might have accomplished even more as a basketball player. But he also might have burned out early in his career. Work ethic is well known to be critical to rising in professional sports and competitive professions. Even so, playfulness might be an underrated contributor to long-term success.

3. Be Playful

Is there any empirical evidence that suggests playfulness is actually good? Swiss psychologist René Proyer has studied adult playfulness more intensely than anyone I know. He found that playfulness is a blend of openness to experience and extraversion, and a relative lack of conscientiousness and neuroticism. It is "an openness to being a fool, which is a combination of not worrying about competence, not being self-important, not taking norms as sacred and finding ambiguity and double edges a source of wisdom and delight." Overall, playful people do not take themselves too seriously, and they seem to know when to take it easy and when to be serious.

In a 2013 paper, Proyer found that playful people are slightly more satisfied with their lives than those who are less playful. He also discovered that happy people enjoyed communing with nature, whereas playful people did not. In contrast, happy people did not particularly enjoy going on vacation, whereas playful people did. A recent study randomly assigned some participants to count the playful things they did every day for one week, whereas others did not receive the instructions to count. Those who tracked their playful experiences reported more life satisfaction and less depression than those in the control group, not only right after the intervention was over but also up to three months later. The authors did not measure meaning or psychological richness, but I suspect that the playfulness intervention would be particularly effective at enhancing psychological richness, as playfulness is likely to bring novel, interesting experiences to one's life.

4. Spontaneity!

Like playfulness, spontaneity can enrich our lives. One of the reasons why sitcoms like *Friends* and *Seinfeld* remain so popular is that they portray a fantasy world where you can pop in and out of a friend's apartment anytime you want, no appointment necessary, and do something unplanned every day. If you aren't naturally spontaneous, making friends like Samantha in *Sex and the City* can bring playfulness and spontaneity to your life.

Here comes a hard question: When was the last time you went out with someone spontaneously? I still go on some spontaneous outings with my wife when we can, but I haven't done anything like that with my friends for years. In graduate school, when most of my friends were at school, I would stop by a lab mate's office and we would go across the street to Espresso Royale for a cup of coffee. Almost every day, I had coffee with someone. Almost every day, I ate lunch with someone unplanned.

When I got a faculty position at the University of Minnesota, I hoped to do the same and dropped by a nearby assistant professor's office. I knocked on the door and said, "Hi, Bob, do you want to grab coffee?" He said, "Nope. I can't. I don't have time right now." Then he searched his pocket and took out a PDA (this was September 2000), looked at his schedule carefully, and said, "What about in two weeks?" I was stunned. This was what it meant to be a professor as opposed to a graduate student, I thought. Professors are not just busy but highly protective of their time. A senior professor later advised me to be stingy with my time. Otherwise, I wouldn't be productive.

We live in a highly scheduled time. Our calendars are packed, leaving few opportunities for spontaneous activities. The pandemic-era shift to remote work has further limited spontaneous interaction. Pamela Hinds, a professor at Stanford Business School specializing in work teams, collaboration, and innovation, wondered if work teams consisting of people at multiple sites collaborate and innovate at the same rate as work teams where everyone is at a single site. Hinds partnered with Mark Mortensen to survey forty-nine teams in the research and development division of a single multinational corporation. The results showed that geographically distributed teams had far less spontaneous communication, less shared identity, and far more task conflict than those in geographically concentrated teams. Hinds and Mortensen concluded that "spontaneous communication contributes to a shared identity, facilitates the creation of shared context, and aids distributed teams in identifying and resolving conflicts before they escalate." With work meetings increasingly held via Zoom and other online formats, it is getting harder and harder to initiate spontaneous interactions with others.

5. Why It's So Hard to Make Friends Over Thirty

Spontaneity poses another challenge when we try to make new friends in adulthood. What is the difference between college friends and post-college friends? College friends are the friends you lived in close proximity to, maybe even in the same dorm room, and with whom you had repeated and unplanned interactions. Your post-college friends might be coworkers or the parents of your children's friends. How close have you become with them? I would be surprised if you were able to make new friends as close as your best friends from college.

In the essay "Why Is It Hard to Make Friends Over 30?" *New York Times* reporter Alex Williams concludes, "No matter how many friends you make, a sense of fatalism can creep in: the period for making B.F.F.'s, the way you did in your teens or early 20s, is pretty much over. It's time to resign yourself to situational friends: K.O.F.'s (kind of friends)—for now." At work, you might get close to someone from being on the same project. But, unless you are on the same project with this person again, it's hard to stay in touch. In the essay, Williams writes about a writer on the NBC series *Up All Night* who became really close with another woman on her team: "But as soon as the pilot was over, it was hard to be as close without that constant day-to-day interaction; there aren't those long afternoons which bleed into evenings hanging out at the beach and then heading to a bar." If you have a partner, then your partner must like any new friends, too, which makes it even harder. When you add a child or two into the equation, making friends later in life can feel nearly impossible. In other words, after college it is really challenging to find someone who lives close by, with whom you can meet up every day and have spontaneous outings.

Of course, we could act spontaneously by ourselves. The philosopher Jason D'Cruz has written about planned vs. unplanned actions using the term "volatile reason." He considers a hypothetical person named Moritz as an example. In this scenario, Moritz has a ticket for a train ride from Berlin to Dresden to meet his friends. His friends are preparing a dinner, and Moritz has tickets to a concert for him and his friends that evening; in other words, he has a plan and responsibilities. On the train, however, he sees the train schedule and realizes that he could go on to the unknown city of Zittau if he stays on past Dresden. When the train arrives at Dresden, he spontaneously decides to stay on and visit Zittau, reasoning that he could just call his friends to cancel their plans and apologize. Right after the train leaves Dresden, Moritz feels an overwhelming euphoria and a powerful sensation of freedom. D'Cruz argues that this was not a well-premeditated deliberate action, but nonetheless this spontaneous action served to fulfill Moritz's deep desire to lead an interesting life. Spontaneity over responsibility. We can and should be like Moritz once in a while.

6. Why Do We Need Playfulness?

Most of us strive to become better at what we do for a living. As a researcher, I try to stay up to date on the latest literature, statistics, data visualization, and so forth. This is all serious business. It requires careful attention, time commitment, and dedication. With this level of focus, it's easy for a lot of time to pass without fun or laughter. That might be one of the reasons why so many of the world's best athletes, such as Michael Phelps, Simone Biles, and Naomi Osaka, have suffered from burnout. They have talent, determination, and a ton of grit. Nevertheless, at some point the sports they loved became their jobs and livelihoods, sucking the fun out of the whole thing. There are, of course, other important factors that caused their mental health issues, such as his parents' divorce, in the case of Phelps, or sexual abuse, in the case of Biles. To be sure, it is not just seriousness and dedication that brought about their burnout and depression. However, the bottom line is that elite athletes' lives are tough. They must train hard. They must constantly compete and perform. Any rare, lackluster performance is recorded and broadcast. No wonder the sports they loved so much and they are so good at could lose their appeal.

To be clear, specialization and professionalism are great for skill acquisition and improvement. But remember the fate of Jack (played by Jack Nicholson) in Stanley Kubrick's movie *The Shining*: all work and no play not only make Jack a dull boy, but also make him go nuts at the end. When winning becomes everything, life gets too heavy. A playful mindset can help people who are psychologically stuck move past their low points and enjoy the journey, not just the outcome. A spontaneous action could help us experience life without prior planning. Some of the most interesting experiences we have are often things we do on a whim. In my case, I was driving my family from Baltimore to Charlottesville one day when I saw a sign for Annapolis. I asked my wife and two kids, "Does anyone want to go to Annapolis?" To my surprise, everyone said, "Why not!" So we went to Annapolis, totally unplanned. We wandered around town and hopped on a cruise that my son still talks about.

In sum, personality traits alone do not determine our capacity for psychological richness: we can all learn to foster psychological richness through playfulness and spontaneity. On this front, a psychologically rich life again stands in contrast to lives oriented around happiness and meaning, which prioritize more serious activities. In order to achieve meaning in life, you must dedicate yourself to an important cause, spending time on often difficult tasks for others' benefit. Happiness is also serious. Psychologists report that being gritty, kind, sociable, and mindful can help you achieve happiness. These are all admirable goals, but being gritty or mindful requires sustained attention and is not always easy. Such endeavors are not for everyone, nor for every day. Like Shaq, there are individuals who prefer playfulness over mindfulness and mischievousness over seriousness. Grit can clearly help a person achieve their goals, but being single-minded *can* suck the fun and richness out of life. Simone Biles withdrew from the Tokyo Olympic Games. Fear and anxiety overwhelmed her. But, after taking some time off, she came back strong and rejuvenated.

As an antidote to too much seriousness, we need playfulness and spontaneity. Hobby over duty. Entertainment over commitment. Relaxation over dedication. Try to be playful at work or at home at least once a day. Try to make your partner, friend, or coworker laugh. Take a detour on your way home. Jump in a puddle. Go for a swim. Get wet; get dirty. Be like a little kid once in a while. When you do something spontaneous, you'll make life rich and memorable.

CHAPTER EIGHT

THE BEAUTY OF DIY

The greatest improvement in the productive powers of labour, and the greater part of the skill, dexterity, and judgment with which it is anywhere directed, or applied, seem to have been the effects of the division of labour.

—Adam Smith, *The Wealth of Nations*

1. Why Productivity Is a Main Concern

So far, I have talked about the factors that facilitate a psychologically rich life such as the mindset of playfulness and the attitude of *expeditus* ("ready to march"). Closely related to the potential harm of early specialization discussed in the previous chapter, I will now talk about another force that could suck psychological richness out of your life, the obsession with productivity, and the counterforce that could fill your life with psychological richness: Do-It-Yourself.

Many of us start the day by looking at our to-do list while fueling ourselves with caffeine. "America Runs on Dunkin'" has become such a successful advertisement campaign in part because it positioned Dunkin' Donuts as a company that helps you get going. We live in a culture that idolizes individuals who are prolific, well organized, and get things done. Productivity gain is great, but at what cost? What might be the unintended psychological consequences of our obsession with efficiency?

I like Adam Smith's *The Wealth of Nations* a lot. The copy I bought has a lovely introduction by the brilliant economist Alan Krueger, in which he says something along the lines of this: economics students are lucky because the foundational book on modern economics was written by a great storyteller. I totally agree. *The Wealth of Nations* was a surprisingly fascinating read. If I had read it before William James's *Principles of Psychology,* I might have chosen economics over psychology. I even named the first book I wrote in English *The Psychological Wealth of Nations.*

Just like any good book, *The Wealth of Nations* starts with a marvelous observation. Imagine a pin factory. If one worker did all the operations necessary to produce a single pin, this worker could produce maybe one pin a day. This means that ten workers, working independently, would produce only ten pins a day. But what if these ten workers each specialized in one or two operations? For example, one person draws out the wire, another straightens it, another cuts it, another sharpens its top, and so forth. Adam Smith estimated that, this way, these ten workers could produce 48,000 pins a day, or 4,800 per worker. Thus, a very simple division of labor would increase productivity by 4,800 times! No wonder modernization is often equated with specialization and the division of labor.

The Wealth of Nations was published in 1776, the year the U.S. declared independence. At that time, the U.S. was largely an agricultural society without any factories. In 1908, Henry Ford started producing the popular Model T. At first, his factory was able to produce only a few models a day. However, after Ford introduced the assembly line—a far more efficient division of labor—in 1913, his factory was eventually able to produce over 10,000 per day. Now, well over one hundred years after this invention, you might think we've reached maximum productivity. After all, how much smaller can we make each operation? Yet companies like Amazon and Target are constantly looking for more ways to improve efficiency, from staffing changes to real-time inventory.

2. When We Did Everything by Ourselves

In the past, the division of labor was mostly limited to workplaces such as factories, farms, and restaurants. At home, most people were cooking, cleaning, and doing laundry by themselves until the 1990s, even as microwaves, laundry machines, and dishwashers made house chores easier and less time-consuming. Over the last two decades, however, economizing habits have thoroughly penetrated our life, resulting in further division of labor. Outsourcing is no longer a term reserved only for multinational corporations or the rich. Many middle-class households outsource home cleaning, lawn care, and even grocery shopping. Busy professionals use AIs for scheduling, planning, and even financial investments.

In academia, big team science is taking over traditional small lab science, requiring a great degree of division of labor. In big team social psychology, someone has to prepare experimental materials, someone else has to run the study, someone else has to clean up the data, someone else has to analyze it, someone else has to interpret it, and so on. Each team member does their part; then the team quickly assembles all the parts and moves on to the next paper. In so doing, they produce dozens of papers every year.

Jerome Kagan, the late Harvard psychologist, lamented this trend, saying that "the typical scientist during my graduate years went to the basement of the university building, with the help of a graduate student, writing and rewriting a paper reporting an interesting result . . . two minds and four hands, often with no outside funds, performed all the work. Under these conditions the pride savored if the experiment were successful, or the blend of frustration and sadness if not, was restricted to a pair of agents. These emotions are seriously diluted when hundreds of experts design experiments to be executed by teams."

3. The Division of Labor and Alienation

To be clear, Kagan was not complaining about the productivity of team scientists. Instead, he was lamenting the psychological and experiential aspects of doing science today. Karl Marx famously speculated about various negative consequences of the division of labor. For instance, he worried that the division of labor would make humans one-dimensional: "Division of labour seizes upon, not only the economic, but every other sphere of society, and everywhere lays the foundation of that all engrossing system of specializing and sorting men, that development in a man of one single faculty at the expense of all other faculties." Marx was further concerned that the division of labor would make laborers simpletons: "It increases the social productive power of labor, not only for the benefit of the capitalist instead of for that of the labourer, but it does this by crippling the individual labourers." Marx argued that the division of labor "mortifies the body and ruins the mind."

In his presidential address to the American Sociological Association in 1985, Kai Erikson discussed how Marx's theory of alienation is still relevant in the modern workplace. Specifically, he argued that the key sources of alienation boil down to "those structures in the modern workplace that subdivide labor into narrower and narrower specialties, and, second, those structures in the modern workplace that limit the amount of control workers exercise over the work they do." Clerical workers are subject to quotas, routines, and constant monitoring by their managers. Erikson encouraged us to think of the modern-day division of labor as a potential agent of "human indifference, brutality, exhaustion, cruelty, [and] numbness."

Sociologist Melvin Kohn found some evidence in support of Marx's speculations. For instance, he looked at survey data from 3,101 Americans employed in civilian occupations. He measured three dimensions of labor: closeness of supervision, routinization of work, and substantive complexity of work, as well as four specific aspects of alienation: powerlessness, self-estrangement, normlessness, and cultural estrangement. Respondents with close supervision, routinized work, and lack of work complexity were more likely to report feeling that they did not have any control over their lives and felt powerless, that they felt aimless and estranged from what most others valued in their lives, and that they didn't care what was right or wrong.

4. Specialization and Its Discontents: Take 1

Kagan's idea of "diluted emotion" is not exactly the same as Marx's idea of alienation; Marx's alienation is much darker. Also, being part of a big team and performing a specialized task such as data analysis is perhaps not as alienating as working in a factory assembly line. It can be fun to be part of something larger than yourself. After reading Kohn's study, I was curious about the psychological consequences of the division of labor, specifically its effects on happiness, meaning, and psychological richness. Does the division of labor take away a full range of emotional experiences in favor of machinelike efficiency? Does specialization reduce psychological richness and increase boredom? Or is everything fine if you just do your job?

To answer these questions, my graduate student Youngjae Cha and I designed an online assembly task. Participants were invited to a designated Zoom link at a prescheduled time, where they were greeted by our research assistant. Each experimental session had three participants, who were told that they would be assembling motorcycles as a team online. They first spent some time coming up with the name of their team as a team-building activity. Then they were told that they had been assigned to either one aspect of the assembly (the division of labor condition) or the whole production by themselves (everyone assembled all parts of a motorcycle; once they finished assembling one motorcycle, they moved on to another one). This assignment was done at the team level. So, one session was the division of labor condition and the next was the whole production condition. We encouraged participants to produce as many motorcycles as possible. At the end of the experiment, we asked them how happy they felt, how meaningful they thought the task was, and how psychologically rich they felt. In terms of productivity, participants in the division of labor condition did far better than those in the whole production condition. When every member completed the whole production by themselves, they were able to assemble only five motorcycles on average. For a three-person team, this meant an average of fifteen motorcycles. In contrast, the division of labor team produced, on average, sixty motorcycles within the same amount of time. The division of labor increased production by four times!

But did the division of labor come at any psychological cost? In terms of happiness, no. Participants in both conditions reported similar levels of enjoyment and happiness. In terms of meaning, there was no cost either. Participants in both conditions reported similar levels of meaningfulness when asked about the task. However, the participants in the division of labor condition reported significantly lower levels of psychological richness than those in the whole production condition. That is, the division of labor made the task more boring, monotonous, and less interesting. Assembling a whole motorcycle by yourself was not efficient. Indeed, it was quite the opposite. Even so, it was a far more interesting experience.

5. Specialization and Its Discontents: Take 2

Imagine working at a consulting firm and being placed on a big collaborative project with many others. Within this team, imagine specializing in one area and repeating similar tasks every day. What would it be like to have a job like this?

Now imagine working in a consulting firm where you work independently. You are assigned to a big project that demands various tasks. Working independently, you have to be a generalist, doing many different tasks by yourself. What would it be like to have a job like this?

In a study to test this, we asked half of a sample of UVA students to imagine the first scenario, and the other half to imagine the second scenario. To our surprise, the students expected that they would be happier in the specialized job on a collaborative project than in the generalist job on an independent project. They predicted similar levels of meaning. But most importantly, the students thought that their life would be psychologically richer in the generalist job than in the specialist job. In this manner, we replicated the results from the online assembly experiment: like those in the division of labor condition, participants in the specialized job thought their job would be less interesting than those in the generalist job.

Of course, participants' predictions about an imagined life are not always correct. To account for this, we ran another experiment, this time measuring behavioral curiosity. We kept the experimental setup for this study the same as for the consulting scenario experiment. However, instead of asking them how they would feel when thinking about their lives working in a consulting firm, we asked participants to complete a trivia task. This task involved questions like: Who was the only U.S. president to also hold a patent for an invention? In this task, after a question was presented, there were two response options: a wait button and a skip button. If participants hit the skip button, then the answer was not shown and they moved on to the next question. If they hit the wait button, they had to wait for a certain amount of time (the precise time was randomized between ten and fifteen seconds) to get an answer (e.g., Abraham Lincoln). Typically, curious people wanted to know the answer, so they were willing to wait. Our experiment consisted of fifteen questions. The more answers someone waited for, the more curious they were.

Participants imagining they were generalists proved behaviorally more curious and more willing to wait for answers than those who were imagining a specialist job, conceptually replicating the psychological richness findings. In other words, when you are assigned to be a specialist, you lose interest in other seemingly irrelevant matters. When you are assigned to be a generalist, you are more curious about other things.

But why? Well, when you specialize in something, you are selectively attending to what is relevant to your specialty and trying to ignore irrelevant information. If you are a healthcare consultant, for instance, you need to learn so much about the healthcare business that you might need to ignore information unrelated to that industry. Specialization gives you deep knowledge in certain topics and marketable skills. But unintentionally, specialization leaves you uninterested in other areas of life. It's like going to the Louvre, being so focused on the *Mona Lisa* that you forget to look to your right, left, and back and miss all the other masterpieces!

6. What About Outsourcing?

Outsourcing is a modern way to live more efficiently. Professionals do jobs such as mowing the lawn and cleaning the gutters much better and more quickly than individuals can. The primary goal of outsourcing in this context is to gain time. For instance, you pay $200 for a person to clean your house. You save a few hours of free time, which presumably translates into more happiness. Ashley Whillans and colleagues found that, across 4,469 respondents, those who spent some money every month to save free time were happier than those who didn't. This was in part explained by time stress measured by prompts such as, "I feel pressed for time today." That is, those who spent money on time-saving services were less stressed about time, and the less stressed about time someone is, the more satisfied they are with their lives overall.

Whillans and colleagues then conducted an experiment to test the causal role of time-saving spending. They gave participants $80 and told them to spend $40 on a time-saving service one weekend and spend the other $40 on a material purchase another weekend. Participants were contacted on the days they spent $40. Participants reported more positive emotions and less negative emotions after the time-saving spending than after the material purchase. Again, participants felt less time pressure after the time-saving service, and the less time pressure they felt, the more happiness they reported.

Unlike division of labor, outsourcing does not involve repetitive tasks and inhumane working conditions (at least not for the person paying). It is all about freeing up time. To the extent that you are paying someone to do the tasks you don't want to do and as a result gaining free time, it should increase your happiness. But does outsourcing detract from psychological richness, just as specialization and division of labor do? We have not empirically tested this, but there is a possibility that outsourcing could reduce psychological richness.

A while ago, my wife and I were thinking about converting our unkempt side yard to a brick patio. After getting a few estimates, the lowest price we found was $9,000. We checked the material cost, which was about $4,000. We thought to ourselves, couldn't we do all the digging and labor ourselves if it meant saving at least $5,000? We watched a couple of YouTube videos, and it seemed doable. Being cheap, we decided to do it ourselves. The rest is your typical DIY story. It was a lot more work than we had ever anticipated. Digging nine inches of a sloped, tree-root-filled, rock-hard clay-soil twenty-by-twenty-four-foot yard was hard. Tamping down the ground to create a firm and level base for bricks was taxing. Our house sat on the top of a hill and our worksite was on the opposite side of the driveway, making transporting three hundred bags of gravel and sand with a wheelbarrow an insanely difficult task. Not to mention carrying 2,000 bricks—it was literally backbreaking. There were many mornings when I was unable to get up because of the back pain. We questioned our decision many times. We blamed each other many times. We regretted not hiring someone else to do it instead. It took us almost three months to complete. In the end, the result was pretty good, but clearly not as good as what $9,000 would have accomplished in three to four days! Given how many hours we spent on the project, we weren't sure if we'd saved much money in the end, either.

And yet, years later, we still talk about memories from our patio project. While digging one day, I saw a snake and screamed! I have a phobia of snakes, so I jumped, though it was just a garden snake in hibernation. Before our project, I had never laid bricks. In general, I am not very handy, so my self-esteem when it comes to handiness is pretty low. But through our endeavors, I discovered that I'm not half bad at brick edging—a new discovery about myself. If we had hired someone to do everything for us, would I still be talking about it? Probably not, because I wouldn't have discovered the snake in hibernation, nor my unknown brick-edging skills. Yes, our patio project produced a lot of stress, physical pain, and unhappiness during those three months. Outsourcing would have increased happiness in the short run. In the long run, however, we now have far more stories that we can tell our friends, as well as the undiluted raw emotion of pride, a sense of accomplishment, and memories of agony and pain.

Outsourcing routine cleaning would have no opportunity cost in terms of psychological richness. After all, cleaning your house by yourself might not generate many interesting stories. So what's the point, other than saving some money? In contrast, outsourcing a project like building a brick patio might be a mistake because it could have some opportunity cost for psychological richness. Hiring someone to do the job might inadvertently rob you of an opportunity to have an interesting experience that could add richness to your life story.

7. Set Yourself Free from the Productivity Trap!

To foster psychological richness in our lives, we must lean into the unfamiliar, the risky, and the challenging. Assembling a whole motorcycle is a lot more difficult and time-consuming than assembling a part of it. Building a brick patio is much harder than hiring someone to do it. Being a generalist requires broader perspectives than being a specialist. Familiarity generates reliable happiness, but it doesn't generate much richness. In contrast, while a challenging project can produce a lot of negative emotions in the short run, it can also add psychological richness in the long run. Before hiring someone else to do a job, ask yourself: Could I do it myself? Would I have an interesting story to tell if I did? Is efficiency everything? Escape the productivity trap once in a while. Think of a *slower* way to do the same thing—bake your own bread; hand-grind your own coffee beans . . . do it yourself, and add some spice to your life.

CHAPTER NINE

DO AESTHETIC EXPERIENCES COUNT?

I was always going to the bookcase for another sip of the divine specific.

—Virginia Woolf, *The Waves*

1. How to Live 4,000 Lives

Most psychologically rich experiences I have discussed so far are firsthand, direct experiences, like study abroad and building a patio. Can aesthetic experiences such as reading novels produce the same kind of psychological richness?

Mohammed Aziz would certainly say yes. Aziz is a seventy-two-year-old bookseller in Rabat Medina, Morocco. He was orphaned at age six. He became a fisherman to try to make a living and achieve his dream of graduating high school. However, at age fifteen, the high cost of textbooks forced him to drop out. He channeled this frustration into a career selling books, starting out with only a rug and nine books set up in the shade under a tree. Now he owns a bookstore and spends six to eight hours a day reading. In an interview, he said, "My life revolves around reading. . . . I've read more than 4,000 books, so I've lived more than 4,000 lives." Aziz works twelve hours a day and rarely takes vacations. All the same, he has accumulated a wealth of psychologically rich experiences by living 4,000 lives through 4,000 books.

In *Swann's Way*, the opening volume of his masterpiece *In Search of Lost Time*, Marcel Proust reflects upon his own reading experiences: "These afternoons were crammed with more dramatic events than occur, often, in a whole lifetime. These were the events taking place in the book I was reading." He went on to describe the magic novelists wield, remarking how "for the space of an hour he [the novelist] sets free within us all the joys and sorrows in the world, a few of which only we should have to spend years of our actual life in getting to know, and the most intense of which would never be revealed to us." So, yes, it is possible to lead a psychologically rich life via books.

To me, Kazuo Ishiguro's *The Remains of the Day* is not just an engrossing novel about Mr. Stevens, a British butler who works for the nobleman Lord Darlington until the end of World War II; it is also about moral dilemmas and the meaning of life. In the novel, Mr. Stevens (played by Anthony Hopkins in the film version) served Lord Darlington as best as he could. At the peak of his career, he managed a staff of twenty-eight as Lord Darlington hosted many important meetings during World War II. His greatest pride was his professionalism and ability to carefully plan and perfectly execute all his duties around the house. After the war, however, Darlington Hall, which had been kept in the Darlington family for many generations, was eventually sold to an American businessman, Mr. Farraday, and Mr. Stevens was reduced to managing a staff of only four. For the first time in his professional life, Mr. Stevens is given a real vacation, and he decides to take a trip to western England. For the first time, he has time to reflect upon his life up to that point and his time serving Lord Darlington.

Mr. Stevens dedicated his whole life to Lord Darlington and Darlington Hall. He had a purpose in life. He had meaning in life—that is, until the war ended and Lord Darlington turned out to be a Nazi sympathizer and a naive, amateur diplomat whose actions ultimately harmed England. Did this render Mr. Stevens's life a complete waste, or was his dedication worth something on its own? At the end of the novel, Mr. Stevens states: "Lord Darlington wasn't a bad man. He wasn't a bad man at all. . . . His lordship was a courageous man. He chose a certain path in life, it proved to be a misguided one, but there, he chose it, he can say that at least. As for myself, I cannot even claim that. You see, I *trusted*. I trusted in his lordship's wisdom. All those years I served him, I trusted I was doing something worthwhile."

While reading this novel, I was mentally transported to Darlington Hall and the events of the 1930s and the early 1940s. For the first time, I wondered, could my dedication to something turn out to be completely misguided and harm humanity more than help? Being Japanese, I have always thought of imperial Japanese colonels and politicians as being pure evil, but I had never considered the morality of those who worked for them, who dedicated their lives to supporting them. *The Remains of the Day* challenged my views of some Japanese colonels during World War II and others in compromised situations: they might have been simply doing their jobs, (falsely) believing that they were serving for a greater good. This book certainly changed the way I view Japanese history. I might have been an evil colonel in their situations, a possibility that I had never entertained before. This was not a happy thought, but nevertheless made the reading experience deeper and richer.

2. Psychologically Rich Films

As the above example shows, it is possible to achieve psychological richness indirectly through books, movies, and art. But not all reading or watching experiences are rich. So what is the key to a psychologically rich aesthetic experience? First, while reading or watching, one gets so immersed in the narrative world described in the story that they don't notice minor changes in the physical world around them (e.g., someone entering the room): a complete melding of attention, imagery, and feeling that psychologists call "transportation." They have to be transported to the narrative world and experience the events in the story as if they were in them themselves. Second, just as in a physical experience, not every immersive experience is psychologically rich. It also has to be memorable. There have been many times when I watched a movie over the weekend, only to forget the plot after just a few days. In order for the reading or watching experience to be rich, it has to remain vivid in one's memory. In other words, unless these experiences are retained in your mind, they are not enriching your life.

Just as material wealth requires the accumulation of money, psychological richness requires the accumulation of interesting experiences, directly or indirectly. Some sensation-seekers go all over the world only to find that these diverse experiences do not seem to add up to a satisfying life. They constantly need new experiences. They are like high-income individuals who spend all the money they earn. Just as high-income individuals need to save money in order to be materially rich, the psychologically rich need to remember and cherish their experiences. The memory is crucial.

Lastly, in order for reading and watching to be rich, it has to have some complexity and eventually change your perspective. The film *Home Alone* is highly immersive, fun, and even memorable. But it was not that psychologically rich, mainly because it did not have much complexity and did not change my perspective in life.

What psychologically rich films have you watched? For me, Akira Kurosawa's 1950 film *Rashomon* falls into this category of a rich aesthetic experience. The film revolves around a single event, the murder of a samurai, but the four main characters each provide completely different accounts of what happened. Each character leads the audience to believe that their version is the truth, but the next version goes on to contradict the previous one just as convincingly. Finally, just as the film seems to end on a depressing note about the cruelty of human nature and fallibility of human memory, a final event epitomizing human goodness emerges out of nowhere. During a time when I came to view the world as a terrible place, the film made me believe that the world is a hopeful place instead. I found *Rashomon* to be a deep, interesting, and psychologically rich film.

If you're too young for *Rashomon,* let's consider *The Matrix* (1999). The film is memorable in many ways: the iconic choice between the red pill and blue pill; the confusion between reality and virtual reality. Morpheus says, "The Matrix is everywhere. It is all around us. Even now, in this very room. You can see it when you look out your window. . . . It is the world that has been pulled over your eyes to blind you from the truth." "What truth?" Neo asks. Morpheus replies: "That you are a slave, Neo. Like everyone else you were born into bondage. Into a prison that you cannot taste or see or touch. A prison for your mind." Gradually, you start to notice what is really happening to all the characters.

If you're too young for *The Matrix,* what about *Parasite* (2019)? This movie is about two families: the poor Kims and the wealthy Parks, both of whom have a son and a daughter. Somehow, all four members of the Kim family start working for the Park family and discover the life of the rich. Contrary to stereotypes that cast the poor as hopeless and incompetent, the two Kim children are smart, stylish, and cunning. They lie to the Parks and claim to be an artist and elite college student in order to be hired as an art tutor and an English tutor, respectively. On the other hand, contrary to the stereotypes that portray the rich as savvy and calculating, the Parks are nice and naive. In a memorable scene, Mr. Kim describes Ms. Park, saying, "She's rich, but still nice." Ms. Kim replies, "Not 'rich, but still nice.' She's nice *because* she's rich. Hell, if I had all this money, I'd be nice, too!" The film gives us a new way of thinking about the rich and the poor, abilities and opportunities, fairness and morality.

3. So End the Chatter

In his *Critique of Judgment,* Immanuel Kant distinguished beautiful arts from pleasant arts. He described pleasant arts as "those that are directed merely to enjoyment. Of this class are all those charming arts that can gratify a company at table . . . to this class belong all games which bring with them no further interest than that of making the time pass imperceptibly." In contrast, "beautiful art is a mode of representation which is purposive for itself, and which, although devoid of [definite] purpose, yet furthers the culture of the mental powers in reference to social communication." Here, Kant defines an aesthetic experience as something greater than the enjoyment of mere sensation but rather the enjoyment of what he calls "reflective judgment," which involves some gap between sensation and reality and a new mental representation and understanding of an object.

When Sonny Rollins, the legendary jazz saxophonist, was asked about art and, more specifically, why art matters, his reply evoked Kantian aesthetic judgments: "Technology is no savior. We can eat, sleep, look at screens, make money—all aspects of our physical existence—but that doesn't mean anything. Art is the exact opposite. It's infinite, and without it, the world wouldn't exist as it does. It represents the immaterial soul: intuition, that which we feel in our hearts. Art matters today more than ever because it outlives the contentious political veneer that is cast over everything. . . . Art, in the same way, both inspires us to go out and find something new and highlights what we don't know."

In his essay "The Power of Art in a Political Age," David Brooks echoes Sonny Rollins's point. Brooks writes, "Like a lot of people, I spend too much of my time enmeshed in politics. . . . So I'm trying to take countermeasures. I flee to the arts." Art, he says, "prompts you to stop in your tracks, take a breath and open yourself up so that you can receive what it is offering, often with a kind of childlike awe and reverence . . . artworks widen your emotional repertoire. When you read a poem or see a piece of sculpture, you haven't learned a new fact, but you've had a new experience." We can open ourselves up to new experiences not just through reading novels and poems, but also by looking at art.

Rollins's and Brooks's takes on the arts remind me of Martin Heidegger's "Das Gerede" (endless chatter). In *Being and Time,* Heidegger argued that we live by "following the route of *gossiping* and *passing the word along,*" and that the endless chatter of everyday life obscures what is truly important. In the world of "Das Gerede," we understand everything without thinking deeply on our own. We are bombarded with "the constant possibility of distraction." Social media is endless chatter. Small talk is endless chatter. This chatter makes life feel uprooted, groundless, and floating. Between our to-do lists and endless distractions, we rarely have a moment to think deeply, or to convene with the sublime.

For me, arts and sports provide rare moments to escape the endless chatter of everyday life. Looking at Mark Rothko's *No. 13 (White, Red on Yellow)* and his other color field paintings is always a unique, visceral experience. The simple color and fuzzy lines are calming, absorbing, even moving, maybe because I know Rothko was depressed and ultimately took his own life. Or maybe it has nothing to do with this background knowledge. I've sat in front of *No. 13* in the Metropolitan Museum of Art many times. It draws me in and I forget about everything else. As Mark Rothko once said, "A painting is not about an experience. It is an experience."

4. Finally Some Data

In his 1971 book, *Aesthetics and Psychobiology,* Daniel Berlyne summarized a series of experiments on aesthetic judgments. His major finding was that there are different, optimal levels of complexity for pleasantness and interestingness. Simple geometric figures are typically perceived to be more pleasant than complex ones, whereas complex ones are typically perceived to be more interesting than simple ones.

In one experiment, Berlyne manipulated two factors of geometric figures: the first was symmetry (i.e., how symmetrical and homogeneous elements were), and the other was the number of elements (i.e., one to five elements vs. numerous elements). Some figures were simple and symmetrical, some were simple and asymmetrical, some were complex and symmetrical, and the others were complex and asymmetrical. Participants rated the simple and symmetrical figures to be the most pleasant, followed by complex and symmetrical, simple and asymmetrical, and complex and asymmetrical. Symmetry was key to pleasantness. Yet, Berlyne found that participants rated simple and symmetrical figures (rated most pleasing) to also be the least interesting. Complexity and asymmetry added interestingness, whereas they detracted from pleasantness.

More recently, Paul Silvia and Samuel Turner Jr. conducted an intriguing experiment on aesthetic judgments. Participants looked at thirteen classical paintings, six of which were calming, such as *Dance Foyer at the Opera* by Edgar Degas and *The Water Lily Pond* by Claude Monet. The other seven were disturbing, such as Francis Bacon's *Figure with Meat* (the pope in horror surrounded by two cow carcasses) and Francisco Goya's *Saturn Devouring His Son* (yes, a god eating human flesh). These paintings are quite shocking and grotesque, particularly in comparison to the famously serene, warm painting by Monet. After looking at each painting, participants reported how interesting or uninteresting, boring or engaging, enjoyable or unenjoyable, pleasing or displeasing, comprehensible or incomprehensible, familiar or unfamiliar each painting was. Results showed that pleasantness ratings were predicted by comprehensibleness, familiarity, and simpleness. In other words, the easier to understand and simpler the paintings were, the more pleasant they were. In contrast, interestingness ratings were predicted by disturbingness and unpleasantness. That is, the more disturbing and unpleasant they were, the more interesting the paintings were.

In another experiment, Silvia explored the role of comprehension. For instance, participants were asked to read Scott MacLeod's famously abstract poem *The Life of Haifisch*. Those who were not provided with any background information could not understand it and did not find it interesting. In contrast, the other participants who read the same poem but with more background information, such as its title and the explanation that *Haifisch* means "shark" in German, found it more comprehensible and far more interesting. There is an intricate line. For art to be appreciated, it must be at least minimally comprehensible.

While at the University of Virginia, I had the chance to work with two students, Erin Westgate and Nick Buttrick, with whom I read the existing literature on experimental aesthetics such as Paul Silvia's. We wondered if reading all kinds of books early on in life helped readers appreciate more complexity and lead an intellectually rich life. So we asked over 5,000 people about their reading habits during childhood, their current cognitive styles, and their perceived levels of psychological richness. We assumed that reading in general would be associated with a more flexible cognitive style and more psychological richness. Our findings were more intricate than we had anticipated.

First, as predicted, individuals who grew up reading a lot of literary fiction were indeed more attributionally complex (i.e., able to think of multiple reasons why someone might behave a certain way) and led a psychologically richer life as adults than those who did not. Second, unexpectedly, those who grew up reading a lot of romance novels were significantly *less* attributionally complex than those who did not. These readers seemed to "essentialize" to a greater degree than those who had read less romance. For instance, early romance readers tended to hold a more simplistic view of the world: Joe is a jerk, Jill is an angel, baseball is a bore, opera is for old people, and so on. In contrast, those who grew up reading a lot of literary fiction were less likely to essentialize and more likely to think that Joe could be a jerk to some but also sweet and generous to homeless people, for example. Third, these findings were replicated using other measures, such as the essentialism scale. The findings remained significant after statistically controlling for participants' age, gender, education, income, and political orientation—the link between reading a lot of literary fiction and cognitive complexity was there but not because those readers were more educated, older, or more politically liberal.

In the end, we found empirical support for Lionel Trilling's main thesis in his 1950 book *The Liberal Imagination:* "Literature is the human activity that takes the fullest and most precise account of variousness, possibilities, complexity, and difficulty." Our studies were correlational, so the causal role of reading literature needs to be tested in the future. Overall, reading literature is associated with more cognitive complexity and better perspective-taking skills (skills and abilities to see another person's behavior from that person's perspective rather than from an observer's perspective), and it appears to help us appreciate the ups and downs of our own lives.

I have repeatedly argued that a perspective change is a key to a psychologically rich experience, though so far I have not provided empirical evidence for this claim. In a series of experi-

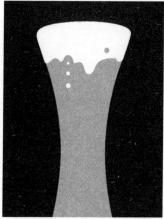

Figure 2. Noma Bar's *Hangover.* Copyright
permission obtained from Noma Bar

ments, Jordan Axt, Hyewon Choi, and I tested whether a figure
with multiple views, like a figure-ground drawing, would be
more visually rich than a figure with one view.

Look at Noma Bar's drawing of a skinny, tall glass filled with
beer (Figure 2, above). The foam on top is shaped so that, when
viewed a certain way, it looks like a face. In one experiment, we
showed this image on screen and asked participants a question:
"What do you see?" After they wrote their answer, they moved
on to another page with a new question: "Now, what else do you
see?" Most see a glass of beer first. But afterward, many see a
face—that is, an eye, nose, and mouth. Depending on your perspective, you see beer or a face.

Another group of participants saw an altered image of the beer
glass (Figure 3). Everything is the same except that the foam in
this glass does not look like a face, because I removed the bubble
that was the "eye" in the first drawing. That is, the altered image
is just a glass filled with beer. We asked the same two questions:
"What do you see?" Then, "What else do you see?" Again, most
of them saw a glass of beer. But none of them saw a face. The first
group of participants saw a series of figure-ground drawings one

at a time and were asked to write about what they saw. The second group saw a series of slightly altered drawings—essentially the same images as the first group saw, but lacking the secondary object—and were asked to write about what they saw. Then all the participants were asked to evaluate the drawings and report their current moods.

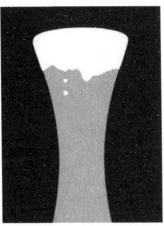

Figure 3. An altered image of
Noma Bar's *Hangover*

In a series of experiments, we found that participants who saw the figure-ground drawings found them psychologically richer—that is, more interesting, intriguing, and refreshing, and less boring and clichéd—than those who saw the drawings with a clear main figure. A subtle visual difference made a huge psychological difference between the two groups. The figure-ground group saw multiple things in one drawing. Perhaps they were puzzled at first, with some vague feeling that something was different. That feeling then turned into a more certain identification of the secondary view. In contrast, the control group saw drawings that were singular, clear, and unambiguous. Notably, the figure-ground drawings did not evoke different moods in any of the experiments. Participants in the control condition were as happy as those in the figure-ground condition. Even so, a slight addition of complexity and unexpectedness enhanced visual and perceptual richness, as if it were an aesthetic spice.

5. Then There Are Sports

For some, sports are simply a pastime, what Kant called "games which bring with them no further interest than that of making the time pass imperceptibly." For others, sports are more than just entertainment. Sports are particularly powerful sources of drama, mainly because the outcome is not scripted. You never really know what will happen. When you think you've won the World Series, a star first baseman could miss a routine ground-ball, letting it go through his legs; the next thing you know, the other team has won the championship (this really happened, in 1986). Then there are impossible passes by Magic Johnson and improbable dunks by Michael Jordan and LeBron James at the least expected moments. There is drama and beauty in high-level sports. Indeed, watching sports could be construed as an aesthetic experience, as philosopher Stephen Mumford describes in detail in his 2012 book *Watching Sport: Aesthetics, Ethics and Emotion.*

To me, one of the real incentives to come to the U.S. was a chance to see the National Basketball Association (NBA) and Major League Baseball (MLB). Here is one of the dramatic turn of events that happened to my favorite team, the Houston Rockets, in 1995. The Rockets won their first NBA championship during the 1993–1994 season, led by my favorite player, Hakeem Olajuwon. The next year, during the 1994–1995 season, the Rockets started out by winning nine games in a row, and it looked to everyone like another championship season.

But then their offense struggled. The Rockets ultimately ended the regular season with a 47-35 record and were the number six seed in the Western Conference playoffs. It was a disappointing end of the regular season. In the first round of playoffs, they faced the number-three-seeded Utah Jazz, who ended the regular season with a 60-22 record and had Karl Malone and John Stockton on their roster. Utah initially led the five-game series 2 to 1. One more win and Utah would move on. However, in game four Houston won: the series was now tied at 2 to 2. For game five, they went back to Utah. Would Utah's home court advantage end the Rockets' season? Nope, Houston beat Utah 95 to 91.

In the second round of playoffs, Houston faced the number two seed, the Phoenix Suns. Phoenix led 3 to 1 in the seven-game series. Again, one more loss and Houston's season would have been over. They had to win three games in a row in order to win the series. Phoenix had a chance to win game five, but their star forward, Charles Barkley, uncharacteristically missed both free throws toward the end of regulation and the game went into overtime. In the end, Houston won game five in Phoenix, and the rest is history. They won game six at home *and* game seven in Phoenix. In the conference finals, Houston beat the number-one-seeded San Antonio Spurs. Then they swept the Orlando Magic in the finals and won their second consecutive NBA championship.

The number-six-seeded team winning it all is truly unbelievable, but coming back from 1-2 in a best of five series AND from 1-3 in a best of seven series is practically unheard of. There were many moments during the playoffs when I thought it was over. But it wasn't. Head coach Rudy Tomjanovich famously proclaimed, "Don't ever underestimate the heart of a champion!" The 1995 playoffs were moving, dramatic, and a whole lot psychologically richer than watching a number one seed win the championship. An underdog victory like this expands your view of what is possible.

6. Why Aesthetic Experiences Matter

So, yes, reading a poem or novel, watching a film, looking at a piece of artwork, or watching an awe-inspiring athletic performance increases psychological richness. It requires our own interpretation of the poet's, novelist's, filmmaker's, or artist's personal beliefs and expression, and recognition of beauty in athletes' extraordinary actions. In this sense, it differs from firsthand experiences gained through personal adventures. Nonetheless, we can still have very real, immediate experiences through arts and sports under the right circumstances.

At the end of *Time Regained,* the final volume of *In Search of Lost Time,* Proust talks about the role of art more generally: "Through art alone are we able to emerge from ourselves, to know what another person sees of a universe which is not the same as our own and of which, without art, the landscapes would remain as unknown to us as those that may exist on the moon. Thanks to art, instead of seeing one world only, our own, we see that world multiply itself and we have at our disposal as many worlds as there are original artists, worlds more different one from the other than those which revolve in infinite space, worlds which, centuries after the extinction of the fire from which their light first emanated, whether it is called Rembrandt or Vermeer, send us still each one its special radiance." In his real life, Proust was often sick and refrained from traveling too far. Even so, he experienced multiple worlds across time and geography thanks to art.

Film critic Roger Ebert watched over 10,000 movies and wrote over 6,000 reviews. He forgot about most of the films eventually, but he remembered those he deemed worth remembering. Ebert explained that "if you pay attention to the movies they will tell you what people desire and fear in their deepest secrets. At least, the good ones will. That's why we go, hoping to be touched in those secret places." The more you are touched in those secret places, the more psychologically rich your inner life becomes. Ebert, who was born in Urbana, Illinois, graduated from the University of Illinois at Urbana-Champaign, and lived all his adult life in Chicago, might not have led a life of physical, geographical exploration, but he certainly led a life of aesthetic and intellectual exploration.

When we are absorbed in a complex narrative world or the unscripted world of sports, we are transported and transformed. It is a transcending experience that is different from our typical everyday experiences, that produces a different set of thoughts and emotions, and that sometimes gives us a glimpse of an unforeseen possibility and a new perspective on life. In short, a psychologically rich experience.

CHAPTER TEN

THE POINT OF EXPLORATION

And the purpose of life, after all, is to live it, to taste
experience to the utmost, to reach out eagerly and without
fear for newer and richer experience. You can do that only if
you have curiosity, an unquenchable spirit of adventure.

—Eleanor Roosevelt, *You Learn by Living*

1. What the Great Tit Knows

A WWE match could be an interesting weekend outing. A visit
to a national park might evoke awe and wonder you rarely experience in your everyday life. *Schindler's List* will make you cry
and cry. "So what?" you might ask (despite reading the last chapter). Aren't these activities all what the philosopher Blaise Pascal
would have called "diversions"? Other than filling people's time
to avoid boredom, do these activities have any genuine benefits?
In other words, what is the point of exploration?

Nature may have an answer. The great tit (*Parus major*) is a bird
in the tit family Paridae, about five inches in length. It is a common species in Europe, North Africa, the Middle East, and Central Asia. English zoologist John Richard Krebs and colleagues
tested whether the great tits will "know" where to forage when
two patches of vegetation differ in terms of availability of food.
When one patch was far better than the other (e.g., 50 percent dif-

ference in food availability), the great tits explored a bit (about ten hops), figured out which one was better, and stuck with the better one, or "exploited" it. When the difference in food availability was small (e.g., 10 percent difference), they explored a lot more (over forty hops on average) before settling on the slightly better one.

The scientists also ran computer simulations and compared simulated optimal results with the actual experimental data from the great tits. Shockingly, the great tits' choices were almost identical to the ideal simulated behaviors. That is, great tits instinctively used an ideal, explore-then-exploit foraging strategy and adjusted the degree of exploration depending on the levels of food availability in different patches.

By definition, a psychologically rich life leans toward "exploration" strategies rather than "exploitation" strategies. Like the great tits, people seem to vary their strategies according to their circumstances. In fall 2019, when we asked 585 UVA students what kind of college life they would like to have, we found that the degree to which they chose the psychologically rich life dramatically differed by what year of college they were in.

	Psychological Richness	Happiness	Meaning
Freshman	**43.4%**	34.1%	22.5%
Sophomore	37.5%	**41.2%**	21.3%
Junior	33.9%	33.9%	32.1%
Senior	13.6%	40.9%	**45.5%**

Figure 4. An Ideal College Life: What College Students Prefer (Forced-Choice Data from UVA).

Among first-year students, a psychologically rich college life was the most popular option, a happy life second, and a meaningful life last. Among sophomores, a happy life was the top answer, followed by a psychologically rich life. Among juniors, all three options were equally attractive. Finally, among seniors, a meaningful life was the most popular, closely followed by a happy life. Early on, many college students prefer exploration. However, just like great tits, once they figure out what they want to do, their priorities seem to shift toward dedicating themselves to achieving a meaningful life. We learned that UVA students tend, like the great tits, to use the explore-then-exploit strategy.

2. Kepler's Choice

But are these UVA students following the optimal strategy? Do humans use the optimal exploration-exploitation strategy in general? Cognitive psychologists Peter Todd and Geoffrey Miller are in a better position than myself to answer these questions, as they are the experts on the optimal explore-exploit strategy in various decision-making situations. They authored a fun and informative article entitled "From Pride and Prejudice to Persuasion: Satisficing in Mate Search."

The chapter starts with the story of Johannes Kepler, a German astronomer and mathematician. His first wife died of cholera in 1611; Kepler did not mourn much, as his first marriage was not a happy one. Soon afterward, he began a methodical search for a new wife. He thoroughly courted and interviewed eleven women over a two-year period. Friends urged him to choose candidate number four, a woman of high status and large dowry. However, she rejected his proposal because he made her wait too long. So he went with his personal favorite, candidate number five. Though she was not from the wealthiest family, she was well educated and is thought to have provided favorable domestic conditions for Kepler to produce four more major works. Kepler took his time, explored widely, brought excitement and vigor to the search, and chose his second wife well. He was happily married.

Kepler was the leading mathematician of his time, so he probably had a very good sense of probability theorems. In statistics, there is a famous problem called the "secretary problem." In this task, you are supposed to make the best possible hiring decision based on a series of interviews. Researchers measure how many candidates from a set pool you interview before deciding to hire a particular individual. You cannot go back to previous interviewees, and you must make binary decisions (yes or no) until you make a yes (hire) decision. Computer simulations show that the optimal strategy here is to interview the first 37 percent of candidates (i.e., saying no to all of them) and from that point on decide whether a new candidate is better than the best of the first 37 percent. This is called the "37 percent rule." How many people actually follow the 37 percent rule? Very few.

If you had 100 potential mates, would you date 37 of them at least once and then start using the 37 percent rule until you find the best available one? Probably not. This is because dating so many people is costly, not only financially but also psychologically. In addition, even when you finally think you have found The One, that person might say no to your proposal. Then your extensive search would be wasted. It makes more sense to settle on the first person you like well enough who likes you back.

Nevertheless, it is interesting to know that psychologists have conducted a lot of secretary problem (SP) experiments that minimize additional search costs (e.g., just flipping another card instead of finding a time and location to meet a date). Even in an artificial lab experiment where the search cost is little, only a fraction of people use the optimal search strategy. For instance, only 30 percent of college students followed the 37 percent rule under experimental conditions, though college students were slightly better than pigeons, of which only 17 percent followed the rule. Herbranson and colleagues concluded as follows: "Across three experiments, pigeons and humans failed to consistently use the optimal solution to the SP. Most importantly, both species failed to do so in the same way: They made selections too soon, before considering the ideal number of options."

If people make a selection too early in a task with little search cost, then they are far more likely to make a selection too early in a real mating task with high search cost and rejection probability. Indeed, economists argue that people make suboptimal choices in mate selection because they do not explore enough. For most people, the more exploration they do, the better choices they make.

3. The "Take a Dozen" Heuristic

Psychologists Samantha Cohen and Peter Todd analyzed nationally representative data collected by the Centers for Disease Control to gain insight into the exploration-exploitation trade-off in real marital decisions. They learned that some people spend a long time dating several people before getting married, whereas others spend a short time dating a few and settle down quickly. In explore-exploit trade-off terminology, the first group explored for a long time before exploiting, whereas the second group explored for a short period before exploiting. The animal behavior literature and computer simulations both suggest that insufficient exploration results in more errors. Of course, if one mate were far better than the rest, there would be no need to explore—the choice would be obvious. But in a real mating context, there are many potential mates with only slight differences in overall value. This means that it is better to explore more before settling down on one mate. The CDC data indicates that those who spend less time exploring (those who get married quickly after starting a serious relationship) are indeed more likely to end their marriage in divorce than those who spend more time exploring before marriage. So, on average, the more exploration, the more marital stability.

The CDC data are consistent with the 37 percent rule. However, Peter Todd and Geoffrey Miller take issue with the 37 percent rule on several grounds. For example, animals can't really tell the difference between the best possible mate and a top 10 percent mate. Also, for animals, finding the best mate isn't critical. Rather, being able to find one of the best options is (e.g., the top 10 percent). What if we change the criterion from the best option to one of the best options? Now a more cursory search—looking at the first 14 percent instead of the first 37 percent—yields the highest probability of success, when the number of potential mates is set to 100. When the number of potential mates is set to 1,000, an even more cursory search of just 3 percent yields the highest probability of finding someone from the top 10 percent. In other words, if there were 100 potential mates, you would only need to look at the first 14 mates carefully and then pick the next mate that is better than the best one from the first 14. In the case of 1,000 potential mates, you would need to look at 30 mates carefully and pick the next one that is better than the best of the first 30. A lot more reasonable than the 37 percent rule.

In the end, Todd and Miller argue that the "take a dozen" heuristic, regardless of the problem set, does a pretty good job of finding a top 10 percent option. This means when you next look for a new romantic partner or a new apartment, you had better consider at least a dozen before making a decision. Though it is a lot easier than the 37 percent rule, the "take a dozen" heuristic is still pretty demanding. How do people have twelve serious relationships before marriage? Kepler did a rather thorough job of considering eleven candidates over two years—pretty close to Todd and Miller's "take a dozen" heuristic.

4. The Geography of Marriage: Cupid's Short Flights

If Kepler and the statisticians above have figured out the optimal solution to many of our decisions, why don't we explore more?

Aside from search cost and rejection probability, what else is key? And can it tell us something about the psychologically rich life?

An answer might lie in sociology and social psychology. James Bossard, a sociologist at the University of Pennsylvania, obtained 5,000 marriage licenses submitted in Philadelphia and surrounding counties in 1931, and examined where the pairs had lived at the time of application. In order to learn about the geography of marriage in Philadelphia, Bossard wanted to see how far people lived from each other before they decided to get married. If bachelors and bachelorettes explored their options widely, many would marry someone who lived far away from them.

It turned out that Philadelphians in the 1930s found their partners nearby. Only 890 couples, or 17.8 percent, were made up of a partner living in Philadelphia and the other living outside the city before marriage. The remaining 82.2 percent of the couples had lived separately in Philadelphia before marriage. The most famous findings from this research were that over half of the couples had lived within twenty blocks of each other before marriage, and that 33.58 percent of them had lived within five blocks or less! Although eligible bachelors and bachelorettes in a large city like Philadelphia have literally hundreds of thousands of potential mates, the majority of them appeared to consider only those who lived close to them. How else would the majority of matches have been made within twenty city blocks? Reflecting upon his findings, Bossard commented, "Cupid may have wings, but apparently they are not adapted for long flights."

Living nearby could indicate many factors. For one thing, in 1931 Philadelphia was ethnically and racially segregated. Thus, proximity also meant shared cultural, linguistic, and religious backgrounds, which was particularly important then. Proximity also meant that people were more likely to have interactions nearby than they would with people who lived farther away. That is, the chance of acquaintanceship was dramatically higher if they lived close by.

You might say, well, the Philadelphia study is great, but that was 1931. A lot has changed, including where people live, how they meet, and whom they marry. In 1931, it was nearly impossible to marry someone of a different race. Even among the white population, people from different religions rarely married each other. Now, with the popularity of online dating platforms, the number of potential mates seems to have exponentially grown. Is the residential proximity effect a thing of the past?

Karen Haandrikman and her colleagues asked this exact question, looking at the vital statistics for the entire population of the Netherlands. Yes, you read that right: the entire population of the Netherlands. More specifically, they selected 289,248 individuals who started cohabitation as domestic partners between January 1, 2004, and December 31, 2004.

First, the researchers looked at where each individual had lived prior to cohabitation. Because there was a chance that those who submitted the cohabitation application as partners during 2004 had already been living together, the researchers also looked at the residential distance between each partner roughly five years prior to cohabitation. Both sets of data showed that the most common residential distance between partners prior to cohabitation was just one kilometer, or .62 miles. Roughly 13 percent of newly cohabiting couples had lived roughly one kilometer away from each other right before they started cohabitating; roughly 10.5 percent of them had lived roughly one kilometer away five years before they started cohabitating. The median distance was 6.2 kilometers (3.85 miles) right before cohabitation, 7.8 kilometers (4.85 miles) five years before, and 22.9 kilometers (14.23 miles) at birth. That is, half of Dutch people who started cohabitating in 2004 chose a partner who had been born less than fifteen miles away from their own birthplace. These statistics suggest an astonishingly small world, even for a quite cosmopolitan European country. Online dating became popular in the early 2000s. Yet Cupid in the Netherlands in 2004 was no different from Cupid in Philadelphia in 1931—not adapted for long flights. What does this tell us?

5. The Propinquity Effect

In the late 1940s, social psychologists Leon Festinger, Stan Schachter, and Kurt Back were also interested in distance and relationships when they set out to examine friendship formation in two MIT residential complexes: Westgate and Westgate West. Unlike the city of Philadelphia, there were no ethnic enclaves—no Chinatown where Chinese immigrants would gravitate, for example—so the selection effect (i.e., a resident choosing to live in a particular area) was kept to a minimum.

Festinger and colleagues knew exactly where all the participants in this study lived, and asked one simple question: "What three people in Westgate or Westgate West do you see most of socially?" In the microcosm of a college dorm, their research replicated the Philadelphia and Dutch findings: 112 out of the possible 187 friendship nominations, or 60 percent, lived next door or in the unit connected directly through staircases. Only seven nominations were made of someone living four units away or more. So, physical distance clearly matters. The other interesting finding from the study was that functional distance also matters. Those who lived close to the staircases were far more likely to become friends with someone living on a different floor than those who lived farther away from the staircases. What this suggests is that physical and functional distance dictate the probability of a chance meeting, and that the more frequently one meets someone informally, the more likely it is that a friendship emerges. In the context of college dorms, where cultural, ethnic, and religious backgrounds are randomized, Festinger's findings point to the surprising power of geography and repeated chance meetings. But why do chance encounters matter?

6. The Mere Exposure Effect

At their best, social psychologists work by identifying an association between two variables in the real world (e.g., residential proximity and friendship), then test causal mechanisms, or what accounts for the observed correlation. What repeated chance meetings do is increase familiarity. Bob Zajonc, one of the greatest social psychologists of all time, zeroed in on the familiarity effect, or what he called the "mere exposure effect," in a series of experiments.

Even before he conducted this series of experiments, Zajonc made an ingenious refinement of previous research on word frequency and its link to perceived "desirability" of a word (i.e., how good or bad a word sounds). Word frequency was measured by how often each word appeared in published books and magazines in the 1920s and 1930s, in painstaking work conducted by Edward Thorndike and Irving Lorge. Desirability was determined by aggregating English speakers' ratings of various English words. Everyone agrees that the word "good" is good, but not as good as the word "better." But, in terms of word frequency, the word "good" is used far more often than the word "better." So, if frequent encounters increase the desirability of a word, then the word "good" should be more desirable than the word "better." Indeed, participants in a psychology experiment reported that the word "good" is more desirable than the word "better"!

The findings from this research on word frequency are fascinating, but they are still correlational. That is, we cannot infer a causal effect between frequency and liking a word. So Zajonc designed an experiment in which participants were presented with nonsense words such as "iktitaf," "afworbu," and "saricik." The experimenter told the participants that these were "Turkish" words (they weren't) and showed them how to pronounce each. The participants were then asked to pronounce each word. Afterward, they were asked to guess the meaning of each "Turkish" word in terms of how good or bad they are. Some words were presented only once or twice, while others were presented ten or twenty-five times. That was how Zajonc manipulated familiarity. He found that all twelve nonsense words were rated higher on goodness when presented more frequently than when presented less frequently. He then replicated this initial finding with Chinese characters. In the next experiment, Zajonc used photos of graduating Michigan State University seniors and replicated again that those same photos were better liked when presented more frequently to the participants than when they were presented less frequently.

The story of the mere exposure effect doesn't stop here. Richard Moreland and Bob Zajonc ran a field experiment in a real college classroom. They selected four female research assistants who were rated as equally attractive to attend an introduction to psychology class with various degrees of frequency. One woman never attended the lecture, the second woman attended five times, the third woman attended ten times, and the fourth one attended fifteen times over the course of the semester. They were instructed to enter the lecture hall, walk the same staircases, and sit in the same area, so that most students could see them. They were all dressed in a casual fashion.

At the end of the semester, students in the class were asked to rate the photos of the four women in terms of attractiveness, familiarity, and perceived similarities (to the rater). The results were very similar to the earlier lab experiments: the attractiveness ratings (on the 1 to 7 point scale) in this field experiment increased linearly as exposure increased: 3.62 for the woman who never showed up in the lecture, 3.88 for the woman who showed up five times, 4.25 for the woman who showed up ten times, and 4.38 for the woman who showed up fifteen times.

Likewise, more exposure was associated with more perceived similarities, as well. Interestingly, the mere exposure effect seems to happen without much awareness. For instance, when students were explicitly asked whether they knew these four women, nobody said yes. Very few people said they had seen them before. Yet, in terms of familiarity, they rated the women who attended the lecture ten and fifteen times more familiar than those who did not attend or attended only five times.

In this series of experiments, Zajonc and colleagues showed that repeated exposure amplifies not only familiarity, but also perceived similarity (to the rater) and favorability. Previous research already convincingly demonstrated that perceived similarity leads to attraction. New experiments showed that residential proximity increases both familiarity and perceived similarity, thereby enhancing the interpersonal attractiveness of those around us. These elegant experiments demonstrate that mere exposure increases favorability, providing a compelling causal claim for the Philadelphia marriage study and the Dutch cohabitation study. Repeated chance meetings do magnify attraction between people, sometimes resulting in a romantic relationship.

7. The Mere Exposure Effect Goes Shopping

These mere exposure effects may influence other aspects of our lives, too. For instance, have you wondered why American cities and suburbs look alike? When I first went to a large shopping mall in Staten Island, New York, I was impressed by the size and number of stores. When I later went to a medium-sized shopping mall in a suburb of Portland, Maine, I was puzzled. Why did these two malls look exactly the same? Why were so many of the stores I'd seen in a Staten Island mall also in Portland's mall?

As a graduate student, I started going to psychology conferences in various cities around the U.S. and experienced a similar feeling. I would fly into a large airport, which was usually located in a faraway suburb of a major city. A taxi then takes a huge multilane highway, passing cookie-cutter housing developments, box stores, and shopping malls before finally reaching the downtown area where the conference usually takes place. Why do all these cities look alike? This was not the case in Japan: Tokyo and Osaka are both large cities with many high-rise buildings and large train stations. Yet they have very different feels, perhaps due to the overwhelming number of local stores, restaurants, and cafés. In American suburbs, whether you're outside of New York or LA, you can expect to see the same stores, like Target and Whole Foods, and the same restaurants, like the Cheesecake Factory and Panera.

When I was in Charlottesville, I would go to a local coffee shop every day and never went to Starbucks. But when I was traveling, I would realize that all of a sudden I loved going to Starbucks. When I was in the psychology building (Gilmer Hall) in Charlottesville and saw a graduate student walking by, I would greet them with a very curt "hey." When I saw the same graduate student at a conference in Las Vegas, I went "Hey, Gary, so nice to see you!" and almost hugged him. Would I ever hug him in Gilmer Hall? No chance. So, a familiar person or store seems to be particularly attractive when you are away from familiar places and surrounded by strangers. Is it possible that the mere exposure effect is even stronger when you're in an unfamiliar setting?

To find out, my students and I decided to use residential mobility data from the U.S. census to approximate how often people meet strangers, based on the reasoning that, in a city where a lot of people move, the chance of being surrounded by strangers is a lot higher than in a city where people don't move. We tested whether there were more national chain stores such as Chili's, Whole Foods, and Payless Shoes in mobile states such as Nevada and Florida than in stable states such as Pennsylvania and West Virginia. The idea is that national chain stores are more familiar than local stores in a new town and offer psychological comfort. If so, national chain stores should be more popular in U.S. states where there are a lot of newcomers, such as Nevada and Florida. Sure enough, there are more national chain stores in mobile states than in stable states. This is true even when controlling for median income and the total population (as richer, more populated states would attract more businesses).

We also found that University of Virginia students who grew up moving more frequently liked national chain stores more than UVA students who grew up in one place. In a final series of experiments, we manipulated the mindset of residential mobility by asking some participants to think about getting a job right after UVA that required them to move to a new city every other year, some to think about getting a job right after UVA that required them to live in the same city for at least ten years, and the others to think about a typical day in their own lives (the control group). We then gave a modified version of Zajonc's mere exposure task, one with Chinese characters and the other with portrait photos.

In all three conditions, we observed the mere exposure effect, replicating the earlier findings. Most importantly, though, we found that in the residential mobility condition participants showed a particularly strong familiarity-liking effect. That is, when they thought about moving around frequently in the future, they liked a familiar Chinese character or a familiar face more than when they thought about staying in one place for a long time or about a typical day. It turned out that those in the mobility condition used more anxiety-related words while describing their future mobile lives than those in the stability or the control conditions, and that the more anxiety-related words participants used, the stronger familiarity-liking effect they showed. In other words, stress and anxiety amplify our tendency to like a familiar object.

The mere exposure effect is a replicable phenomenon and fun to read about. But let's think about its implications critically. What about the secretary problem as it applies to finding a partner? You are supposed to explore unfamiliar candidates before settling down in order to make an optimal decision. You are supposed to seriously consider a dozen potential mates if you want to have a really good partner. These are stressful processes. Psychological research shows that our tendency to like a familiar object and our aversion to extra effort makes us settle down prematurely. Our own research further shows that this bad mental habit gets worse when we are under stress. Ironically, when you are in a new place, the conservative mindset kicks in in full force and makes you search for familiarity.

When I studied abroad at Bates, there were only three other Japanese students: Yoko, Kiyomi, and Mariko. I am ashamed to say that I hung out with those three Japanese students far more than I probably should have. Why did I go all the way from Tokyo to Lewiston, Maine, to hang out with other Japanese people? It doesn't make rational sense, but psychologically it does. We can commiserate and understand each other. Familiarity is a powerful force. It gives us comfort. It's a psychological teddy bear. The mere exposure effect exerts its strongest effect, and a psychological teddy bear is most attractive, paradoxically and unfortunately, when we are exploring the world and putting ourselves in uncomfortable situations.

8. Love It or List It

Take house hunting, for example. When you moved to a new city, where did you rent first? If you eventually bought a house in that city, where was it? In Japanese, there is a proverb, *Sumeba Miyako:* once you live somewhere, whatever city you land in (even an undesirable one) becomes your capital (best) city. When I first moved to the University of Minnesota, we rented an apartment in downtown Saint Paul for one year. Most folks recommended

Uptown Minneapolis. Indeed, at first we found downtown Saint Paul less convenient than Uptown. But we found a coffee shop we liked. We found a Japanese restaurant we liked. By October of that year, we were looking for a condo in the downtown Saint Paul area. We then moved to Charlottesville and immediately bought a small house in North Downtown. After ten years, the first house became too small for a family of four. So we moved to a larger house in what neighborhood? North Downtown!

In the popular HGTV series *Love It or List It,* the couples featured have houses that need major renovations. One of the hosts, Hilary, is a designer who helps the couple renovate their house. The other host, David, is a real estate agent who helps the couple find a new home in a new neighborhood. David shows three houses that meet the couple's wish list. Objectively speaking, the houses shown by David typically appear to be more attractive than the renovated old house. Yet every time I've watched the show, the couple has loved the renovation and opted not to list it to move to a new house—they loved their neighborhood too much to leave. This is a prime example of the familiarity bias that we've discussed previously.

The behavioral economist Richard Thaler discovered a related phenomenon known as the "endowment effect." Let's say I was selling a coffee mug for $5, and you were nice enough to buy it from me. Then, a week later, I asked you if I could buy it back from you, and if so, how much I would have to pay for it. Logically speaking, the value of the coffee mug should not have increased during that week—if anything, the now "used" coffee mug should be worth less than $5. However, in experiments like this one, it turns out that most people want a lot more than $5! Typically, the lowest price participants were willing to sell a possession of their own was twice as much as the highest price they were willing to pay to purchase that same object. For the same mug they paid $5 for, they wanted others to pay $10. This is the psychology of ownership, or the endowment effect. Once you own something, the value of that object increases to you. This is why most people overestimate how valuable their houses are. Because they own it and are familiar with it, they like it and think it is more valuable than most others would—another reason why *Love It or List It* couples tend to love it more than they list it.

The draw of familiarity is often stronger than that of variety, too. In a study where consumers were asked to plan a snack for each of the next three days, they tended to choose three different snacks: for instance, a matcha Kit-Kat for day one, Reese's Peanut Butter Cups for day two, and Hershey's Milk Chocolate for day three. Their reasoning was that they didn't think they would want the same thing for three straight days; that would be too boring. They wanted variety! Amazingly, however, when consumers were asked to actually buy snacks for the next three days at once, they tended to buy three of their favorite snack—in my case, three matcha Kit-Kats—instead of three different snacks.

The lesson here is that we like the *idea* of variety, but in the end we tend to choose the same old products. We like the idea of going to a different restaurant every week, but we actually tend to stick with our favorite restaurant again and again. In the planning phase, we seek variety. Imagining different snacks is exciting! Imagining a hike in the Alps is exciting! In the implementation phase, however, we tend to seek familiarity and ease, because we become aware of other practical factors (e.g., a long flight to Switzerland). When faced with an actual choice, we tend to choose a sure "winner" rather than a risky product. We'll settle for something familiar because trying something new is too much work. In the long view, we want novelty; in the short term, we want security. Familiarity is warm and fuzzy, and it has a surprising power over us, steering us away from psychological richness.

This is also related to a larger human tendency: loss aversion. Daniel Kahneman and Amos Tversky asked subjects: Given a

50 percent chance of winning £1,000 vs. a 100 percent chance of winning £450, which would you prefer? Logically, we are supposed to choose the former because its expected value is £500, which is greater than the expected value of the latter, £450. Nevertheless, most of us would choose the latter. We want a sure gain rather than a hypothetical gain, even when the hypothetical gain could be larger than the sure gain. A sure win is pleasant and comfortable. A hypothetical win is risky, anxiety-provoking, and uncomfortable. Loss aversion makes us conservative in many decision-making situations. But if we always chose a sure bet, we would never venture outside of our comfort zone. If we never ventured outside of our comfort zone, we would never encounter anything unexpected.

There is endless empirical and real-life evidence for the mere exposure effect and the power of familiarity or certainty, which seems to spell doom for psychological richness. At the same time, there is an interesting twist here. We may not know what we want. We tend to think it won't be fun to talk to a stranger. But when we actually interact with a stranger, we tend to enjoy it far more than we think. In other words, we tend to underestimate how enjoyable doing something unfamiliar, like talking to a stranger, is. Social psychologists Nick Epley and Juliana Schroeder tested how much people enjoy talking to strangers in a clever field experiment on a commuter train. Their research assistants approached 118 commuters at the Homewood Metra station, one of the first stations on the express line to the Millennium Station in downtown Chicago. One third of the commuters were told to "have a conversation with a new person on the train today, try to make a connection, find out something interesting about the person." One third were told to "keep to yourself and enjoy your solitude on the train today." The last third were told not to make "any changes to your normal commute." They were all given an envelope with a survey and told to complete the survey at the end of their train ride and mail it back with the return envelope with a stamp. Out of 118 commuters, 97 returned the survey. The commuters randomly assigned to talk to a stranger reported that their commutes were significantly happier and more pleasant than those assigned to the solitude or control conditions.

Interestingly, Epley and Schroeder recruited another 105 commuters from the Homewood Metra station and asked them simply to imagine how they would feel if they were in the talk-to-a-stranger condition, the solitude condition, and the control condition. Contrary to the actual participants, those in the imagined experiment predicted that they would report feeling significantly less happy and less pleasant when talking to a stranger than in the other two conditions. We are clearly mistaken to think that not making any changes to our commute and keeping to ourselves would be better than talking to a fellow commuter. We think sticking to a routine commute is better than making a new social connection: a clear familiarity bias. We settle on a job candidate or potential mate before exploring enough. We need to overcome this familiarity bias in order to explore the new and unknown.

9. The Many Benefits of Exploration

Steve Jobs didn't suffer from a familiarity bias—he was eager to explore the unknown world of India at age nineteen. Unfortunately, he got sick and lost a lot of weight. Yet, years later, he credits his experiences in India for giving him confidence to trust his intuition. He made a lot of brilliant choices and some questionable ones thanks to his unique decision-making style, which balanced rationality and intuition.

Steve Jobs was idiosyncratic, a true one and only. Is there anything generalizable from his experience in India? Or is it specific only to him? Social psychologists Angela Ka-yee Leung, William

Maddux, Adam Galinsky, and Chi-yue Chiu have amassed evidence showing that multicultural experiences seem to increase creativity. For instance, participants were asked to solve the Duncker candle problem. You have a candle, a pack of matches, and a box of tacks. Can you attach a candle to a wall so that the candle will burn properly and won't drip wax on the table or floor? (The answer is in the endnotes.) This is a widely used task for testing creativity. Among MBA students, those with more experience living abroad were more likely to solve the Duncker candle problem than those with less foreign experience. These findings were also replicated using different types of creativity tasks.

So, why should multicultural experiences be associated with creativity? Leung and colleagues speculate that people acquire novel ideas and concepts from multicultural experiences. One new concept I learned about when I moved to the U.S. was the possibility of building or renovating your own house. For an American reader, this is an ordinary idea. To me, it was a radical idea. To be clear, DIY does exist in Japan, but it typically involves small projects like building shelves or bookcases. I had never imagined that nonprofessionals would try to renovate or build a whole house by themselves. That aspiration, that frontier spirit, was new to me. American balloon framing is a genius invention that makes constructing houses easier. These concepts were totally out-of-box thinking to me, but now seem quite normal. I bet my college friends in Tokyo would think I was crazy if I decided to build my own house.

Leung and colleagues also speculate that multicultural experiences teach us to recognize that the same behavior can have different meanings. A smile is a good example. I was raised not to smile in front of people because it could come across as impolite. But when I came to the U.S., everyone told me to smile more because it would be more polite! Now, when I go back to Japan,

I have to consciously try not to smile. For example, I went to a fancy department store in Ginza, Tokyo, on one trip. I entered an elevator and looked at the others already in it. I noticed that their faces froze; they were scared of me. Why would they be scared of me? I am a friendly Japanese person! A moment later, though, it suddenly hit me that I was making eye contact and smiling at them—how rude! Here is what you are supposed to do in Japan: You enter an elevator. Never look at anyone directly. No eye contact. You look down and don't bother anyone. Leung and colleagues argue that experiences like this help us understand multiple meanings of the same form of behavior, which in turn helps us think of multiple uses for one tool or idea.

A recent review of studies also shows that the benefits of multicultural experiences go beyond creativity. For example, time spent living abroad also helps individuals gain a clearer sense of who they are and the lives they want to pursue. Individuals who have more foreign experiences trust others more and are better able to understand and relate to others. Those who have explored the world tend to hold fewer negative stereotypes and prejudices, and they discriminate against outgroup members less than those who have not.

It should be noted that there are some undesirable outcomes correlated with multicultural experience as well. For instance, individuals with more multicultural experiences are more likely to believe in moral relativism—the idea that morality, or what is good or bad, is not absolute, but relative. Furthermore, when there was a chance to cheat on a performance task, those with more cross-cultural experiences cheated more than those with fewer cross-cultural experiences.

After all, Steve Jobs did lie to the audience about particular device functions in several product launches. He regularly parked his car in the handicapped section at Whole Foods. He showed signs of moral relativism. But Jobs was also creative. He helped design the Mac, iPod, iPad, and iPhone. Referring to Bob

Dylan and the Beatles, the musicians he loved, Jobs said, "They kept evolving, moving, refining their art. That's what I've always tried to do—keep moving. Otherwise, as Dylan says, if you're not busy being born, you're busy dying." So keep moving. Keep exploring, despite the psychological biases holding you back. You might earn a prize or two: creativity, experiential wisdom—and a top 10 percent mate.

CHAPTER ELEVEN

TURN ADVERSITY INTO A PSYCHOLOGICALLY RICH EXPERIENCE

For a typically healthy person, conversely, being sick can even become an energetic *stimulus* for life, for living *more*. . . . He exploits bad accidents to his advantage; what does not kill him makes him stronger.

—Friedrich Nietzsche, *Ecce Homo*

1. Nietzsche: What Doesn't Kill You Makes You Stronger

Most psychologically rich experiences are intentional. One usually makes the choice to study abroad. One chooses to read Marcel Proust; one chooses to watch an Agnès Varda film; one chooses to take up a DIY project. But what about unintentional experiences? A natural disaster such as an earthquake or hurricane or an illness is an unexpected and challenging experience. These experiences typically provide victims with new perspectives. So, do unintentional, adverse experiences add psychological richness to our lives?

The philosopher Friedrich Nietzsche thought of earthquakes as a sort of catharsis, saying, "Earthquakes bury many wells and leave many languishing, but they also bring to light inner powers and secrets." As an expert on classical philosophy, Nietzsche was cognizant of the ancient world. In ancient Greeks he saw the greatest human strength at a time of crisis: the will to live and to re-create. The best of humanity often comes out of the worst conditions.

Nietzsche wrote essays comically entitled "Why I Am So Wise," "Why I Am So Clever," and "Why I Write Such Good Books." He was a funny guy. How did he have so many insights? Nietzsche credited his illness. In 1869, at age twenty-four, he was appointed chair of classical philology (the study of the history of languages) at Basel University, the youngest ever appointed to the post. In 1876, an illness forced him to take leave from Basel. This prolonged illness gave him a chance to change his habits completely. It helped him detach himself from typical conventions. He later recalled that "it permitted, it *commanded* me to forget; it bestowed on me the necessity of lying still, of leisure, of waiting and being patient. But that means, of thinking." In his sickness, he stopped reading and started thinking. Looking back on his life, Nietzsche said that he was never happier with himself than in the sickest and most painful periods of his life. During illness, he felt that he was returning to his natural self. "Looking from the perspective of the sick toward healthier concepts and values and, conversely, looking again from the fullness and self-assurance of a rich life down into the secret work of the instinct of decadence . . . Now I know how, have the know-how, to reverse perspectives." Nietzsche credited his illness as a source of perspective change and wisdom, suggesting that adversity has the potential to generate psychological richness.

2. Kahneman's "Interesting" Life

Daniel Kahneman won the 2002 Nobel Prize in economics. With Amos Tversky, he published a series of influential papers in the 1970s and 1980s, establishing himself as one of the most prominent psychologists in the world. His papers changed not just how psychologists think about human cognition, but also how economists think about rationality, the foundational assumption in much of modern economics. For instance, in one widely cited 1974 paper, Tversky and Kahneman described three heuristics: the representativeness heuristic, the availability heuristic, and the anchoring and adjustment heuristic, each of which has generated thousands of further research papers. (This 1974 *Science* paper was cited by 4,851 papers published in 2022 alone, an indication of its enduring influence.)

But Kahneman, who died at age ninety in 2024, was not just a Nobel laureate. He had an extraordinary personal story. He escaped Nazi-occupied Paris when he was seven. In his Nobel biography, Kahneman recalled a scary incident: "It must have been late 1941 or early 1942. Jews were required to wear the Star of David and to obey a 6 p.m. curfew. I had gone to play with a Christian friend and had stayed too late. I turned my brown sweater inside out to walk the few blocks home. As I was walking down an empty street, I saw a German soldier approaching. He was wearing the black uniform that I had been told to fear more than others—the one worn by specially recruited SS soldiers. As I came closer to him, trying to walk fast, I noticed that he was looking at me intently. Then he beckoned me over, picked me up, and hugged me. I was terrified that he would notice the star inside my sweater. He was speaking to me with great emotion, in German. When he put me down, he opened his wallet, showed me a picture of a boy, and gave me some money." It was a close call. Kahneman went on to say, "I went home more certain than ever that my mother was right: people were endlessly complicated and interesting." He credited his mother for inspiring him to become a psychologist.

Kahneman's father was interned in Drancy and was supposed to be sent to an extermination camp. However, his employer intervened, and he was released. Then his family escaped to Vichy, but after the Germans arrived, they had to escape once more to the center of France. His father died in 1944, and his family moved to Palestine after the war.

Kahneman graduated from Hebrew University and served in the Israeli army as a platoon leader for one year, then as an officer in the psychology branch of the Israel Defense Forces for another year before starting his graduate work at UC Berkeley. Many different subjects interested him, so he studied an eclectic mix of topics including subliminal perception, optical benches, personality assessments, Ludwig Wittgenstein, and the philosophy of science. Before he started his famous collaboration with Amos Tversky on cognitive biases, Kahneman studied psychoanalysis, memory, vision, and motivation. After his collaboration with Tversky was over, Kahneman went on to study pleasure and pain, then happiness and life satisfaction, and made foundational contributions at each stop.

With his diverse contributions to society as a military leader, teacher, and scholar, you might expect Kahneman to think his life was extremely meaningful, right? Wrong. Kahneman didn't characterize his life as meaningful. In a 2018 interview, he said, "I recall a conversation with Martin Seligman, the founder of positive psychology, in which he tried to convince me I had a meaningful life. I insisted—and I still think this today—that I had an interesting life. 'Meaningful' isn't something I understand."

Neither did Kahneman view his life as wholly happy. In the same interview, he said, "There were four years when I worked alone on a book. That was terrible, and I was miserable." Kahneman—who escaped Nazi-occupied Paris, was on the run for three or four years during World War II, and would later go on to win the Nobel Prize—experienced many ups and downs in his life. He said his life was best described as "interesting"; I would call it psychologically rich.

3. When a Hurricane Hit New York City

On October 29, 2012, Hurricane Sandy hit New York City. Takashi Fujimoto, age sixty-four, was living alone in a basement apartment in Staten Island. Water began to gush into his apartment while he was working with photographic lighting equipment. When he tried to unplug the cords, he was electrocuted. He spent all night floating in and out of consciousness in his flooded apartment. The next morning, his landlord found him in a puddle of water and called for an ambulance. Fujimoto was hospitalized for the next thirty-seven days, as he had suffered a stroke and burns. Most of his possessions were ruined. But Catholic Charities provided him with a $500 grant to buy a winter jacket, clothes, and shoes. As recounted in *The New York Times,* "Mr. Fujimoto became misty-eyed as he talked about the people who helped him recover after the storm. 'It changed my perspective for life.'"

Fujimoto's experience with Hurricane Sandy was far from intentional. Though he was proud to have lived independently for the previous thirty-six years, this near-death experience changed him. It was terrible, but it reaffirmed his belief in community, to the point that he even continued to live in the same basement apartment with the same landlord and neighbors afterward.

While New York City recovered from Hurricane Sandy fairly quickly, New Orleans suffered for years after Hurricane Katrina. In 2018, Joe Bridges and his son Jordan reflected on the effects of Katrina thirteen years after it happened. They evacuated to Atlanta first, then to Washington D.C. In January 2006, they returned to New Orleans. Joe said, "It kind of threw me off a little bit because we were living in D.C., where everything is beautiful. It's nice. And then I would come back to New Orleans to where it was like a bomb had went off." In 2018, Jordan could still see abandoned homes from Katrina, describing the storm as a "veil" that still covered the city. Despite the long-lasting damage, Jordan said, "I think we're a better city because of it. Much stronger, closer knit. Going through something as significant as Katrina with your loved ones and friends. Those bonds, you know, those are the things that are gonna last forever." Hurricanes Katrina and Sandy destroyed many people's lives. But, as Nietzsche pointed out, they brought to light one of the greatest human strengths, compassion.

4. When an Earthquake Hit Kobe

On January 17, 1995, a magnitude 7.3 earthquake shook Kobe and the surrounding areas of Japan. Known as the Hanshin-Awaji earthquake, its epicenter was close to downtown Kobe, a city with a population of 1.42 million people. Collapsed houses, ruined highways, and fires made it look like a war zone. Over 100,000 homes were completely destroyed and over 6,400 people died. In Japan, the Tokyo and Tohoku areas are known for frequent earthquakes, whereas the Kobe and Kansai areas are not. So this earthquake surprised and devastated Kobe residents.

How deep are the psychological scars that these experiences leave? To investigate, I spent my sabbatical year (2012–2013) in Kobe. I analyzed the Hyogo Life Recovery Surveys, which were conducted across the city of Kobe and its surrounding areas in 2001, 2003, 2005, and 2011. Insurance companies examined damaged homes and classified them into four categories: complete damage, half, partial, and none. By 2001, all the physical damage in Kobe and its surrounding areas was fully repaired, meaning that, at the time of the first survey, the current living conditions of the respondents whose houses had been completely destroyed in 1995 were not substantially different from those whose houses had been spared by the earthquake.

Yet psychological scars were still visible for those who had lost their homes. For instance, in 2001 Kobe residents whose houses were completely destroyed by the 1995 earthquake were significantly less satisfied with their lives and reported more negative emotions and more physical illnesses than those whose houses had suffered no damage in 1995. Time did not heal everything, because the results in 2003, 2005, and even 2011—sixteen years after the earthquake—were similar to those from 2001. The psychological immune system was not enough for the devastation of the earthquake. The victims were still significantly less satisfied with their lives and reported more negative emotions and physical illnesses after all these years.

Our surveys also indicated the more home damage they had incurred, the more likely it was that they had lost a loved one. This human loss could also have a lingering negative effect on well-being. So, we examined housing damage simultaneously with human losses. Our analyses showed that housing damage and human loss each had an independent effect on well-being, such that the more housing damage and human loss respondents incurred, the less life satisfaction and more negative emotions and health problems they reported. In short, the Kobe earthquake was a tragic case where time did not heal everything.

5. Does the Experience of Natural Disaster Make Us More Prosocial?

In *A Paradise Built in Hell,* Rebecca Solnit documents numerous examples of prosocial actions among disaster victims. For instance, right after the 1906 San Francisco earthquake, Anna Holshouser started a makeshift soup kitchen in an evacuation camp. With the support from Oakland across the bay, she served two to three hundred people a day. Solnit concludes: "Surrounding them [the wounded, killed, orphaned], often in the same city or even neighborhood, is a periphery of many more who are largely undamaged but profoundly disrupted—and it is the disruptive power of disaster that matters here, the ability of disasters to topple old orders and open new possibilities. . . . The very depth of emotion, the connecting to the core of one's being, the calling into play one's strongest feelings and abilities, can be rich, even on deathbeds, in wars and emergencies." Solnit seems to argue that a natural disaster reveals one's true colors, reaching the deepest part of our existence, and even helps us realize what's best within us. In contrast, she points out that "what is often assumed to be the circumstance of happiness sometimes is only insulation from the depths, or so the plagues of ennui and angst among the comfortable suggest."

So, according to Solnit, even devastating natural disasters such as the 1995 Hanshin-Awaji earthquake should have some silver linings. I remember watching surviving children who were interviewed on TV back in 1995. They were asked what they wanted to become. Many said nurses, firefighters, and doctors. As with Takashi Fujimoto in Staten Island, is it possible that the devastating earthquake changed these children's perspectives on life and made them more prosocial?

The best, most direct evidence for this can be found in studies conducted by Jean Decety and his colleagues. They collected data on altruistic giving from six- and nine-year-old Chinese children living in Sichuan, China, in April 2008. Just one month later, on May 12, 2008, a magnitude 7.9 earthquake hit Sichuan. One month after the earthquake, the researchers collected data from a new group of six- and nine-year-olds from the same schools. This created a sort of natural experiment where participants in the pre- and post-earthquake conditions were chosen as if randomly (meaning the children in the pre-earthquake study were presumably no different from the children in the post-earthquake study in any other ways except for having experienced the major earthquake).

The experiment went like this: One child at a time was invited to a quiet room in their school, where they were greeted by a female researcher who told them they could pick ten stickers for themselves out of a hundred stickers. After the children picked their favorite ten, they were told that some of their classmates had not been selected to play this game and would not receive any stickers. However, if they wanted to donate some stickers out of the ten they had received, they could. They were given an empty envelope for any stickers they wanted to donate to an anonymous classmate. After the session was over, the researcher counted how many stickers each child donated as a behavioral measure of altruistic giving. Before the earthquake, nine-year-olds gave, on average, slightly more than one out of the ten stickers. One month after the earthquake, nine-year-olds gave, on average, about four out of the ten stickers.

Is there other evidence that shows the long-term effect of experiencing natural disasters on victims' values and occupational preferences? To explore this question, we looked at trends in job applications at the municipality level from 1989 to 2000 in the Kobe and Tokyo areas, which were distinguished in that Kobe had experienced the major earthquake in that period, whereas Tokyo had not. We looked at how many people applied to become social workers, firefighters, and kindergarten teachers (jobs hired at the municipal level in Japan). We found that the number of applicants per position soared in 1995 in the Kobe area, but not in the Tokyo area. These findings suggest that the earthquake made prosocial jobs more desirable.

Recall that, even sixteen years after the Hanshin-Awaji earthquake, Kobe residents who had lost their houses in the quake were less satisfied with their lives and reported more physical symptoms than those whose houses had not been damaged. These findings show that the negative effects of natural disasters on the well-being of survivors are long-lasting. The tragedy becomes ingrained in their identities and life stories and can rob them of happiness and normalcy. No one wishes to suffer such a tragedy. Yet, even if happiness is impossible in the aftermath, survivors can still lead a good life. Indeed, some of the best qualities of humankind emerge as antidotes to grief in these difficult times: many survivors become more prosocial. The change of perspective experienced by earthquake survivors could mean that their lives are now psychologically richer than before. They discovered "a treasure amidst ruins."

6. The Surprising Results of COVID-19

The COVID-19 pandemic disrupted all of our lives, changing the way we live and work. Has it changed the way we view the world? Has it enhanced psychological richness? One study examined whether individuals who were exposed to COVID-19 (that is, respondents themselves, a family member, or an acquaintance diagnosed with or died from COVID-19) during the early phase of the pandemic showed more prosocial behaviors than those who were not exposed. Participants were given an unexpected monetary bonus: $5 in the U.S. and €4 in Italy. Then they were asked if they would like to donate some of the money to a charity in the state/region where they lived, a national charity, or an international charity. They were told that the amount they donated would be doubled by the researcher. Both American and Italian participants exposed to COVID-19 not only were more likely to donate to a charity than those who were unexposed, but also donated more. These findings indicate that personal experience with COVID-19 made the victims change their values in a prosocial direction.

Did an unusual experience of COVID-19 increase psychological richness? Micael Dahlen and Helge Thorbjørnsen directly tested this question. During the second week of April 2021, 973 Swedes anonymously filled out a questionnaire that asked about their COVID-19 status as well as whether they felt they were living a psychologically rich life. It turned out that those who had

had COVID-19 reported more psychological richness than those who had not been infected. Respondents with the experience of having COVID-19 were also *less* likely to say that they would like to erase the pandemic time period from their life than those without the experience of having the virus. That is, those who'd had COVID-19 regretted *less* than those who had not.

Dahlen and Thorbjørnsen then conducted a second survey from a representative sample of Swedes in June 2021. Replicating the results from the first study, those who'd previously caught COVID-19 reported that their lives were psychologically richer than those who had not. Furthermore, the COVID-19 respondents reported lower levels of death anxiety than those who had not had the illness. So it appears that the experience of COVID-19 made them less afraid of death and helped them live without fear. (Though, of course, the reverse causality is possible here: people who were getting out and about without death anxiety had more psychologically rich lives and were also more likely to get COVID.)

7. The World Is Richer for Having the Devil in It

Clearly, I am not arguing that tragic events like war and pandemics are positive. Beyond the events themselves, some disasters trigger even worse consequences, such as massacre or mass violence. A day after the Great Kanto earthquake in 1923, a rumor that Koreans were looting and rioting spread quickly. A panic ensued, and at least 6,000 Koreans were killed in the greater Tokyo area. Likewise, right after Hurricane Katrina, there was an "elite panic," or excessive fear of social disorder. Vigilantes were formed and they inflicted unprovoked violence on Black residents. Incidents like this should not have happened. Some people are traumatized for a long time; others decide to end their lives after a natural disaster.

However, research shows that most people are remarkably resilient. Most people do move on. Ann Masten, the world authority on psychological resilience, summarized decades of resilience research as follows: "Early images of resilience in both scholarly work and mass media implied that there was something remarkable or special about these children, often described by words such as *invulnerable,* or *invincible.* . . . The idea of resilient children as remarkable individuals possessing extraordinary strength or inner resilience has lingered, even in scholarly work. . . . The great surprise of resilience research is the ordinariness of the phenomena. Resilience appears to be a common phenomenon that results in most cases from the operation of basic human adaptational systems." Research provides empirical evidence for a popular Japanese proverb: "Fall seven times, stand up an eighth time" (七転八起).

During hard times, when happiness feels out of reach, there are other values with which we can frame our lives. One way to think about an unfortunate event is that it might unintentionally enrich our lives, even when the "enriching" experience is far from a happy one. A painting by Guido Reni shows St. Michael putting his foot on Satan's neck. William James commented on this painting, saying that "the world is all the richer for having a devil in it, *so long as we keep our foot upon his neck.*" Psychological richness and misfortune can coexist, so long as the misfortune is kept in check.

CHAPTER TWELVE

A STORY WE TELL

How often do we tell our own life story? How often do we adjust, embellish, make sly cuts? And the longer life goes on, the fewer are those around to challenge our account, to remind us that our life is not our life, merely the story we have told about our life. Told to others, but—mainly—to ourselves.

—Julian Barnes, *The Sense of an Ending*

1. An Interesting Life vs. an Interesting Story

In the previous chapter, I showed how the experience of a natural disaster tends to make victims become more concerned about the welfare of others and gives them a new perspective on life. However, whether their experiences truly enrich their lives or not depends on the story people tell themselves. Some stories are dramatic, memorable, and ultimately uplifting, while others are hopeless, depressing, and dark. In this chapter, I will delve into the role of storytelling in psychological richness.

Psychological richness is inherently intertwined with the quantity and quality of your stories. The more interesting stories you have, the more psychologically rich your life is. But, as Julian Barnes points out, we tell our own life story differently at different times. How do you tell your life story? More generally, how much do storytelling abilities matter in creating psychological richness? How much does the structure of a story matter? For example, a story of George W. Bush could be told in terms of his illustrious family line and the fact that he followed in his father's and grandfather's footsteps, an obedient first son of a prominent political family. Alternatively, you can tell G.W.'s story in a different way. You could add his rebellious years and the fact that George H. W. Bush, his father, did not have high expectations: the narrative of a rich, spoiled kid turning into a Bible-loving, sober, compassionate, conservative politician. My question to you is this: Can we make a life sound like a psychologically richer one?

2. *Redirect:* The Art of Story Editing

In his book *Redirect,* the renowned psychologist Tim Wilson discusses this exact process, which he calls "story editing." Story editing is "a set of techniques designed to redirect people's narratives about themselves and the social world." For instance, one way you could edit your story would be to highlight all the challenges you faced in your life. G.W., who probably did not face tough challenges at Yale as a multigenerational Yalie, could say that Yale was going through a time of grave change during his college years (1964–1968)—as antiestablishment feelings grew, legacy students like him were despised for the first time. He had to prove his own worthiness and did so in a counterproductive way, by drinking and partying too much. He could reframe his Yale years as a prelude to becoming a mature man in his thirties. By emphasizing how terrible he was in his teens and twenties, he could also highlight his improvements.

This is quite a healthy way of thinking about yourself. Indeed, in one study by Anne Wilson and Michael Ross, parents of college students taking an intro to psychology class were asked to report how broadminded, self-confident, socially skilled, and so forth they were relative to other people of the same age on an 11-point scale, ranging from 0 (much less than most) to 5 (same as most) to 10 (much more than most). The parents were asked to answer these questions about themselves right now (average age of forty-nine) and then again applying them to when they were sixteen years old, when they were their children's age (average age of twenty), and at the midpoint between their age and their children's age (average age of thirty-five). For the desirable traits such as broadmindedness, self-confidence, and being socially skilled, parents' average ratings steadily increased from 5.87 when they were sixteen, meaning they were slightly above average, to 6.67 when they were their children's age (roughly age twenty), to 7.21 when they were roughly thirty-five years old, to 7.47 now (roughly forty-nine years old)—a lot more broadminded, self-confident, and socially skilled than the average forty-nine-year-old. As it turns out, most Americans think they score above average on many desirable traits such as leadership skills and social skills (though not on concrete ability traits such as musical skills and math abilities). But what is more interesting about this study is that parents seem to underestimate their skills as young people—in this way, they get to feel like they have improved a lot.

However, the parents in the study might have indeed been less socially skilled and lacking self-confidence when they were young. There's no way to know for sure. To gain more insight into this phenomenon, Wilson and Ross ran a longitudinal study. At the beginning of the school year in September, they asked undergraduate participants to evaluate how independent, self-confident, and socially skilled they currently were, relative to their same-age peers in college. About two months later, in November, they were asked to indicate again how independent, self-confident, and socially skilled they currently were, relative to their same-age peers. At time two, the students were also asked to look back at the beginning of the semester and evaluate how independent, self-confident, and socially skilled they were. By assessing their current selves, as well as how they remembered themselves in the past, they were able to compare their recollections with their actual ratings two months earlier. In September, they rated their desirable traits as 6.35 on the same 11-point scale (way above average). In November, they rated themselves on the desirable traits as 6.05 on the same 11-point scale. Their September ratings were significantly better than their November ratings. Yet, in November, they *remembered* their September selves to be significantly *worse* than their November selves: the remembered September self-rating was 5.74!

Wilson and Ross entitled their paper "From Chump to Champ: People's Appraisals of Their Earlier and Present Selves." By seeing our old selves as not particularly self-confident, socially skilled, or independent, we can see our current selves as much stronger in those areas. To borrow Tim Wilson's terminology, we are constantly story editing. The derogation of the past self is one editing method. I am still shy, but I was terribly shy when I was young (I think). So I can say that, compared to my youth, I have become far less shy. I am not a good writer, but I was a terrible writer when I was young. Compared to when I was twenty-five, I have become a better writer. In this way, I can feel that I have grown as a person over time.

3. What We Can Learn from Others' Struggles

We can derogate our past self in many domains, from maturity to writing skills to morality. One area where story editing is difficult to implement is in objective performance. For instance, if you are a marathon runner of my age, you know exactly how you did ten years ago, five years ago, and last month. The record might look something like 2:31 ten years ago, 2:39 five years ago, and 2:48 last month. If you are in the second semester of your first year in college, you remember exactly how you did academically in your first semester. If your grades haven't improved, it's hard to employ a "chump to champ" narrative.

But, even on more objective measures, people are drawn to a narrative about personal growth. Tim Wilson and Patricia Linville carried out an intriguing experiment to show how that can take place. They recruited second-semester first-year students at Duke who did not do well in the first semester of college. Half of them watched an interview with upper-class students talking about how they did poorly in their first year but improved over time. One interviewee said his GPA increased from 2.0 to 2.6 to 3.2. Participants in the experimental condition were also shown the survey results of upper-class students: "67% said their freshman grades were lower than they had anticipated; 62% of the students said their GPA had improved significantly from the first semester of their freshman year to their upper-class years." The other half of the participants did not receive any information. All the participants completed a questionnaire, then a brief version of GRE reading comprehension and anagram problems, and another version of GRE reading comprehension and anagram problems one week later.

The GRE performance of the participants in the GPA information condition improved significantly more from week one to week two than the GRE performance of those in the control condition without GPA information. The participants in the experimental condition also expected that their GPA would improve from the first to the second year to a greater extent than those in the control condition. Strikingly, those in the GPA information condition actually improved their GPA by .34 from the first semester of their first year to the second semester of their sophomore year, whereas those in the no-information condition saw their GPA drop by .05. Finally, 25 percent of students in the no-information condition transferred out of Duke by the end of their sophomore year, whereas 5 percent in the GPA information condition did.

Wilson and Linville's experiment shows that having a role model—knowing someone who went through similar, tough experiences but ended up successful—can provide the idea and hope that it is possible to improve and survive. The key example of story editing here was how the students viewed their bad academic performance in the first semester. Instead of saying, "I am not smart enough to be at Duke," they learned to say, "First year is tough for everyone; even smart kids struggle."

Similarly, for most of us, physics is a tough subject. When we think about geniuses such as Galileo, Newton, and Einstein, we think that everything comes naturally to them and they are totally different from us. So, when we must learn $E = mc^2$, it is hard for us to identify with Einstein. But what if you were told that Einstein struggled too? He was dissatisfied with his theory of relativity because it did not include electromagnetism. He tried to integrate electromagnetic and gravitational phenomena. Unfortunately, he was never able to do this, despite the fact that he spent the last twenty-five years of his life on it. Knowing this, Huang-Yao Hong and Xiaodong Lin-Siegler carried out an experiment telling one group of tenth-grade students about the struggles of Galileo, Newton, and Einstein, while telling another group only about their extraordinary accomplishments. All the students then attended three identical physics lessons.

Amazingly, the students who heard about the struggles of the greatest scientists were more interested in science at the end of the study than those who heard only the major accomplishments of the greatest scientists. Furthermore, they remembered the key concepts learned during the three subsequent lessons better than those in the accomplishment condition. They also thought that Galileo, Newton, and Einstein had to work hard, whereas those in the accomplishment condition thought they were born geniuses. The students who learned about the struggles of the scientists must have normalized the challenges they faced, just as Duke students learned to see that even smart kids struggle in their first year of college. Overall, learning about the scientists' struggles increased high school students' class engagement and performance. There have been numerous intervention studies of this sort conducted in diverse settings since Wilson and Linville's seminal 1982 paper.

For me, the main lesson of *Redirect* is that our story is in our control. You can see your struggles from a different perspective, and the new interpretation of those struggles becomes a foundational step toward self-understanding and further transformation. Edit your story, drop the old version of yourself, and come to believe in the new version of your narrative. I am not saying that you should edit out all the bad experiences to create a happier version of your life story. Not at all. You should keep most, if not all, of the bad experiences, but use them as a springboard for later transformation, as a point of redirection in your life story.

You can't make an uneventful life psychologically rich. I bet even Virginia Woolf couldn't. But if you've had some unusual experiences such as an earthquake or hurricane or tough periods in your life, you could edit them to make them more interesting to you and others. That will then become part of your story and who you are. At the heart of a psychologically rich life is experience itself. Unless you have a life full of interesting experiences, it is not going to be a psychologically rich one. But if you become a better "story editor," you can extract the most interesting aspects of your experiences and make your story psychologically richer. Another benefit of story editing is that the well-edited story is easier to remember.

4. Key to Narrative Complexity

Over the last forty years, the psychologist Dan McAdams has studied "narrative identity," or how people tell their life stories, using a method called the "Life Story Interview." An interview begins with this prompt: "Please begin by thinking about your life as if it were a book or novel. Imagine that the book has a table of contents containing the titles of the main chapters in the story. To begin here, please describe very briefly what the main chapters in the book might be. What does a table of contents for your book look like? How many chapters are there in your book? How would you name each chapter?"

Once the interviewee answers these questions, they are asked to think of a few key scenes that stand out in their story: What was the high point of your life? What was the low point? What was the turning point? Can you name a positive childhood memory? Can you name a negative childhood memory?

Then the interviewee is asked to imagine their future: What is the next chapter of your life? What are your dreams, hopes, and plans? Then there are questions about challenges, religious and political ideology, and values. Finally, the interviewee is asked to reflect upon their life story and extract a main theme. As you can imagine, this interview typically takes a few hours.

There are many ways to classify narratives, but two main types are the redemption narrative and the contamination narrative. George W. Bush's story is a typical redemption narrative that goes from good to bad before it hits a turning point and concludes with a happy ending. G.W.'s story was so prototypical that McAdams even wrote a book entitled *George W. Bush and the Redemptive Dream*. The other archetype is a contamination narrative, where people tell a story that starts out good but goes south after a certain point.

Narrative identity, or how we tell our life stories, is associated with various personality traits. For example, individuals who tell a redemptive story report themselves to be more conscientious, agreeable, extraverted, and less neurotic than those who do not. The emotional tone of a life narrative is more positive among agreeable, conscientious, and non-neurotic people than among disagreeable, unconscientious, and neurotic people. Individuals high in openness to experience tend to tell more complex stories than those low in openness. So, one's personality colors how they tell their life story.

Recent studies also show that the perspective of a life story changes the way people tell it. For instance, Benjamin Rogers and colleagues asked half of a group of participants a series of questions such as: "What makes you *you*?" "What change of setting or novel experience prompted your journey to become who you are today?" "What overall goal were you striving for that led to who you are today?" "What challenges or obstacles, such as a nemesis/rival or negative event, stood in the way of your journey?" "How did you personally grow as part of your journey to become who you are today?" "In what ways has your journey left a legacy?" These are the prompts that presumably lead a person to think of themselves as the hero of their story. The other half of participants were asked a series of mundane questions such as, "Tell us various features of your life . . . such as your work and home." Telling their stories as a hero made people feel that their lives were more meaningful and flourishing. Ultimately, the way you view your role in your own life—whether you see yourself as a hero of the story or as an observer—does make a difference in terms of how the story is told and whether your life sounds more satisfying, more meaningful, and, most likely, psychologically richer.

5. Build Your Portfolio of Psychological Richness

Memory is key to a psychologically rich life. If we forget a past event, we miss out on the chance to add that experience to our portfolio of psychological wealth. But how do we remember? Looking to cognitive science, it's clear that deep processing, rehearsal, and consolidation are the keys. In other words, we need to pay attention to what is happening, think about an event frequently, and elaborate on it in order to remember it.

Some people are naturally more reflective. If you reflect on the events of the day every night, you are much more likely to remember events than those who don't. One of the reasons why sensation-seekers might not lead a far more psychologically rich life than non-sensation-seekers—despite the fact that sensation-seekers seek out more diverse, novel experiences than non-sensation-seekers—is that they don't reflect upon their experiences. In one study, sensation-seekers did poorly in short-term memory and working memory tasks, relative to non-sensation-seekers. Without reflection, experience serves as a momentary thrill. After a while, these people need more excitement. Sensation-seekers are like millionaires who party and spend all the money they have earned; they are wasting their adventures and not accumulating psychologically rich experiences.

If you are not naturally inclined to be introspective, though, what can you do? Having someone test your memory in everyday life is one way. For instance, my wife once asked me, "Shige, do you remember that exhibition at the Guggenheim? A Swedish woman . . . what was her name?" "I have no idea what you are talking about. When did we go?" "First year in New York. In winter. Super abstract." "Uh . . . huge, pink paintings? Af Klint or something?" "Yes, Hilma!" Then we can remind ourselves that Hilma af Klint created her amazing, abstract pieces before Piet Mondrian and Wassily Kandinsky, without any direct association with any major avant-garde artists. Unlike most artists, af Klint did not want the public to see her work until after her death.

Without my wife asking these questions, I would not have thought about the Klint exhibition, let alone remembered her paintings. So, having people ask you questions about your past experiences is really helpful. My wife, children, and students have fulfilled that role for me. They are also good listeners. If you have a captive audience, you are much more likely to tell them what happened each day. Retelling, in turn, helps you remember what happened (even if the stories themselves are not accurate recollections of exactly what happened).

A good listener not only asks the right questions and listens, but also helps you craft a story and see the point of your story. For example, Sixo, a character in Toni Morrison's *Beloved*, explains why he walks thirty miles to meet his woman: "She is a friend of my mind. She gather me, man. The pieces I am, she gather them and give them back to me in all the right order. It's good, you know, when you got a woman who is a friend of your mind." A good therapist can also help put confusing pieces together. Finding someone with whom you can talk about your past experiences on a regular basis helps you digest, remember, and accrue your experiences.

Some of you might not like company. After all, some people are like Daniel Plainview (played by Daniel Day Lewis) in the movie *There Will Be Blood*, who says, "I see the worst in people . . . I want to earn enough money, so I can get away from everyone." If you prefer a solitary solution, keeping a journal and rereading it is an excellent way to keep track of your experiences. Ernest Hemingway spent his twenties in Paris and kept detailed journals. Before he left Paris in 1930, he put them in a trunk and stored them in the basement of the Ritz Hotel. In 1956, he was having lunch with the manager of the Ritz, who told him that his trunk was still stored in the basement! So Hemingway went to the basement, retrieved his trunk, and, in it, discovered his journals from the 1920s. He read and wrote about his experiences in Paris later in his memoir, *A Moveable Feast*. Under the title, he wrote, "If you are lucky enough to have lived in Paris as a young man, then wherever you go for the rest of your life, it stays with you, for Paris is a moveable feast." Hemingway had so many extraordinary life experiences, ranging from World War I to World War II to the Spanish Civil War. His journalistic habits of recordkeeping helped him remember and cherish those unique experiences for years to come. As a result, Hemingway collected many moveable feasts.

I was too lazy to do this myself, but diaries and journals are building blocks of your future psychological richness. However, the benefits of journal keeping are not limited to memory. James Pennebaker discovered that by writing you can organize your thoughts and overcome a traumatic event. You can start to see why you did this, or why that happened, and what it all means. Likewise, you can look at old photo albums to refresh your memory.

In sum, the same series of events can be related in different ways, made more interesting by story editing. By emphasizing struggles and challenges, you can give your narrative a structure and transform it. You can make the same story more like a hero's journey by focusing on crises and how you overcame them. Alison Gopnik's *Atlantic* story in Chapter 4 is fascinating because it starts with a sudden crisis that prompts a long, unexpected intellectual journey. Toni Morrison's *Song of Solomon* is so good because the main character, Macon Dead III, nicknamed "Milkman," is totally clueless at the beginning, and readers slowly figure out his family mysteries and what the "Song of Solomon" really means alongside him. The bottom line is not how you tell a story per se, but what kinds of experiences you actually have, whether you reflect on them, and whether you can keep them in your psychological memorabilia box.

CHAPTER THIRTEEN

TWO REMAINING QUESTIONS

*Too Much Richness? Is It Possible to
Find Richness in the Familiar?*

Too much mystery is merely an annoyance. Too much
adventure is exhausting. And a little terror goes a long way.

—Dean Koontz

Before reaching the book's conclusion, I want to touch on two remaining questions. I hope by now you agree that there is a point to a life of exploration, curiosity, and psychological richness. But, first, you might be wondering if there is such a thing as too much psychological richness? I do, too. Second, most of the facilitators of psychological richness that I have discussed so far are on the side of "go" rather than "stay." Can we also gain psychological richness by staying, or from familiar objects and people?

1. Too Many Moves?

Most people agree that you cannot be too rich when it comes to material wealth. But can your life be too psychologically rich? I started my book with The Clash's "Should I Stay or Should I Go?" Here I assumed that moving is a more psychologically enriching experience than staying. But what if someone moves more than ten times over the course of their childhood?

Uli Schimmack and I analyzed the Midlife in the United States (MIDUS) data that were collected in 1995 and again in 2005. MIDUS, organized by the prominent well-being researcher Carol Ryff, included multiple indicators of well-being as well as information regarding how many times participants moved in childhood. We wondered if excessive childhood moves would be associated with unhappiness in adulthood.

The key takeaway from our paper was that excessive childhood moves could have a lingering negative effect on subjective well-being in adulthood among introverts because they tend to have a harder time making social connections in new places and end up with few close relationships in adulthood.

Our paper was published in June 2010. On July 9, 2010, *The New York Times* reported on our paper. In response, I received numerous emails from *Times* readers and others. At that point, we had not articulated the concept of psychological richness. So we were unable to test whether excessive childhood moves might affect psychological richness. But personal experiences shared by readers were highly informative in regard to happiness. Many who moved around as children reported continued difficulties in adulthood. For instance, here is an email from Mary.

> I read with much interest the *New York Times* article in the Sunday, July 11 edition. It was fascinating to me as I have been in and out of therapy for many years and I always seem to come back to one place—the fact that I moved and changed schools 12 times in 12 years—from 1st grade to 12th grade. It has always seemed like such an unlikely thing to have impacted my life in such a way and sometimes I even feel guilty bringing it up. It hardly compares to real trauma and yet I cannot let it go. Many thanks for a bit of validation and understanding. Mary

Many others expressed similar struggles. Like Mary, Liz went to eleven schools in multiple countries, called herself "one of those children . . . it was a constant move, move, move." She also went in and out of psychiatric units, but psychiatrists could not find anything wrong. She could not settle down, put down roots, and find any sort of contentment. Twenty-year-old Gus faced similar issues. From kindergarten to eighth grade, he was a new kid at a different school every year. He was never close to anyone. At the end of his email, he wrote, "I feel so lost." Peggy, a sixty-three-year-old mother of three children, had thirteen childhood moves, and she wondered if her inability to fit in was caused by this lack of stability. Finally, Jim, sixty-one years old, went to eight grade schools and three high schools. He told me that he has very few friends and has a "problem with getting attached to people" as well as drugs, fights, and jail. Jim said, "I wish I could get past being angry about all the moving and missing all the things you are supposed to do as a kid growing up. I know there are others out there like me."

Their difficulties are in part due to the fact that the moves were initiated by their parents. They did not get to decide whether to stay or go, yet they had to suffer the consequences of the moves. As Mary and Liz mentioned, they do not have any particular diagnosable psychopathologies: rather, difficulty forming relationships with others seems to be at the core of most of these readers' problems. They are like trees transplanted too many times. It is hard to be uprooted from a familiar soil and then grow roots in a new soil once, let alone being uprooted again and again. Yet, they blame themselves for their struggle.

I am not a clinical psychologist, so my suggestions might be off target. But here are a few suggestions for people struggling with childhood instability. A first step is to embrace the fact that this is fundamentally not their fault. A second step is to find someone who can understand their predicament, perhaps someone else who had similar difficulties early on, like a sibling who experienced the same repeated moves, or an adult child of a military or diplomat family. My hope is that once they find someone who can understand and validate their childhood difficulties and sub-sequent struggles, they might be able to focus on some positive aspects of having lived in diverse environments.

Indeed, some emails I received show just that. Here is an email from Tom.

> I read with interest this morning a report on your recent paper dealing with children who move frequently (*UVA Today*). I have been interested in this topic for quite a while as I grew up in a Navy family and moved, during my child-hood years, every 2–3 years. Once we actually lived in the same house for 4 years, but I changed schools 3 times dur-ing that period. . . .
>
> I found, quite consciously while growing up, that it was very important to gain rapid peer respect among some group at each new school and in each new neighborhood. I found the safest and best way for me was to excel in school—go to the head of the class. Start day one each fall letting them know there was a new guy in town who was serious competition—and have no doubt, among the top echelon of students in each school, there is always competi-tion. . . . I'm not sure how valuable anecdotal information like mine is to you, but I'd be happy to trade thoughts about it with you anytime.

Similarly, Erin wrote, "I moved a lot and I do regret not hav-ing close friends," but she also thanked her parents for giving her opportunities to have "a wide variety of experiences with people from different places" and "[see] our country, not just visiting but immersing myself in it."

Finally, D.J. moved over forty-five times in his life and went to eleven different schools in twelve years. He compared his life to that of a friend from third grade in Colorado, who still lives in the same area and only left to serve in the air force for a few years before returning. His friend thinks he is crazy for moving so much, and D.J. thinks his friend is crazy for staying in the same place. D.J. sees that both sides have their drawbacks and their perks. His friend has a hard time remembering particular years or when things happened to him. D.J. can easily track years based on where he was living at the time. D.J. says, "I have re-created myself so many times and had the opportunity to change how people perceived me." Most revealingly, he summarizes his views: "I think satisfaction can be found in both lifestyles. For me staying in one place would have been torture, for him [his Colorado friend] moving would be unthinkable."

With as many moves as D.J. has experienced, for him there is no such thing as too many moves or too much richness. In contrast, for Mary, Liz, Gus, Peggy, and Jim, eight to thirteen moves were definitely too much. When asking the question of whether there can be too much richness, one's personality, family situation, and many other contextual factors clearly play an important role.

2. A Twenty-Four-Hour Live Concert: Too Much Stimulation?

Speaking of extremity, have you heard of a twenty-four-hour concert? No, it is not a recorded concert that you can listen to anytime you want. It is a twenty-four-hour live concert! Taylor Mac performed *A 24-Decade History of Popular Music* at St. Ann's Warehouse in Brooklyn in 2016, singing and dancing for twenty-four hours straight, from noon on Saturday to noon on Sunday. The critic Wesley Morris praised the show in *The New York Times*: "Mr. Mac gave me one of the great experiences of my life. . . . It wasn't simply the physical feat. . . . He remembered all the lyrics . . . he *sang* them—in every imaginable style, at every tempo, with every possible facial expression and every register of his handsome, protean voice."

My first impression was that this was a ridiculous idea. Who would voluntarily deprive themselves of sleep and sit on an uncomfortable chair all day? I was surprised to learn that 850 people were crazy enough to pay to be there. And this was a uniquely transformational experience for Morris: "Early on, he made a stirring case for the British homophobia of 'Yankee Doodle,' and lets you think its standing as an American staple is an early example of American *re*-appropriation. Anyway, I'll never hear the song the same way again." The audience was asked to actively participate in a war scene, among others, and act like racists and homophobes to feel what hate actually feels like. They felt love, empathy, and, according to Morris, "the shredding of shame."

Morris was not alone. Arts editor Alex Needham wrote in *The Guardian* on the same day: "Staying up for such a long time has a strange effect on one's state of mind. I've never had strong feelings about 'You Keep Me Hangin' On' by the Supremes, but Mac's version, sung by an imaginary bus of gay people going to support the civil rights movement's 1963 March on Washington, brings sudden tears to my eyes. . . . At 7am, the Brooklyn United Marching Band, a troupe of black boys in pink caps, file on to the stage and batter the hell out of their drums to provide a seismic conclusion to 'Move on Up,' Curtis Mayfield's anthem of African American pride and self-determination. . . . This combination of sound, spectacle and a spirit of joyful activism against injustice is so powerful it all but tears the roof off, and as the audience roars for what seems like about five minutes, Mac laughs: 'We still have five hours.'" Concertgoers at Taylor Mac's concert did unusual things and felt unfamiliar emotions, which resulted in changes in perspective.

This is a prime example of a psychologically rich experience.

But who wants to spend all night doing it? I am all for psychological richness, but even I would still hesitate to sign up for this concert. There are good reasons why a typical concert lasts only a few hours. Again, for people like Wesley Morris and Alex Needham, this was a supersized rich experience. For others, however, this might be too much, even dangerous to their health.

In the end, though, we can't know what is too much for us until we try. We have an instinct to run away from risks, which helps us survive. But too much running away makes us too timid to truly live. We need to push ourselves beyond our comfort zones every once in a while. The film director and writer Sarah Polley published a book entitled *Run Towards the Danger,* describing a series of tragedies and dangerous situations she experienced. Next time you encounter danger, you might consider challenging yourself and running toward it.

3. Finding Richness in the Familiar?

The remaining question is whether we can find richness in the familiar, not just in the unfamiliar. Søren Kierkegaard's 1843 *Either/Or* is all about the conflicts between stability and instability, boredom and excitement, long term and short term, rationality and passion, planning and spontaneity. As summarized earlier, this book juxtaposes Author A (presumably a young man) with Author B (presumably the retired judge). "A" promotes an aesthetic life, or a life of beauty and adventure, whereas "B" promotes a life of commitment. So far, I have argued for embracing A's priorities: novelty, passion, spontaneity, going with the flow. Indeed, by trying new things in life, you constantly learn and grow. But is that the only path to a psychologically rich life? Is it also possible to gain psychological richness from B's perspective, by digging deep into one person or object?

Some of the richest experiences in life involve finding something new in a familiar person, object, or place. I met my wife in 1991 and we got married in 1999. I spent a lot of time with her before marriage. Even so, there were many things that I didn't know about her until after we were married. For instance, after years of leaving most of the walls in our house empty, I finally wanted to hang some paintings on the living room wall. This was around 2010, nearly twenty years after I first met her. "What should I buy?" I asked. My wife replied, "I can paint." "What?" I did not know she could paint. And boy could she paint. She has painted so much that most of our walls are now graced by her paintings.

My wife is a friendly but very anxious person. She worries about the many things that could go wrong in life. She is also a meticulous person who does everything very methodically and slowly. She sometimes spends more than thirty minutes writing a simple reply to an email. She's that kind of person. So I expected her paintings to be rather dark and to take a while to finish. I was surprised to see her paint pears in pink and sky blue and create Mondrian-style canvases in pastel colors, all very, very quickly. Her paintings were so happy. She went about making them so decisively. Deep down, she must be a very happy person. Yet, if I had never wanted a painting for our living room wall, I might have never discovered this aspect of my wife's personality. Learning something new about my wife, two decades into our relationship, was enriching for both of us. There are some things you only learn from knowing one person for a long time.

"B" in *Either/Or* argues that a sense of novelty, passion, spontaneity, even adventure can be sustained within the institution of marriage, stating that "for me this is a matter of the continual rejuvenation of our first love. . . . This rejuvenation . . . is not just a sad backward glance, or the poetic memory of an experience. . . . This is an activity." So what is the activity? The answer is an internal action, or reflection, including gratitude to God. "A thanksgiving of this kind, like all prayer, is combined with an element of action, not in an external but an internal sense, in this case to want to hold on to this first love." According to B, grateful reflection in the context of religion helps you maintain your love toward your partner.

Is there any evidence for B's assertion about the continual rejuvenation of first love? Frank Fincham and colleagues did a fascinating study on prayer in the context of romantic relationships. In one study, participants who were currently in an exclusive romantic relationship were recruited. One group of participants was randomly assigned into the prayer condition. In this condition, they were asked to pray at least once a day for the well-being of their partner for four weeks. The other group was simply asked to take some time each day to think about what they had done that day. Four weeks later, they all reported whether they had engaged in infidelity as well as on their level of relationship satisfaction. Those randomly assigned to the prayer condition were less likely to engage in infidelity than those in the control condition. Furthermore, those in the prayer condition felt that their romantic relationship was more holy and sacred than those in the control condition.

In *Either/Or,* B also argues that the element of history, or the remembrance of shared experiences, is something that marital love has but first love lacks: "The historical nature of marital love is apparent from its being a process of assimilation; it tries its hand in what it experiences and refers its experience back to itself . . . love emerges tested and purified from this movement and assimilates the experience." Couples often tell each other the same stories. My wife and I often recite a Halloween story about when our first son dressed as Thomas the Tank Engine when he was three years old. My wife made a Thomas costume, a cardboard train decorated with blue felt fabric and yellow and red tape, while I made a chimney-shaped hat. He looked super cute. We brought him to UVA's big Halloween trick-or-treat on the university's grounds. It was fun until our son had a little accident—I'll spare you the details.

B talks about the development of fellowship in *Either/Or*. Marital love is not just passion and thrill, but also shared memory of adversity. Fellowship emerges out of repeated shared experiences over an extended period of time. Couples who have children can bond over parenthood and learn something new from raising them. As B says, "The whole of life is lived again in the children; only then does one come to some understanding of one's own life." When your kids go to elementary school, you will reexperience your elementary school days from a parental perspective. When they go to high school, you will reexperience being in high school, noticing both similarities and differences. B uses poetic reproduction of music as a metaphor for marital love: "In music an even tempo may have much beauty and great effect"—even if it is monotonic. That is, marital love might suffer from monotony, but monotony can be an even tempo that, played properly, produces beauty and great effect. According to Kierkegaard's B, marital love can be like Maurice Ravel's *Boléro* and Philip Glass's *Metamorphosis*: very monotonic on the surface but rich and beautiful deep down.

4. How to Keep the Fire

Marital monotony can be beautiful, as Kierkegaard's B suggests. But for most, like Kierkegaard's A, it can also be boring. How can we continue to rejuvenate our long-term romantic relationships, beyond prayer? Art Aron and colleagues conducted one of the most famous relationship experiments, which can help us answer this question. In the experiment, dating and married couples were randomly assigned into one of two conditions. Those assigned to a "novel-arousing" task condition were instructed to travel the length of several gym mats and back (roughly thirty feet), remaining on their hands and knees at all times and returning to the starting point, where they were to cross over a rolled-up gym mat approximately three feet high. In addition, they were asked to carry a pillow without using hands, arms, or teeth, even while going over the barrier. They were asked to do this three times in under one minute. In the control condition, couples simply rolled a ball in turn.

As Aron predicted, couples completing the novel-arousing task reported significantly higher levels of relationship quality than those completing the mundane task after the activity. The researchers then replicated these findings with a new sample of sixty-three married couples. In a final study, the researchers added two discussion tasks before and after the activity. Couples in the novel-arousing task condition not only reported higher levels of relationship quality but also exhibited more loving gestures during the later discussion task than those in the mundane condition.

Aron and colleagues found that engaging in novel and challenging activities could rekindle love, and even passion. In a separate line of research, they also found that 40 percent of those married over ten years reported being "very intensely in love." It turns out that it is possible to keep love alive over many years. In another study, the researchers used a neuroimaging technique, showing participants facial images of their partner as well as images of a close friend and a stranger. Participants had been married for an average of 21.4 years, yet they showed far stronger activation in the brain regions associated with the dopamine-rich reward system, such as the ventral tegmental area and dorsal striatum, when they saw their partner's image than when they saw a close friend or a stranger. Kierkegaard's B was right in that it is possible to maintain passion over a long period of time.

Aron's well-known "self-expansion theory" of romantic relationships posits that, at the beginning of a relationship, two individuals engage in intense conversations with a lot of self-disclosure; as time passes, their partner becomes part of themselves, essentially expanding the self. However, after the initial phase of mutual self-disclosure, opportunities for further expansion are limited. Aron theorizes that the typical decline in marital satisfaction over the course of a marriage is due in part to this lack of new opportunities to expand the self, and that engagement in novel activities could provide further opportunities for self-expansion. In this way, couples can experience "continuous rejuvenation."

In an interview, Art Aron said he and his wife, Elaine, took their findings to heart: They took walking trips in Japan, Italy, Serbia, and New Zealand. They painted pictures of each other, attended horse races, rafted down the Colorado River in the Grand Canyon, and went whale watching. Novelty is effective for long-term romantic couples, as is shared reflection.

5. Jiro: The Art of Lifelong Devotion

Jiro Dreams of Sushi was the title of David Gelb's 2011 documentary about Jiro Ono, a then eighty-five-year-old sushi chef in Tokyo. Jiro is obsessed with sushi, constantly trying to improve his techniques. He fusses about the temperature of sushi rice to the extreme; it must be the perfect temperature to maximize the taste of the fish. He uses a massage technique to make his octopus more tender. He started off by massaging the octopus for thirty minutes; when he experimented with even longer massages, customers seemed to enjoy the sushi even more. Even though Jiro had already earned three Michelin stars with the thirty-minute massage, now he massages the octopus for forty-five minutes before cooking. He could have been satisfied with the methods he had already developed to get to the pinnacle of culinary art. Nonetheless, he always looks for ways to improve. He pays close and critical attention to each customer's facial expressions after each bite. The selection of fish is as meticulous. His fifty-something son goes to the Tsukiji fish market to source all the ingredients from specialty merchants: shrimp from the same trusted shrimp merchant, eel from the same trusted eel merchant, and so forth. Every aspect of the preparation and cooking is exact, assessed every day, and improved over time. Jiro even cares about whether a customer is right-handed or left-handed, so that a right-handed customer would not be seated next to a left-handed customer, or vice versa: instead, a left-handed person would sit in the corner seat, where no one sits on their left.

Because of war and poverty, Jiro left home at age nine. He did an apprenticeship in a sushi restaurant for many years, and finally opened up his own at age forty. At that point, he started training three to five apprentices at any given time. An apprentice starts out cleaning the restaurant and doing dishes. After ten years of cleaning work, Jiro finally allows an apprentice to cook a tamago sushi (egg custard sushi). Even Nakazawa, now a renowned sushi chef in New York, made two hundred tamagoyakis as an apprentice before Jiro finally deemed one usable. In the world of sushi shokunin (the professional sushi chef), as in any artisanal profession in Japan, there has always been a long and demanding training period. People go through this brutal apprenticeship because in the end they want to open up their own restaurants and succeed.

In Chapter 7, I talked about how Michael Phelps and Simone Biles, arguably the best swimmer and gymnast of all time, suffered from depression and lost interest in the sports they excelled at. So, why didn't Jiro also burn out after doing the same thing every day for over sixty years? First, Jiro's quest for perfection is private and personal, whereas Phelps's and Biles's were public and in the context of competition with other athletes. What is so tough about being an elite athlete is that every defeat is objectively recorded and becomes public. While Jiro has had many competitors, Jiro's performance was not closely watched against the performances of others. Second, like all sushi chefs in Japan, Jiro faced diverse, unexpected challenges over time. As some popular sushi fish disappeared from Tokyo Bay, Jiro had to adjust the type of sushi he served over the years. All these environmental changes have forced him to change the way he creates his menu. These challenges as well as economic challenges keep him on his toes. Whereas some elite athletes tend to ruminate on their performance and need to motivate themselves to train hard every day, Jiro has been preoccupied with various daily decisions and demands. Because of all the challenges, he hasn't had time to really ruminate on his mistakes (I assume even a master makes them now and then). Third, going back to the theme of Chapter 7, Jiro is playful. He was a very mischievous boy, according to an interview with his elementary school friends in the documentary. He has carried his sense of lightheartedness well into his eighties, still joking around with his customers.

After all, sushi is a creative art. Jiro can come up with any number of ways to create a new nigiri or a new way to cook eel if he ever gets bored with the extant menu. He thinks that he can still improve as a sushi chef. Jiro opened Sukiyabashi Jiro in 1965. That is a long time to be the head chef of the same restaurant in the same location. But even after so many years, he hates holidays when he has to close his restaurant. He always looks forward to working at his restaurant. Even if you do the same things every day for many decades, you can still find something new to try regularly.

The work of a shokunin, like Jiro, is different from that of an amateur because it requires lifetime devotion. It changes over time as a shokunin acquires new techniques and perspectives. Jiro somehow finds a way to feel the continuous rejuvenation of his first love for sushi. One way to reach psychological richness is to follow Jiro's path: devotion to one career, provided that the chosen career is deep enough for lifelong exploration.

6. Why the Beatles?

Why are the Beatles so much more popular than the Beach Boys? Looking at Spotify, the Beach Boys have an astonishing 11,861,427 monthly listeners, as of this writing. However, the Beatles have a mind-blowing 30,561,926 monthly listeners, almost three times that of the Beach Boys. They were both extremely popular worldwide in the 1960s. The two bands were active for similar periods and released comparable numbers of albums. Yet today I see more college students listening to the Beatles than the Beach Boys. Why?

One possible explanation is that the Beatles' popular songs are very diverse, ranging from simple love songs such as "All You Need Is Love" and "I Want to Hold Your Hand," to nostalgic and gentle songs such as "Yesterday" and "Hey Jude," to highly philosophical and spiritual ones such as "Let It Be," "Nowhere Man," and "Across the Universe," to rebellious ones such as "Revolution" and "Come Together." The Beatles had an initial "goody-goody" boy band phase, then a countercultural phase, a spiritual phase, and a discontentment phase. They had three members composing songs, John, Paul, and George, giving them more variety than the Beach Boys, with Brian Wilson as a solo composer. Wilson is famously innovative and experimental, so the Beach Boys did produce diverse songs. But for a casual music lover, the Beach Boys are often equated with "Surfin' U.S.A.": "Everybody's gone surfin', surfin' U.S.A." If the Beach Boys' *Pet Sounds* had been played more often than *Surfin' U.S.A.*, more people might have been interested in the Beach Boys.

In the summer of 2020, when it was increasingly clear that the pandemic was here to stay, I felt as though there was no way out, a sense of stuckness, and I stayed shut inside all day. When would we be able to eat out and hang out? When could I go back to Japan and see my aging parents? Being locked down at home, we watched a lot of movies. One of them was the 2019 movie

Yesterday. The protagonist, a struggling singer, realizes that he is the only person who remembers the Beatles and starts singing the Beatles' songs and becomes famous. The movie was OK. Still, it was memorable for a completely different reason other than the plot. When the main character sings "The Long and Winding Road," I just could not stop crying. I was watching it with my wife and two teenage kids, so it was very embarrassing. But its lyrics captured how I felt during COVID.

With the Beatles, Bob Dylan, and Aretha Franklin, you can go deep and always find something new, as they left abundant, diverse bodies of work. Still, it is important to distinguish between nostalgia and psychological richness. Many people keep listening to the same bands because of nostalgia. Here the main activity is the reenactment of the past, returning to the same familiar comfort zone. To be clear, nostalgia—sentimental longing for one's past—has a number of benefits, ranging from a sense of connection between one's past and present, to social connectedness, to helping us find meaning in our lives. However, listening to the same band for the sake of nostalgia does not increase psychological richness. In contrast, if you keep listening to the same band because you keep noticing something you didn't notice before, that is a psychologically rich experience, one of finding richness in a familiar object.

7. Then There Is Virginia Woolf

Like the Beatles, Virginia Woolf has enthusiastic fans across generations. The novelist Jenny Offill wrote an essay entitled "A Lifetime of Lessons in *Mrs. Dalloway*" for *The New Yorker.* She summarizes why it's possible to read *Mrs. Dalloway* many times and discover many new things on each read. When she first read it, she was seventeen or eighteen years old. She was captivated by Septimus Warren Smith, the war veteran with a deep trauma. Woolf introduced him as "aged about thirty, pale-faced, beak-nosed," adding, "The world has raised its whip; where will it descend?" Offill thought, "Yes, this. Exactly this." Then, in her thirties, she read it again. This time she was intrigued by Clarissa Dalloway, who noticed things like "the laughing girls taking their absurd woolly dogs for a run." Finally, Offill read it again as she became Mrs. Dalloway's age, "just broken into her fifty-second year." This time, she was moved by Peter Walsh, Clarissa's old flame, who finds relief in self-distancing; everything becomes less personal.

When I read *Mrs. Dalloway*, I was Clarissa Dalloway and Peter Walsh's age. That made it easy to identify with those characters: all the obligations of daily life, ennui, and the past obsessions and obsession with the past. Peter Walsh talks about his own failure, saying, "He had been a Socialist, in some sense a failure—true. Still the future of civilisation lies, he thought, in the hands of young men like that; of young men such as he was, thirty years ago; with their love of abstract principles; getting books sent out to them all the way from London to a peak in the Himalayas; reading science; reading philosophy." At the end of the party, Sally, Clarissa's close friend in adolescence who used to deride Richard, Clarissa's husband, as not smart enough, says, "Richard has improved. You are right. I shall go and talk to him. I shall say good-night. What does the brain matter . . . compared with the heart?" Old Peter, in the end, reflects, "What is this terror? What is this ecstasy? . . . What is it that fills me with extraordinary excitement?" His answer was Clarissa, his old flame.

For a well-educated and well-traveled person, Peter is truly clueless as to what he wants in his life. When he was young, he thought he would be a writer. Sally asked, "Have you written?" Peter replied, at age fifty-two, "Not a word!" and laughed. Throughout the novel, Peter thinks about Clarissa, Clarissa in childhood, adolescence, and adulthood. Although he found love in India, he could not keep his eyes off her. What is so attractive about Clarissa? That is largely a mystery to me. But here is a fifty-two-year-old man still madly in love with his old girlfriend. No boredom here, but pure, genuine, endless curiosity about one woman. As Offill finds a lifetime of lessons from *Mrs. Dalloway*, Peter keeps finding old and new appeal in Clarissa.

8. Why You Learn Something New from the Old

There is a popular proverb in Japan, 温故知新. The first character means "warm," the second "old," the third "knowledge," and the last "new." *Warm the old, then you will learn something new.* We often learn something new from studying something very old.

Kierkegaard's B in *Either/Or* believes in the sanctity of marriage, and with the right mindset of gratitude, we could all learn more about ourselves and our partner. Art Aron's research shows that an occasional infusion of novelty in a long-term romantic relationship is key to relationship longevity. Jiro Ono has been busy perfecting his sushi art for six decades, even after getting a three-star rating from Michelin. The Beatles, Bob Dylan, Aretha Franklin, Miles Davis, Picasso, Yayoi Kusama, Hilma af Klint, Kara Walker—all have embraced experiment, tried new styles, and evolved over time. You can learn something new from each of these artists by digging deeper and deeper into their work over a long period of time. If you don't feel like reading, listening to, or studying something new, you might try old favorites that you haven't engaged with for a long time. You might discover something new and rich.

CHAPTER FOURTEEN

A GOOD LIFE WITHOUT REGRETS

Final Thoughts on a Life in Three Dimensions

I really like familiarity. It's not something to be proud of, but it's just who I am. I think there's probably a lot of people out there that feel the same way. . . . It's really been a good show for me, kind of facing a lot of demons, being able to crawl out of my comfort zone.

—Eugene Levy, on his new show *The Reluctant Traveler*

In this book, I introduced the new concept of a *psychologically rich* life, adding to the two better-known paths to a good life: a happy life and a meaningful life. Now that you know the ingredients of a happy life, a meaningful life, and a psychologically rich life, let's see if you can start seeing the world through a new lens: life in three dimensions.

1. The Way You Want It

Toward the end of Toni Morrison's *Jazz,* Violet, the main character, recalls a conversation with her hairdresser. Her hairdresser says, "What's the world for you if you can't make it up the way you want it?" Violet is surprised by the question; the thought had never crossed her mind. "What's the point? I can't change it." The hairdresser insists, "That's the point . . . [I] forgot it was mine. My life."

If you don't think of the world the way you want it, you forget it is your life. So, let us not forget that this is our life and that we want something more than what it is. Maybe more happiness, more meaning, or more psychological richness. Instead of waiting until you've reached your deathbed, perhaps try to reflect after each milestone: What would you say about your high school life at the end of high school? What about your college life at the end of college? At the end of your first job? What about parenting when your child graduates from high school? The triad model of a good life—happiness, meaning, and psychological richness— gives you three dimensions with which you can evaluate your experiences.

2. What Is a Good Job?

In 1890, William James invented the self-esteem equation in *The Principles of Psychology,* which is written as follows: "self-esteem = success/pretentions." By pretentions, James meant one's aspirations. So, self-esteem is high if one has fulfilled most of their aspirations, and low if they haven't. According to this formula, there are two ways to increase self-esteem. One is to increase the amount of success. The other way is to reduce aspiration. James's self-esteem equation could be applied to happiness as well. To simplify to the extreme, happiness could be stated as the function of two factors: success (personal, interpersonal, or societal) / (divided by) aspirations. One could increase happiness by increasing success or by reducing aspirations. The American cultural emphasis is on enhancing the amount of success by working harder, whereas the Danish cultural emphasis, for instance, is on minimizing aspirations.

That being said, what kinds of success are we talking about?

Sigmund Freud said that the two main tasks of humans are to work and to love. If you are successful in work and love, you have likely succeeded in life. So let's look at success at work. There are many ways to define success at work; one way is to ask workers how satisfied they are with their jobs. Those who say they are satisfied with their jobs are those who are succeeding. I analyzed Payscale's survey of over two million people in 502 job categories. According to this data, what predicts job satisfaction? More precisely, what kinds of workers have higher-than-average job satisfaction?

For instance, 80 percent of actuaries are satisfied with their jobs. Similarly, 78 percent of computer and information scientists are satisfied with their jobs. In contrast, only 65 percent of police officers are satisfied with their jobs. Social workers were even worse, at only 59 percent satisfied. Why are actuaries and computer scientists more satisfied at work than social workers and police officers? Pay might be one reason. Given the difficult jobs that social workers and police officers do every day, their pay is not that great. Perhaps they feel they are not fairly compensated for what they do. Indeed, across 502 jobs, median salary was strongly correlated with average job satisfaction.

Just as happiness is not the only way to a good life, job satisfaction is not the only way to define success at work. What about meaning in one's job? Interestingly, Payscale measured this. Although the vast majority of actuaries and computer scientists are satisfied with their jobs, many of them do not find their jobs to be very meaningful. For instance, only 36 percent of actuaries find meaning in their jobs, and only 45 percent of computer and information scientists do. In contrast, although social workers and police officers are not super satisfied with their jobs, they find them to be meaningful. Indeed, 73 percent of social workers and 81 percent of law enforcement officers find their jobs to be meaningful.

Are there good jobs that are not high in job satisfaction or meaning, though? The Payscale data show an interesting pattern. While 65 percent of editors find their jobs to be satisfying, only 42 percent find them meaningful. Similarly, 67 percent of art directors are satisfied with their jobs, but only 35 percent find their work meaningful. Writers and authors are very similar to art directors, scoring 67 percent in satisfaction and 30 percent in meaning. Funeral directors are an interesting comparison group. They are similar in terms of job satisfaction: 68 percent of funeral directors are satisfied with their jobs. However, 87 percent of them find their jobs to be meaningful.

If satisfaction and meaning were the only metrics of good jobs, then we might tell art directors, editors, and writers to consider becoming funeral directors. Realistically, we wouldn't, because we know that editors, art directors, and writers have something that funeral directors don't have: self-expression and creativity. Payscale did not ask survey respondents how interesting their jobs were, how much creativity mattered in their jobs, or other questions pertaining to psychological richness. My guess is that many art directors, editors, and writers would say that their jobs are interesting, creative, and psychologically rich. This may be a reason why people continue in such professions. The benefit of the three-dimension framework for defining a good life is that it can be applied to the professional sphere, explaining why some jobs low in happiness or meaning could still be good—psychologically rich—jobs.

3. What Is a Good Vacation?

For your next vacation, would you like to take an all-inclusive luxury tour or a low-key backpacking trip? The all-inclusive tour is easy. All you have to do is pay and show up. The tour company has a plan. They'll entertain you from morning to night—you can just sit back and enjoy. The backpacking trip would be a lot harder. You don't know what kind of accommodations you'll end up with. You have to plan pretty much everything by yourself. It's all on you: it could be great, but it could also be a disaster.

In the podcast *Two Psychologists Four Beers,* Yoel Inbar and Alexa Tullett used those trip metaphors to describe a happy life and a psychologically rich life. A happy life is like a Caribbean cruise. Everything is planned. You get fed, and everything is taken care of. When we asked participants from nine countries to describe an ideal life, many Americans wrote about a life that resembled a luxury cruise. For instance, an eighteen-year-old University of Virginia student wrote, "On a beach with lots of money and a happy family. I would not want to worry about working as I would have been successful enough so I would not have to work anymore." For many, a vacation (and an ideal life) is for relaxation and rejuvenation, for being served and entertained.

A psychologically rich trip is like a backpacking trip. You have to plan it all by yourself. You can choose what you want to do. At the same time, you never know what to expect, and you might encounter something bad. When I was a college freshman in Tokyo, my friend and I went on a backpacking trip in the U.S. We got the cheapest tickets available (Malaysia Airlines for about $700) from Tokyo to LA, and a thirty-day Greyhound pass, which was about $250. We did a thirty-day Greyhound bus trip from LA to San Francisco to Seattle to Mount Rushmore, South Dakota to Chicago to Niagara Falls to New York City to Washington D.C. By the time we were in D.C., we realized we were almost out of time, so the final three days were an almost nonstop bus ride from D.C. to LA. A seventy-hour bus ride . . . not exactly fun.

We didn't have any reservations for hotels in advance, so we looked for somewhere to stay once we arrived in Los Angeles, then in San Francisco, then in Seattle. All we could afford were youth hostels. The Greyhound stations were almost always in downtown areas, which were not the safest back in 1988. With our limited budget and minimal English, we encountered many scary moments. In New York City, a guy just outside our youth hostel on Forty-Second Street approached me and asked if he could borrow $20. A Citibank was right there. He said he would just go to the bank, get cash, and pay me back. "Follow me," he said. So I followed him to the bank and queued in line. After a while, he disappeared. That's how I was scammed out of $20 in Times Square, which was my daily budget!

Our bus from New York arrived in Washington D.C. in the early morning and we ended up falling asleep on a park bench near the White House. It wasn't long before a group of police officers on horseback appeared. They thought we were homeless and literally and physically kicked us out. Yet that same day, we were able to go inside the White House on a tour. We also went on the Capitol Hill tour for free.

When we were in Chicago, there was a huge festival in Grant Park. My friend went to see a White Sox game, but I wanted to go to this festival. So I went alone and ended up meeting three other young people there. They asked me to take a picture of them, so I did. Then we started talking. Before long, they were so nice that they invited me to a party at one of their houses. I didn't have a clue where the house was, nor did I have a change of clothes with me, but I said yes. It was the only time I had any alcohol during that trip. I fell asleep at the party house. The next morning, one of the people I'd met gave me a ride back to the downtown YMCA where I was staying. It turned out I had been somewhere in Wisconsin that night! I couldn't believe it.

Now, I can't say that Greyhound was the way to travel across the entire U.S. My butt certainly hurt from hours of sitting. But I came away from it with a memorable thirty days and the chance to see many sides of the U.S.

Some vacations are more about meaning. In Jonathan Safran

Foer's *Everything Is Illuminated*, the main character (also named Jonathan Safran Foer) travels to Ukraine in search of Augustine, a woman who saved his grandfather's life during World War II. The main purpose of such a trip is to learn more about your family's heritage: where and how they lived, what happened over the course of their lives. By learning about your family's heritage, you learn about yourself. A clear sense of your heritage also gives you a sense of coherence and significance: two key components of meaning in life.

Others opt for volunteer tourism, such as trips to support women's education in Nepal, medical volunteerism in Guatemala, or wildlife conservation in Kenya. Instead of a typical spring break beach trip, some college students volunteer for Habitat for Humanity. Just like a job, vacation can be catered toward increasing happiness, meaning, or psychological richness.

In sum, you can evaluate pretty much anything in terms of happiness, meaning, and psychological richness. Academic courses can be happy, meaningful, or psychologically rich courses. Some friends are fun to be with. Other friends are useful and helpful. Other friends help you expand your horizons. Some places, like Disneyland, help us forget all our troubles and be happy. Some places, such as Jerusalem and Rome, help us remember the past and think about the meaning of life. Other places encourage us to explore and gain psychological richness. New York, for instance, is where "there's nothing you can't do . . . these streets will make you feel brand-new, big lights will inspire you," according to Jay-Z and Alicia Keys in "Empire State of Mind." When you know what you want to maximize (happiness, meaning, or richness), you can start structuring your life and curating experiences that align your goals.

In this book, I have showcased a new path to a good life: psychological richness. To be clear, I am not arguing that a psychologically rich life is the best life, or that it's always better than a happy life or a meaningful life. Rather, I am arguing that prioritizing psychological richness is one way to lead a good life. Like Goldmund in *Narcissus and Goldmund,* even if you aren't happy and don't find your life to be meaningful, you can still lead a good life if you fill it with diverse, interesting, and perspective-changing experiences. And we've seen it is possible to benefit from more than one type of good life. For instance, Oliver Sacks seemed to be very happy at the end of his life. His life was also meaningful, since he touched and changed many patients' and caretakers' lives, and he certainly had many stories to tell. Sacks had all three forms of a good life after all. Linda, the taxi driver we met in Chapter 4, seems to have had it all, too. She is enjoying her retirement, having made a difference in the world over the span of a life filled with many unusual experiences.

So, it's fair to wonder: are there any other paths to a good life? Remember that empirical research into the question of a good life started in earnest only in the 1980s. The first thirty years of the endeavor produced two viable dimensions of a good life: happiness and meaning. Now we have discovered a third dimension: psychological richness. There might be other paths to a good life; new research might soon reveal a fourth (or more). Future research is likely to find cultural differences in the paths to a good life. In the end, this is a story of diverse paths to a good life. Knowing who you are and what you value will guide you in pursuing the right one.

4. Lessons of Psychological Richness

A psychologically rich life is a life with twists and turns, stops, detours, and turning points; a dramatic and eventful life instead of a familiar and cozy one; a life with complexity and multiplicity; a life of *expeditus,* or spontaneity, rather than a life of *deliberatio,* or careful deliberation; a life of long, winding journey rather than a simple and straightforward one. Before Jon Stewart's *The Daily*

Show, there was David Letterman's *Late Show.* I loved his quirky sense of humor. My favorite was his Top Ten lists. So, in the spirit of playfulness, I end my book with my own Top Ten list on psychological richness (see Appendix 3 for an alternative summary).

#10. LIFE WITHOUT REGRETS: Later in life, people tend to regret the things they could have done but did not: not taking a job offer, not moving to Boston when given the chance, not going back to school. It's easy to come up with an excuse for inaction, but when faced with a question of "Should I stay or should I go?" ask yourself: "In ten years, would I regret if I stayed?" Remember, we may regret what we do in the short run, but in the long run, our biggest regrets come from what we didn't do.

#9. FREEDOM OVER SECURITY: In an essay in *The New York Times Magazine,* poet Ada Calhoun recalls how her parents often told her growing up that "most choices could be boiled down to security or freedom, and that it was always better to choose freedom." She followed her parents' advice: she chose a job that allowed her more freedom, even though she hasn't had job benefits in years, and she chose to have a baby despite having no childcare plan. She now feels that "there is no greater security than being out on the right limb, with the right voice in your head." Ultimately, being able to choose freedom over security, possibility over responsibility, and challenge over ease is key to a psychologically rich life.

#8. DON'T BE A SPECIALIST; BE A GENERALIST: Most of us live in a highly specialized world with a meticulous division of labor. Professionally, specialization often leads to success. But too much specialization may lead us to miss the beauty of the forest for a tree. Stay curious in life, be a generalist, maybe even do it yourself once in a while!

#7. "TAKE A DOZEN": Both pigeons and humans don't explore enough. The comfort of familiarity is so powerfully attractive that we forget the joy of exploration, eating the same snack, going to the same chain, and sitting quietly on our commute. But acknowledge this bias and we can overcome it; the "take a dozen" heuristic reminds us to explore at least twelve potential mates, apartments, restaurants, etc., before we take our pick. We make a better decision when we explore more.

#6. FIND RICHNESS IN THE FAMILIAR: But if you are a Daniel Plainview ("I want to earn enough money, so I can get away from everyone") or a Eugene Levy ("I really like familiarity"), you can find richness in the familiar. Revisit a favorite band, author, book, film, or person, and you will discover new in the old.

#5. DON'T BE AFRAID OF NEGATIVE EVENTS: Many of us fall into the happiness trap. We fear negative events, try to avoid them at all costs, and blame ourselves for our discontent. But it is a fact of life: bad things happen. It's OK to fail; it's OK to feel negative emotions. Remember Nietzsche: these challenges will make you wiser. Remember James Joyce: *Per aspera ad astra*—through hardship to the stars. This is all part of your story. Embrace the richness it brings and let your psychological immune system kick in.

#4. WRITE AND TELL: Richness is the accumulation of interesting stories. It's important to remember them, and writing is an excellent way to do it. Telling a story is also a great way to remember. As you write and tell, you can edit your story. Keep the bad stuff but use it as a springboard for growth. Remember Hemingway's moveable feast and find your own. Just as wealth can be transferred across generations and help the next generation become materially rich, your stories can be transferred to the next generation and help them become psychologically rich.

#3. BE SPONTANEOUS: We live in a highly scheduled time. Most of us need an appointment to hang out with our friends. Next time you are bored, text your friends to see if they are free. Deviate from routines from time to time. Be Alice in *Alice in Wonderland*! Seek the unknown. Stop by a gallery, a used bookstore, or a Goodwill store. You never know what you will find.

#2. BE PLAYFUL! We all have a lot of obligations, from doing the dishes to filing our taxes. When we are so focused on getting things done, many things—especially enjoyable experiences, like reading a novel—appear to be a waste of time. Yet it is in playful moments and when you are "on vacation from social and economic reality" that we may discover something unexpected, learn something new, and gain new insight into our goals. "Be open to be a fool!"

#1. JUST DO IT! Beyond important life decisions, a mindset of psychological richness can help us make small, everyday decisions, too. Should I go to a new exhibition or stay home? Should I go on a hike? If you are the type of person who likes to stay within your comfort zone, then I suggest you take a chance and try something new—just do it! On days when people do something new, they feel that the day is psychologically richer, as well as happier and more meaningful.

In the poem "Ed," Louis Simpson introduces his title character Ed as a young man in love with a waitress named Doreen. His family and friends do not approve. So, instead he marries another woman. Years later, his wife leaves Ed. Ed complains to his friends and family that he should have married Doreen. His family and friends reply, "Well, why didn't you?" So I borrow from Simpson to give my last words to you: "Well, why don't you?"

Writing a book is like doing the biggest DIY project. At first, you think it is fairly straightforward. There are five steps: 1. Write a book proposal. 2. Find an agent. 3. Find a publisher. 4. Write. 5. Be surprised when it's published! But just like any DIY project, it is far more complicated than you think it will be. You get stuck. You blame yourself for getting involved in this project. You see no progress at all for the longest time. But then there is a turning point. All of a sudden it seems doable. Then one day it magically, actually ends, and you have a tangible product and a very rich experience.

Writing is typically a pretty lonely process. But all my family members got actively involved and made it less lonely. They were looking out for relevant materials for the book. Kai found a story about the Moroccan bookseller who read 4,000 books. Jin found Raymond Carver's poem "Happiness." Jae found the story about Joy Ryan, the national park enthusiast. So, it was a family book project.

I started my research on psychological richness in the summer of 2015. All the lab members at that time contributed to the initial psychological richness project: Erin Westgate, Hyewon Choi, Liz Gilbert, Jane Derk (formerly Tucker), Jordan Axt, Nick Buttrick, Samantha Heintzelman, Kosta Kushlev, Charlie Ebersole, Brandon Ng, and many undergraduate students at the University of Virginia. They also provided the book's foundational materials. For instance, Hermann Hesse's *Narcissus and Goldmund* was recommended by Jane Derk. Alison Gopnik's *Atlantic* article was Liz Gilbert's suggestion. Rebecca Solnit's *A Paradise Built in Hell* was Nick Buttrick's recommendation. Other former and current graduate students such as Jaime Kurtz and Youngjae Cha were involved in the richness studies included in this book. Colleagues and friends also gave me a lot of encouragement and suggestions. For instance, Tim Wilson and Jerry Clore gave thoughtful feedback on my first talk on psychological richness in September 2017. Michael Morris, who was the action editor of our *Psychological Review* article, suggested that I read Kierkegaard's *Either/Or* and James Joyce's *A Portrait of the Artist as a Young Man*.

I asked many to read my first complete draft in the summer of 2023. Tim Wilson was the first to read and comment on it. Jordan Axt, Lindsey Juarez, Liz Gilbert, and Jane Derk followed. Their constructive feedback (e.g., less detail; more signposting and solutions) was crucial to improve the book to its current form, which I think is quite readable, at least compared to the first draft.

My career started in 1995 at the University of Illinois at Urbana-Champaign under the guidance of Ed Diener. He founded happiness research in psychology. He was also an amazing advisor, mentor, and collaborator. Ed was at every milestone of my adult life; at my wedding in 1999, when I was a fourth-year PhD student, he said I would get a good job, which made Jae's parents happy. In 2006, when I gave a distinguished scientist lecture in Chicago, he and his wife, Carol, took our kids to the Lincoln Park Zoo afterward. In 2018, when I received the midcareer award from the Society for Personality and Social Psychology, he was there to help celebrate it. Ed passed away in April 2021. I miss him. He had a happy, meaningful, and psychologically rich life. I dedicate this book to Ed Diener.

I was lucky that my editor at Doubleday, Kris Puopolo, was already familiar with my work on a psychologically rich life and interested in publishing it. So I didn't have to sell the idea. She already understood its value. But that doesn't mean she just accepted whatever I wrote uncritically. She did have a lot of questions! Her questions helped me clarify the key features of a psychologically rich life. My book agent, Esmond Harmsworth, read my book proposal and helped me sharpen the central messages. Without their help, this project could not begin or end. I was also lucky to get grants from the John Templeton Foundation (via Dan Haybron) and the Templeton World Charity Foundation, which supported the psychological richness studies. I also made substantial progress on my book project during the 2022–2023 academic year, when the University of Chicago (Katie Kinzler, chair; Amanda Woodward, dean) gave me some time off from teaching. Kai Oishi, Jae Lee, Christine Yu, Cynthia Zhang, Charlotte Giff, Molly Rathbun, Gabriella Cordelli, Noura Abousy, Sae Kim helped me with proofreading. Finally, the biggest thanks goes to you, the reader. Thank you for reading it!

Chapter 1: Should I Stay or Should I Go?

3 in her novel *The Goldfinch:* Donna Tartt, *The Goldfinch* (New York: Little, Brown, 2013).

3 "even at the expense of one's own happiness?": Donna Tartt interview, *Charlie Rose,* February 7, 2014.

4 trying to make others happy will make you happy: Keiko Otake, Satoshi Shimai, Junko Tanaka-Matsumi, Kanako Otsui, and Barbara Fredrickson, "Happy People Become Happier Through Kindness: A Counting Kindness Intervention," *Journal of Happiness Studies* 7, no. 3 (2006): 361–75; Oliver Scott Curry, Lee Rowland, Casper Van Lissa, Sally Zlotowitz, John McAlaney, and Harvey Whitehouse, "Happy to Help? A Systematic Review and Meta-Analysis of the Effects of Performing Acts of Kindness on the Well-Being of the Actor," *Journal of Experimental Social Psychology* 76, no. 5 (2018): 320–29; Kristin Layous, S. Katherine Nelson, Jaime Kurtz, and Sonja Lyubomirsky, "What Triggers Prosocial Effort? A Positive Feedback Loop Between Positive Activities, Kindness, and Well-Being," *Journal of Positive Psychology* 12, no. 4 (2017): 385–98; Bryant Hui, Jacky Ng, Erica Berzaghi, Lauren Cunningham-Amos, and Aleksandr Kogan, "Rewards of Kindness? A Meta-Analysis of the Link Between Prosociality and Well-Being," *Psychological Bulletin* 146, no. 12 (2020): 1084–116, https://doi.org/10.1037/bul0000298.

4 trying to make yourself happy sometimes fails: June Gruber, Iris Mauss, and Maya Tamir, "A Dark Side of Happiness? How, When, and Why Happiness Is Not Always Good," *Perspectives on Psychological Science* 6, no. 3 (2011): 222–33.

4 prosocial spending: Elizabeth Dunn, Lara Aknin, and Michael Norton, "Spending Money on Others Promotes Happiness," *Science* 319, no. 5870 (2008): 1687–88; Lara Aknin, Elizabeth Dunn, Jason Proulx, Iris Lok, and Michael Norton, "Does Spending Money on Others Promote Happiness? A Registered Replication Report," *Journal of Personality and Social Psychology* 119, no. 2 (2020): e15–e26, https://doi.org/10.1037/pspa0000191; Iris Lok and Elizabeth Dunn, "Under What Conditions Does Prosocial Spending Promote Happiness?," *Collabra: Psychology* 6, no. 1 (2020): 5.

4 writing gratitude letters: Martin Seligman, Tracy Steen, Nansook Park, and Christopher Peterson, "Positive Psychology Progress: Empirical Validation of Interventions," *American Psychologist* 60, no. 5 (2005): 410–21, https://doi.org/10.1037/0003-066X.60.5.410; Christina Armenta, Megan Fritz, Lisa Walsh, and Sonja Lyubomirsky, "Satisfied Yet Striving: Gratitude Fosters Life Satisfaction and Improvement Motivation in Youth," *Emotion* 22, no. 5 (2022): 1004–1016, https://doi.org/10.1037/emo0000896; Kathryn Adair, Larissa Rodriguez-Homs, Sabran Masoud, Paul Mosca, and J. Bryan Sexton, "Gratitude at Work: Prospective Cohort Study of a Web-Based, Single-Exposure Well-Being Intervention for Health Care Workers," *Journal of Medical Internet Research* 22, no. 5 (2020): e15562.

4 a satisficer (i.e., happy with good enough) mindset: Barry Schwartz, Andrew Ward, John Monterosso, Sonja Lyubomirsky, Katherine White, and Darrin Lehman, "Maximizing Versus Satisficing: Happiness Is a Matter of Choice," *Journal of Personality and Social Psychology* 83, no. 5 (2002): 1178–97, https://doi.org/10.1037/0022-3514.83.5.1178; Sheena Iyengar, Rachael Wells, and Barry Schwartz, "Doing Better but Feeling Worse: Looking for the 'Best' Job Undermines Satisfaction," *Psychological Science* 17, no. 2 (2006): 143–50.

4 not going back to school: Thomas Gilovich and Victoria Husted Medvec, "The Temporal Pattern to the Experience of Regret," *Journal of Personality and Social Psychology* 67, no. 3 (1994): 357–65, https://doi.org/10.1037/0022-3514.67.3.357; Thomas Gilovich and Victoria Husted Medvec, "The Experience of Regret: What, When, and Why," *Psychological Review* 102, no. 2 (1995): 379–95, https://doi.org/10.1037/0033-295X.102.2.379; Neal Roese and Amy Summerville, "What We Regret Most . . . and Why," *Personality and Social Psychology Bulletin* 31, no. 9 (2005): 1273–85.

5 "bad faith": Jean-Paul Sartre, "Bad Faith and Falsehood," *Essays in Existentialism,* translated by Wade Baskin (New York: Citadel Press, 1965), 147–86.

5 Morrison's novel *Sula:* Toni Morrison, *Sula* (New York: Knopf, 1973).

5 neurologist and writer Oliver Sacks: Oliver Sacks, *On the Move: A Life* (New York: Knopf, 2015).

6 paper entitled "Subjective Well-Being": Ed Diener, "Subjective Well-Being," *Psychological Bulletin* 95, no. 3 (1984): 542–75, https://doi.org/10.1037/0033-2909.95.3.542.

6 a series of papers on subjective well-being: Ed Diener and Robert Emmons, "The Independence of Positive and Negative Affect," *Journal of Personality and Social Psychology* 47, no. 5 (1984): 1105–117, https://doi.org/10.1037/0022-3514.47.5.1105; Ed Diener and Randy Larsen, "Temporal Stability and Cross-Situational Consistency of Affective, Behavioral, and Cognitive Responses," *Journal of Personality and Social Psychology* 47, no. 4 (1984): 871–83, https://doi.org/10.1037/0022-3514.47.4.871; Robert Emmons, "Personal Strivings: An Approach to Personality and Subjective Well-Being," *Journal of Personality and Social Psychology* 51, no. 5 (1986): 1058–68.

6 hope, optimism, and flow: Martin Seligman and Mihaly Csikszentmihalyi, "Positive Psychology: An Introduction," *American Psychologist* 55, no. 1 (2000): 5–14, https://doi.org/10.1037/0003-066X.55.1.5.

6 an alternative model of a good life: Carol Ryff, "Happiness Is Everything, or Is It? Explorations on the Meaning of Psychological Well-Being," *Journal of Personality and Social Psychology* 57, no. 6 (1989): 1069–81, https://doi.org/10.1037/0022-3514.57.6.1069.

7 self-determination theory: Richard Ryan and Edward Deci, "Self-Determination Theory and the Facilitation of Intrinsic Motivation, Social Development, and Well-Being," *American Psychologist* 55, no. 1 (2000): 68–78, https://doi.org/10.1037/0003-066X.55.1.68.

7 called the "hedonic approach": Daniel Kahneman, Ed Diener, and Norbert Schwarz, eds., *Well-Being: The Foundations of Hedonic Psychology* (New York: Russell Sage Foundation, 1999); Daniel Gilbert, *Stumbling on Happiness* (New York: Knopf, 2006); Sonja Lyubomirsky, Kennon Sheldon, and David Schkade, "Pursuing Happiness: The Architecture of Sustainable Change," *Review of General Psychology* 9, no. 2 (2005): 111–31.

7 their lives are meaningful: Roy Baumeister, Kathleen Vohs, Jennifer

Aaker, and Emily Garbinsky, "Some Key Differences Between a Happy Life and a Meaningful Life," *Journal of Positive Psychology* 8, no. 6 (2013): 505–16.

7 they feel more engaged: Karoline Hofslett Kopperud and Joar Vittersø, "Distinctions Between Hedonic and Eudaimonic Well-Being: Results from a Day Reconstruction Study Among Norwegian Jobholders," *Journal of Positive Psychology* 3, no. 3 (2008): 174–81.

7 different epigenetic patterns: Barbara Fredrickson, Karen Grewen, Kimberly Coffey, Sara Algoe, Ann Firestine, Jesusa Arevalo, Jeffrey Ma, and Steven Cole, "A Functional Genomic Perspective on Human Well-Being," *Proceedings of the National Academy of Sciences* 110, no. 33 (2013): 13684–89; see also Nicholas Brown, Douglas MacDonald, Manoj Pratim Samanta, Harris Friedman, and James Coyne, "A Critical Reanalysis of the Relationship Between Genomics and Well-Being," *Proceedings of the National Academy of Sciences* 111, no. 35 (2014): 12705–09.

7 they are virtually the same thing: David Disabato, Fallon Goodman, Todd Kashdan, Jerome Short, and Aaron Jarden, "Different Types of Well-Being? A Cross-Cultural Examination of Hedonic and Eudaimonic Well-Being," *Psychological Assessment* 28, no. 5 (2016): 471–82, https://doi.org/10.1037/pas0000209; B. M. L. Baselmans and Meike Bartels, "A Genetic Perspective on the Relationship Between Eudaimonic and Hedonic Well-Being," *Scientific Reports* 8 (2018): 14610.

7 no point debating which is more important: Todd Kashdan, Robert Biswas-Diener, and Laura King, "Reconsidering Happiness: The Costs of Distinguishing Between Hedonics and Eudaimonia," *Journal of Positive Psychology* 3, no. 4 (2008): 219–33; Ed Diener, Derrick Wirtz, William Tov, Chu Kim-Prieto, Dong-won Choi, Shigehiro Oishi, and Robert Biswas-Diener, "New Well-Being Measures: Short Scales to Assess Flourishing and Positive and Negative Feelings," *Social Indicators Research* 97 (2010): 143–56; Martin Seligman, *Flourish: A Visionary New Understanding of Happiness and Well-Being* (New York: Free Press, 2011).

8 How we think about our intelligence: Carol Dweck, *Mindset: The New Psychology of Success* (New York: Random House, 2006).

9 frequent small, pleasant social interactions: Ed Diener, Ed Sandvik, and William Pavot, "Happiness Is the Frequency, Not the Intensity, of Positive Versus Negative Affect," in *Subjective Well-Being: An Interdis-*

ciplinary Perspective, eds. Fritz Strack, Michael Argyle, and Norbert Schwarz (Oxford: Pergamon Press, 1991), 119–39.

9 "To begin with, how *can* things": William James, *The Varieties of Religious Experience: A Study in Human Nature* (New York: Longmans, Green, 1902), 136.

9 The fragility of happiness: Mohsen Joshanloo, Dan Weijers, Ding-Yu Jiang, Gyuseog Han, et al., "Fragility of Happiness Beliefs Across 15 National Groups," *Journal of Happiness Studies* 16 (2015): 1185–210.

9 "yet I could give no reasonable meaning": Tolstoy cited in James, *Varieties of Religious Experience*, 154.

9 The precariousness of meaning: Ronnie Janoff-Bulman, *Shattered Assumptions: Towards a New Psychology of Trauma* (New York: Free Press, 1992).

Chapter 2: The Happiness Trap

12 "Despite whatever's going on": Julie Scelfo, "Suicide on Campus and the Pressure of Perfection," *New York Times,* July 27, 2015.

12 the ultimate goal of goals: Aristotle, *Ethics*, trans. J. A. K. Thomson (New York: Penguin Classics, 1976).

12 "What is human life's chief concern?": William James, *The Varieties of Religious Experience: A Study in Human Nature* (New York: Longmans, Green, 1902), 78.

12 a large international study: Ed Diener, "Subjective Well-Being: The Science of Happiness and a Proposal for a National Index," *American Psychologist* 55, no. 1 (2000): 34–43, https://doi.org/10.1037/0003 -066X.55.1.34.

12 better workers, and they live longer: Sonja Lyubomirsky, Laura King, and Ed Diener, "The Benefits of Frequent Positive Affect: Does Happiness Lead to Success?," *Psychological Bulletin* 131, no. 6 (2005): 803– 55, https://doi.org/10.1037/0033-2909.131.6.803; Julia Boehm and Sonja Lyubomirsky, "Does Happiness Promote Career Success?," *Journal of Career Assessment* 16, no. 1 (2008): 101–16.

13 a "popular, attractive, and talented": Scelfo, "Suicide on Campus."

13 suicide among Americans increased: "Suicide Data and Statistics," Centers for Disease Control and Prevention; 2020 National Survey on Drug Use and Health (NSDUH), Substance Abuse and Mental Health Services Administration (SAMHSA).

13 college students were asked to write: Luo Lu and Robin Gilmour, "Culture and Conceptions of Happiness: Individual Oriented and Social Oriented SWB," *Journal of Happiness Studies* 5, no. 3 (2004): 269–91, https://doi.org/10.1007/s10902-004-8789-5.

14 college students tend to equate: Yukiko Uchida and Shinobu Kitayama, "Happiness and Unhappiness in East and West: Themes and Variations," *Emotion* 9, no. 4 (2009): 441–56, https://doi.org/10.1037/a0015634.

14 iconic 1959 *New Yorker* cover: Condé Nast Store (online), "New Yorker, January 17th, 1929."

14 a victory rarely results in everlasting: Richard Lucas, Andrew Clark, Yannis Georgellis, and Ed Diener, "Reexamining Adaptation and the Set Point Model of Happiness: Reactions to Changes in Marital Status," *Journal of Personality and Social Psychology* 84, no. 3 (2003): 527–39, https://doi.org/10.1037/0022-3514.84.3.527; Maike Luhmann, Wilhelm Hofmann, Michael Eid, and Richard Lucas, "Subjective Well-Being and Adaptation to Life Events: A Meta-Analysis," *Journal of Personality and Social Psychology* 102, no. 3 (2012): 592–615, https://doi.org/10.1037/a0025948.

14 effect of a major accomplishment: Eunkook Suh, Ed Diener, and Frank Fujita, "Events and Subjective Well-Being: Only Recent Events Matter," *Journal of Personality and Social Psychology* 70, no. 5 (1996): 1091–102, https://doi.org/10.1037/0022-3514.70.5.1091.

14 "affective forecasting error": Timothy Wilson and Daniel Gilbert, "Explaining Away: A Model of Affective Adaptation," *Perspectives on Psychological Science* 3, no. 5 (2008): 370–86; Kennon Sheldon, Alexander Gunz, Charles Nichols, and Yuna Ferguson, "Extrinsic Value Orientation and Affective Forecasting: Overestimating the Rewards, Underestimating the Costs," *Journal of Personality* 78, no. 1 (2010): 149–78.

14 if they were denied tenure: Daniel Gilbert, Elizabeth Pinel, Timothy Wilson, Stephen Blumberg, and Thalia Wheatley, "Immune Neglect: A Source of Durability Bias in Affective Forecasting," *Journal of Personality and Social Psychology* 75, no. 3 (1998): 617–38.

15 Happiness is the frequency, not the intensity: Ed Diener, Ed Sandvik, and William Pavot, "Happiness Is the Frequency, Not the Intensity, of Positive Versus Negative Affect," in *Subjective Well-Being: An Interdisciplinary Perspective,* eds. Fritz Strack, Michael Argyle, and Norbert Schwarz (Oxford: Pergamon Press, 1991), 119–39.

15 happiness is the product of close relationships: Ed Diener and Martin Seligman, "Very Happy People," *Psychological Science* 13, no. 1 (2002): 81–84; Robert Emmons and Ed Diener, "Factors Predicting Satisfaction Judgments: A Comparative Examination," *Social Indicators Research* 16, no. 2 (1985): 157–67.

15 not personal success, but *interpersonal* success: Jonathan Haidt, *The Happiness Hypothesis: Finding Modern Truth in Ancient Wisdom* (New York: Basic Books, 2006).

15 Quentin Tarantino: Alex Fletcher, "Ten Things You Never Knew About Quentin Tarantino," *Digital Spy,* August 12, 2009.

16 mimic either smiling or not smiling: Fritz Strack, Leonard Martin, and Sabine Stepper, "Inhibiting and Facilitating Conditions of the Human Smile: A Nonobtrusive Test of the Facial Feedback Hypothesis," *Journal of Personality and Social Psychology* 54, no. 5 (1988): 768–77, https://doi.org/10.1037/0022-3514.54.5.768.

16 failed to replicate the original findings: Maarten Derksen and Jill Morawski, "Kinds of Replication: Examining the Meanings of 'Conceptual Replication' and 'Direction Replication,'" *Perspectives on Psychological Science* 17, no. 5 (2022): 1490–505; Nicholas Coles, David March, Fernando Marmolejo-Ramos, Jeff Larsen, et al., "A Multi-Lab Test of the Facial Feedback Hypothesis by the Many Smiles Collaboration," *Nature Human Behaviour* 6 (2022): 1731–42.

16 others were able to replicate: Tom Noah, Yaacov Schul, and Ruth Mayo, "When Both the Original Study and Its Failed Replication Are Correct: Feeling Observed Eliminates the Facial-Feedback Effect," *Journal of Personality and Social Psychology* 114, no. 5 (2018): 657–64, https://doi.org/10.1037/pspa0000121; Abigail Marsh, Shawn Rhoads, and Rebecca Ryan, "A Multi-Semester Classroom Demonstration Yields Evidence in Support of the Facial Feedback Effect," *Emotion* 19, no. 8 (2019): 1500–1504.

16 asked to behave like extraverts: William Fleeson, Adriane Malanos, and Noelle Achille, "An Intraindividual Process Approach to the Relationship Between Extraversion and Positive Affect: Is Acting Extraverted as 'Good' as Being Extraverted?," *Journal of Personality and Social Psychology* 83, no. 6 (2002): 1409–22, https://doi.org/10.1037/0022-3514.83.6.1409; J. Murray McNiel and William Fleeson, "The Causal Effects of Extraversion on Positive Affect and Neuroticism on Negative Affect: Manipulating State Extraversion and State Neuroticism in an Experimental Approach," *Journal of Research in Personality* 40, no. 5

(2006): 529–50; Mariya Davydenko, John Zelenski, Ana Gonzalez, and Deanna Whelan, "Does Acting Extraverted Evoke Positive Social Feedback?," *Personality and Individual Differences* 159 (2020): 109883.

16 far happier than they had anticipated: Nicholas Epley and Juliana Schroeder, "Mistakenly Seeking Solitude," *Journal of Experimental Psychology: General* 143, no. 5 (2014): 1980–99.

16 These findings have been replicated: Juliana Schroeder, Donald Lyons, and Nicholas Epley, "Hello, Stranger? Pleasant Conversations Are Preceded by Concerns About Starting One," *Journal of Experimental Psychology: General* 151, no. 5 (2022): 1141–53, https://doi.org/10.1037/xge0001118.

16 unhappiness is a sign of failure: Iris Mauss, Maya Tamir, Craig Anderson, and Nicole Savino, "Can Seeking Happiness Make People Unhappy? Paradoxical Effects of Valuing Happiness," *Emotion* 11, no. 4 (2011): 807–15, https://doi.org/10.1037/a0022010; Emily Willroth, Gerald Young, Maya Tamir, and Iris Mauss, "Judging Emotions as Good or Bad: Individual Differences and Associations with Psychological Health," *Emotion* 23, no. 7 (2023): 1876–90, https://doi.org/10.1037/emo0001220.

17 there was no pressure to be happy: Lucy McGuirk, Peter Kuppens, Rosemary Kingston, and Brock Bastian, "Does a Culture of Happiness Increase Rumination Over Failure?," *Emotion* 18, no. 5 (2018): 755–64, https://doi.org/10.1037/emo0000322.

17 Americans on average feel far more pressure: Egon Dejonckheere, Joshua Phee, Peter Baguma, Oumar Barry, et al., "Perceiving Societal Pressure to Be Happy Is Linked to Poor Well-Being, Especially in Happy Nations," *Scientific Reports* 12, no. 1 (2022): 1514.

17 more strongly associated with good luck: Shigehiro Oishi, Jesse Graham, Selin Kesebir, and Iolanda Costa Galinha, "Concepts of Happiness Across Time and Cultures," *Personality and Social Psychology Bulletin* 39, no. 5 (2013): 559–77.

18 In *Brave New World:* Aldous Huxley, *Brave New World* (1932; reprint, New York: Vintage, 2007), 46.

18 try to positively reinterpret the event: James Gross, "Emotion Regulation in Adulthood: Timing Is Everything," *Current Directions in Psychological Science* 10, no. 6 (2001): 214–19, https://doi.org/10.1111/1467-8721.00152.

18 try to distance themselves: Ethan Kross and Ozlem Ayduk, "Making Meaning out of Negative Experiences by Self-Distancing," *Current*

Directions in Psychological Science 20, no. 3 (2011): 187–91, https://doi
.org/10.1177/0963721411408883; Ethan Kross and Ozlem Ayduk, "Self-
Distancing: Theory, Research, and Current Directions," *Advances in
Experimental Social Psychology* 55 (2017): 81–136.

18 a tiny bump in the road: Emma Bruehlman-Senecal, Ozlem Ayduk,
and Oliver John, "Taking the Long View: Implications of Individual
Differences in Temporal Distancing for Affect, Stress Reactivity, and
Well-Being," *Journal of Personality and Social Psychology* 111, no. 4
(2016): 610–35, https://doi.org/10.1037/pspp0000103; Dylan Benkley,
Emily Willroth, Ozlem Ayduk, Oliver John, and Iris Mauss, "Short-
Term Implications of Long-Term Thinking: Temporal Distancing and
Emotional Responses to Daily Stressors," *Emotion* 23, no. 2 (2023):
595–99, https://doi.org/10.1037/emo0001140.

19 the psychological immune system: Daniel Gilbert, Elizabeth Pinel,
Timothy Wilson, Stephen Blumberg, and Thalia Wheatley, "Immune
Neglect: A Source of Durability Bias in Affective Forecasting," *Journal
of Personality and Social Psychology* 75, no. 3 (1998): 617–38.

19 Schwartz found the power of "good enough": Barry Schwartz, Andrew
Ward, John Monterosso, Sonja Lyubomirsky, Katherine White, and
Darrin Lehman, "Maximizing Versus Satisficing: Happiness Is a Matter of Choice," *Journal of Personality and Social Psychology* 83, no. 5
(2002): 1178–97, https://doi.org/10.1037/0022-3514.83.5.1178.

20 A study featuring a similar scenario: Sheena Iyengar, Rachael Wells,
and Barry Schwartz, "Doing Better but Feeling Worse. Looking for
the 'Best' Job Undermines Satisfaction," *Psychological Science* 17, no. 2
(2006): 143–50.

20 If you did not get into your top school: Sonja Lyubomirsky and Lee
Ross, "Changes in Attractiveness of Elected, Rejected, and Precluded
Alternatives: A Comparison of Happy and Unhappy Individuals,"
Journal of Personality and Social Psychology 76, no. 6 (1999): 988–1007,
https://doi.org/10.1037/0022-3514.76.6.988.

20 Jim Clark, who cofounded Netscape: Michael Lewis, *The New New
Thing* (New York: W. W. Norton, 2000), 259.

21 individuals who do not engage in upward: Sonja Lyubomirsky and Lee
Ross, "Hedonic Consequences of Social Comparison: A Contrast of
Happy and Unhappy People," *Journal of Personality and Social Psychol-
ogy* 73, no. 6 (1997): 1141–57.

22 discourages you from embracing: Joar Vittersø and Yngvil Søholt,
"Life Satisfaction Goes with Pleasure and Personal Growth Goes with

Interest: Further Arguments for Separating Hedonic and Eudaimonic Well-Being," *Journal of Positive Psychology* 6, no. 4 (2011): 326–35, https://doi.org/10.1080/17439760.2011.584548; Tenelle Porter, Diego Catalán Molina, Lisa Blackwell, Sylvia Roberts, Abigail Quirk, Angela Lee Duckworth, and Kali Trzesniewski, "Measuring Mastery Behaviours at Scale: The Persistence, Effort, Resilience, and Challenge-Seeking (PERC) Task," *Journal of Learning Analytics* 7, no. 1 (2020): 5–18.

22 "Well, I'd rather be unhappy": Huxley, *Brave New World,* 156.

22 "They would laud and lure me": Friedrich Nietzsche, *Thus Spoke Zarathustra: A Book for All and None,* trans. Walter Kaufmann (1883–1892, translated 1954; reprint, New York: Penguin, 1978), 169–70.

22 "I am a wanderer": Nietzsche, *Thus Spoke Zarathustra,* 152, 155–56.

23 These emotions add: Jordi Quoidbach, June Gruber, Moïra Mikolajczak, Alexsandr Kogan, Ilios Kotsou, and Michael I. Norton, "Emodiversity and the Emotional Ecosystem," *Journal of Experimental Psychology: General* 143, no. 6 (2014): 2057–66, https://doi.org/10.1037/a0038025.

Chapter 3: The Meaning Trap

24 Jobs, Stanford University commencement speech: "'You've Got to Find What You Love,' Jobs Says," *Stanford Report,* June 12, 2005.

24 "To be stupid, selfish, and have good health": Francis Steegmuller, *The Letters of Gustave Flaubert: 1830–1857* (Cambridge, Mass.: Harvard University Press, 1980), 62.

24 "'Happy' people are some of the dullest people": Tony Schwartz, "Happiness Is Overrated," *Harvard Business Review,* October 5, 2010.

24 Silverstein's poem "The Land of Happy": Shel Silverstein, "The Land of Happy," *Where the Sidewalk Ends* (New York: Harper and Row, 1974), accessible at https://allpoetry.com/The-Land-Of-Happy.

25 a happy life might be a selfish one: Carol Ryff, "Happiness Is Everything, or Is It? Explorations on the Meaning of Psychological Well-Being," *Journal of Personality and Social Psychology* 57, no. 6 (1989): 1069–81, https://doi.org/10.1037/0022-3514.57.6.1069.

25 evidence that suggests otherwise: Sonja Lyubomirsky, Laura King, and Ed Diener, "The Benefits of Frequent Positive Affect: Does Happiness Lead to Success?," *Psychological Bulletin* 131, no. 6 (2005): 803–55, https://doi.org/10.1037/0033-2909.131.6.803.

25 spending money on others: Elizabeth Dunn, Lara Aknin, and Michael Norton, "Spending Money on Others Promotes Happiness," *Science* 319, no. 5870 (2008): 1687–88, https://doi.org/10.1126/science.1150952.

25 Happy people volunteer more: Shigehiro Oishi, Ed Diener, and Richard Lucas, "The Optimum Level of Well-Being: Can People Be Too Happy?," *Perspectives on Psychological Science* 2, no. 4 (2007): 346–60, https://doi.org/10.1111/j.1745-6916.2007.00048.x.

25 scholars call a "meaningful life": Michael Steger, Patricia Frazier, Shigehiro Oishi, and Matthew Kaler, "The Meaning in Life Questionnaire: Assessing the Presence of and Search for Meaning in Life," *Journal of Counseling Psychology* 53, no. 1 (2006): 80–93, https://doi.org/10.1037/0022-0167.53.1.80; Paul Bloom, *The Sweet Spot: The Pleasures of Suffering and the Search for Meaning* (New York: HarperCollins, 2021); Emily Esfahani Smith, *The Power of Meaning: Crafting a Life That Matters* (New York: Crown, 2017).

25 significance, purpose, and coherence: Michael Steger, "Experiencing Meaning in Life: Optimal Functioning at the Nexus of Well-Being, Psychopathology, and Spirituality," in *The Human Quest for Meaning: Theories, Research, and Applications,* 2nd ed., ed. Paul Wong (New York: Routledge, 2012), 165–84.

25 Graeber, in his book *Bullshit Jobs:* David Graeber, *Bullshit Jobs: A Theory* (New York: Simon & Schuster, 2018).

26 "Be great": Michelle Obama, "CCNY Commencement 2016," Commencement Archive, City College of New York.

26 As she shared with *PBS:* "Brief but Spectacular: Dr. Donna Adams-Pickett, Obstetrician and Gynecologist," *PBS NewsHour,* February 5, 2023.

27 90 percent of Americans said they have meaning: Samantha Heintzelman and Laura King, "Life Is Pretty Meaningful," *American Psychologist* 69, no. 6 (2014): 561–74, https://doi.org/10.1037/a0035049.

27 Another Gallup survey that focused on purpose: Heintzelman and King, "Life Is Pretty Meaningful."

28 self-reported meaning in life is correlated: Steger, Frazier, Oishi, and Kaler, "The Meaning in Life Questionnaire."

28 Religious people were better able: Nicole Stephens, Stephanie Fryberg, Hazel Rose Markus, and MarYam Hamedani, "Who Explains Hurricane Katrina and the Chilean Earthquake as an Act of God? The Experience of Extreme Hardship Predicts Religious Meaning-Making," *Journal of Cross-Cultural Psychology* 44, no. 4 (2013): 606–19.

29 tend to be optimistic about the future: Steger, Frazier, Oishi, and Kaler, "The Meaning in Life Questionnaire."

29 "Well, Mr. President, I'm helping": John Nemo, "What a NASA Janitor Can Teach Us About Living a Bigger Life," *Business Journals,* December 23, 2014.

29 Conscientious people achieve more: Brent Roberts, Nathan Kuncel, Rebecca Shiner, Avshalom Caspi, and Lewis Goldberg, "The Power of Personality: The Comparative Validity of Personality Traits, Socioeconomic Status, and Cognitive Ability for Predicting Important Life Outcomes," *Perspectives on Psychological Science* 2, no. 4 (2007): 313–45.

29 the majority of Americans: David Schmitt and Jüri Allik, "Simultaneous Administration of the Rosenberg Self-Esteem Scale in 53 Nations: Exploring the Universal and Culture-Specific Features of Global Self-Esteem," *Journal of Personality and Social Psychology* 89, no. 4 (2005): 623–42, https://doi.org/10.1037/0022-3514.89.4.623.

29 optimistic about their futures: Matthew Gallagher, Shane Lopez, and Sarah Pressman, "Optimism Is Universal: Exploring the Presence and Benefits of Optimism in a Representative Sample of the World," *Journal of Personality* 81, no. 5 (2012): 429–40.

29 say they are extraverted, non-neurotic: David Schmitt, Jüri Allik, Robert McCrae, and Verónica Benet-Martínez, "The Geographic Distribution of Big Five Personality Traits: Patterns and Profiles of Human Self-Description Across 56 Nations," *Journal of Cross-Cultural Psychology* 38, no. 2 (2007): 173–212.

29 Others derive meaning in life: Roy Baumeister, *Meanings of Life* (New York: Guilford Press, 1991); Melissa Grouden and Paul Jose, "Do Sources of Meaning Differentially Predict Search for Meaning, Presence of Meaning, and Wellbeing?," *International Journal of Wellbeing* 5, no. 1 (2015): 33–52.

30 associated with right-wing authoritarianism: Jake Womick, Brendon Woody, and Laura King, "Religious Fundamentalism, Right-Wing Authoritarianism, and Meaning in Life," *Journal of Personality* 90, no. 2 (2022): 277–93, https://doi.org/10.1111/jopy.12665.

30 political conservatives: Ronnie Janoff-Bulman, "To Provide or Protect: Motivational Bases of Political Liberalism and Conservatism," *Psychological Inquiry* 20, nos. 2–3 (2009): 120–28; Jesse Graham, Jonathan Haidt, and Brian Nosek, "Liberals and Conservatives Rely on Different Sets of Moral Foundations," *Journal of Personality and Social Psychology* 96, no. 5 (2009): 1029–46, https://doi.org/10.1037/a0015141.

30 higher levels of meaning in life as well as happiness: David New-man, Norbert Schwarz, Jesse Graham, and Arthur Stone, "Conservatives Report Greater Meaning in Life Than Liberals," *Social Psychological and Personality Science* 10, no. 4 (2019): 494–503, https://doi.org/10.1177/1948550618768241.

31 "Terrorist groups provide an important source": Simon Cottee and Keith Hayward, "Terrorist (E)motives: The Existential Attractions of Terrorism," *Studies in Conflict and Terrorism* 34, no. 12 (2011): 963–86.

31 happiness and meaning as paths to a good life: Lyubomirsky, King, and Diener, "Benefits of Frequent Positive Affect"; Katarzyna Czekierda, Anna Banik, Crystal Park, and Aleksandra Luszczynska, "Meaning in Life and Physical Health: Systematic Review and Meta-Analysis," *Health Psychology Review* 11, no. 4 (2017): 387–418, https://doi.org/10.1080/17437199.2017.1327325.

Chapter 4: A Life of Exploration

33 "The world is a great book": Thomas Fielding, *Select Proverbs of All Nations* (London: Longman, Hurst, Rees, Orme, Brown, and Green, 1824), 216.

34 "Did all this make sense?": Hermann Hesse, *Narcissus and Goldmund*, trans. Ursule Molinaro (1930, translated 1968; reprint, New York: Bantam, 1971), 297.

34 "better, righter . . . better than Goldmund's life?": Hesse, *Narcissus and Goldmund*, 214.

35 "The so-called social pleasures": Søren Kierkegaard, *Either/Or: A Fragment of Life*, trans. Alastair Hannay (1843, translated 1992; reprint, London: Penguin, 2004), 240–41.

35 marriage as "a school for character": Kierkegaard, *Either/Or*, 415.

35 Stephen Dedalus in James Joyce's *A Portrait:* James Joyce, *A Portrait of the Artist as a Young Man* (1916; reprint, New York: Penguin, 2003), 158.

36 In a 2015 *Atlantic* essay: Alison Gopnik, "How an 18th-Century Philosopher Helped Solve My Midlife Crisis: David Hume, the Buddha, and a Search for the Eastern Roots of the Western Enlightenment," *The Atlantic,* October 2015.

38 "Coming back to America": Walter Isaacson, *Steve Jobs* (New York: Simon & Schuster, 2011), 48.

38 "Tell me, what was": Bowers cited in Isaacson, *Steve Jobs,* 537.

39 She married in 1949 and raised three children: "Brad Ryan and His Grandma Joy Tour National Parks Together," *Morning Edition*, NPR, August 13, 2019.

40 Watching Brad and Joy in an interview: "Why a Grandmother and Grandson Are Visiting Every U.S. National Park," *PBS NewsHour*, October 1, 2022.

41 Marsh's research on extraordinary altruists: Abigail Marsh, "Extraordinary Altruism: A Cognitive Neuroscience Perspective," in *Positive Neuroscience*, eds. Joshua Greene, India Morrison, and Martin Seligman (New York: Oxford University Press, 2016), 143–56, https://doi.org/10.1093/acprof:oso/9780199977925.003.0010.

Chapter 5: Ingredients of Psychological Richness

43 "Read, every day": "Christopher Morley, 1890–1957," Poetry Foundation.

45 In his poem "Happiness": Raymond Carver, "Happiness," *All of Us: The Collected Poems* (New York: Knopf, 1998).

46 Kenyon writes about her routines: Jane Kenyon, "Otherwise," *Collected Poems* (Saint Paul, Minn.: Graywolf Press, 2007).

46 Oliver in her poem "Wild Geese": Mary Oliver, *Wild Geese: Selected Poems* (Tarset, UK: Bloodaxe Books, 2004).

46 Hyewon Choi and I asked: Shigehiro Oishi, Hyewon Choi, Ailin Liu, and Jaime Kurtz, "Experiences Associated with Psychological Richness," *European Journal of Personality* 35, no. 5 (2021): 754–70.

47 a psychologically rich day was one in which they felt more: Shigehiro Oishi, Erin Westgate, Youngjae Cha, Hyewon Choi, Samantha Heintzelman, and Nick Buttrick, "The Emotional Tone of a Happy Life, a Meaningful Life, and a Psychologically Rich Life." Paper under review (2023).

50 study abroad students reported more: Oishi, Choi, Liu, and Kurtz, "Experiences Associated with Psychological Richness."

51 "light and dark, birth and death": Susan Cain, *Bittersweet: How Sorrow and Longing Make Us Whole* (New York: Crown, 2022), xxii.

51 In six studies, we explored: Oishi et al., "The Emotional Tone of a Happy Life." Paper under review (2024).

Chapter 6: Who Is Rich, Psychologically Rich?

53 "It is better to live rich than die rich": James Boswell, *The Life of Samuel Johnson* (1791; reprint, London: Verlag, 2023), 205.

53 Our lab set out to quantify psychological richness: Shigehiro Oishi and Erin Westgate, "A Psychologically Rich Life: Beyond Happiness and Meaning," *Psychological Review* 129, no. 4 (2022): 790–811, https://doi .org/10.1037/rev0000317.

57 identify all the words describing personality: Gordon W. Allport and Henry S. Odbert, *Trait-Names: A Psycho-Lexical Study* (Princeton: American Psychological Association and Psychological Review Company, 1936).

58 "If many human beings": Allport and Odbert, *Trait-Names,* 19.

58 Goldberg had 187 college students: Lewis Goldberg, "An Alternative 'Description of Personality': The Big-Five Factor Structure," *Journal of Personality and Social Psychology* 59, no. 6 (1990): 1216–29, https://doi .org/10.1037/0022-3514.59.6.1216.

58 These factors, known as the "Big Five": Robert McCrae and Paul Costa, "Validation of the Five-Factor Model of Personality Across Instruments and Observers," *Journal of Personality and Social Psychology* 52, no. 1 (1987): 81–90, https://doi.org/10.1037/0022-3514.52.1.81.

59 early 1990s: Paul Costa and Robert McCrae, "Four Ways Five Factors Are Basic," *Personality and Individual Differences* 13, no. 6 (1992): 653–65; Oliver John and Richard Robins, "Determinants of Interjudge Agreement on Personality Traits: The Big Five Domains, Observability, Evaluativeness, and the Unique Perspective of the Self," *Journal of Personality* 61, no. 4 (1993): 521–51.

59 we collected data from over 5,000 respondents: Shigehiro Oishi, Hyewon Choi, Nicholas Buttrick, Samantha Heintzelman, Kostadin Kushlev, Erin Westgate, Jane Tucker, Charles Ebersole, Jordan Axt, Elizabeth Gilbert, Brandon Ng, and Lorraine Besser, "The Psychologically Rich Life Questionnaire," *Journal of Research in Personality* 81 (2019): 257–70, https://doi.org/10.1016/j.jrp.2019.06.010.

59 the correlation between heights of fathers: Karl Pearson and Alice Lee, "On the Laws of Inheritance in Man: I. Inheritance of Physical Characters," *Biometrika* 2, no. 4 (1903): 357–462.

60 Students who are open to experience: Julia Zimmermann and Franz Neyer, "Do We Become a Different Person When Hitting the Road? Personality Development of Sojourners," *Journal of Personality and*

Social Psychology 105, no. 3 (2013): 515–30, https://doi.org/10.1037 /a0033019.

61 psychologists have classified openness: Colin DeYoung, Lena Quilty, Jordan Peterson, and Jeremy Gray, "Openness to Experience, Intellect, and Cognitive Ability," *Journal of Personality Assessment* 96, no. 1 (2014): 46–52; Scott Barry Kaufman, "Opening Up Openness to Experience: A Four-Factor Model and Relations to Creative Achievement in the Arts and Sciences," *Journal of Creative Behavior* 47, no. 4 (2013): 233–55.

62 They talk to many new people: Daniel Feiler and Adam Kleinbaum, "Popularity, Similarity, and the Network Extraversion Bias," *Psychological Science* 26, no. 5 (2015): 593–603.

63 One factor is their confidence: Helen Cheng and Adrian Furnham, "Personality, Peer Relations, and Self-Confidence as Predictors of Happiness and Loneliness," *Journal of Adolescence* 25, no. 3 (2002): 327–39.

63 Instead, you are thinking about the benefits: Andrew Elliot and Todd Thrash, "Approach-Avoidance Motivation in Personality: Approach and Avoidance Temperaments and Goals," *Journal of Personality and Social Psychology* 82, no. 5 (2002): 804–18, https://doi.org/10.1037/0022 -3514.82.5.804.

63 extraverts were involved with more: Jerry Burger and David Caldwell, "Personality, Social Activities, Job-Search Behavior and Interview Success: Distinguishing Between PANAS Trait Positive Affect and NEO Extraversion," *Motivation and Emotion* 24, no. 1 (2000): 51–62.

64 Anglim and colleagues' meta-analysis: Jeromy Anglim, Sharon Horwood, Luke Smillie, Rosario Marrero, and Joshua Wood, "Predicting Psychological and Subjective Well-Being from Personality: A Meta-Analysis," *Psychological Bulletin* 146, no. 4 (2020): 279–323, https://doi .org/10.1037/bul0000226.

64 a happy life is the preponderance: Ed Diener, Eunkook Suh, Richard Lucas, and Heidi Smith, "Subjective Well-Being: Three Decades of Progress," *Psychological Bulletin* 125, no. 2 (1999): 276–302, https://doi .org/10.1037/0033-2909.125.2.276.

64 Primarily because the quality of social: Ed Diener and Martin Seligman, "Very Happy People," *Psychological Science* 13, no. 1 (2002): 81–84.

67 strong convictions: Robert P. Abelson, "Conviction," *American Psychologist* 43, no. 4 (1988): 267–75, https://doi.org/10.1037/0003 -066X.43.4.267. Linda J. Skitka, Christopher W. Bauman, and Edward G. Sargis, "Moral Conviction: Another Contributor to Atti-

tude Strength or Something More?," *Journal of Personality and Social Psychology* 88, no. 6 (2005): 895–917, https://doi.org/10.1037/0022 -3514.88.6.895. Keith J. Yoder and Jean Decety, "Moral Conviction and Metacognitive Ability Shape Multiple Stages of Information Processing During Social Decision-Making," *Cortex* 151 (2022): 162–75.

68 Even if you are neurotic: Mirjam Stieger, Christoph Flückiger, Dominik Rüegger, Tobias Kowatsch, Brent Roberts, and Mathias Allemand, "Changing Personality Traits with the Help of a Digital Personality Change Intervention," *Proceedings of the National Academy of Sciences* 118, no. 8 (2021): e2017548118.

Chapter 7: Playfulness

69 Robert McCrae and Paul Costa asked 240 men: Robert McCrae and Paul Costa, "Openness to Experience and Ego Level in Loevinger's Sentence Completion Test: Dispositional Contributions to Developmental Models of Personality," *Journal of Personality and Social Psychology* 39, no. 6 (1980): 1179–90, https://doi.org/10.1037/h0077727.

70 "on vacation from social and economic reality": Erik Erikson, *Childhood and Society* (1950; reprint, New York: W. W. Norton, 1985), 212.

70 already training at eight years old: Mitch Bowmile, "Michael Phelps: The Making of a Champion," *SwimSwam,* May 8, 2020.

70 Biles is another extraordinary athlete: Simone Biles website, Simone biles.com/about/.

71 humans have an extraordinarily long childhood: Alison Gopnik, "Childhood as a Solution to Explore-Exploit Tensions," *Philosophical Transactions of the Royal Society B* 375, no. 1803 (2020): 20190502, https://doi.org/10.1098/rstb.2019.0502.

71 a time of play, which is crucial for learning: Brenna Hassett, *Growing Up Human: The Evolution of Childhood* (London: Bloomsbury Sigma, 2022).

71 A recent study examined whether: Arne Güllich, Brooke Macnamara, and David Hambrick, "What Makes a Champion? Early Multidisciplinary Practice, Not Early Specialization, Predicts World-Class Performance," *Perspectives on Psychological Science* 17, no. 1 (2022): 6–29, https://doi.org/10.1177/1745691620974772.

72 Another study compared forty-eight German Nobel: Angela Graf, *Die Wissenschaftselite Deutschlands. Sozialprofil und Werdegänge zwischen 1945 und 2013* [Germany's scientific elite. Social profile and careers

from 1945 to 2013] (Frankfurt: Campus Verlag, 2015), cited in Güllich et al., "What Makes a Champion?"

73 the essay "Human, All Too Human": Friedrich Nietzsche, *On the Genealogy of Morals and Ecce Homo,* trans. Walter Kaufmann and R. J. Hollingdale (1887 and 1908 [1888]; reprint, New York: Vintage, 1989), 287.

73 story of William James Sidis: Amy Wallace, *The Prodigy: A Biography of William James Sidis* (New York: Dutton, 1986).

74 Ohtani jokingly gave his bat CPR: Stephanie Apstein, "Angels Star Shohei Ohtani Is a Legendary Hitter, Pitcher and Prankster," *Sports Illustrated,* May 13, 2022.

74 interview with Patrick Bet-David: "Shaq Opens Up About Kobe, Creating Wealth and Life," *PBD Podcast,* September 12, 2022.

75 playfulness is a blend: René Proyer, "A New Structural Model for the Study of Adult Playfulness: Assessment and Exploration of an Understudied Individual Differences Variable," *Personality and Individual Differences* 108 (2017): 113–22, https://doi.org/10.1016/j.paid.2016.12.011.

75 "an openness to being a fool": Maria Lugones. "Playfulness, 'World'-Travelling, and Loving Perception," *Hypatia* 2, no. 2 (1987): 17.

75 Proyer found that playful people: René Proyer, "The Well-Being of Playful Adults: Adult Playfulness, Subjective Well-Being, Physical Well-Being, and the Pursuit of Enjoyable Activities," *European Journal of Humour Research* 1, no. 1 (2013): 84–98, https://doi.org/10.7592/EJHR2013.1.1.proyer.

75 A recent study: René T. Proyer, Fabian Gander, Kay Brauer, and Garry Chick, "Can Playfulness Be Stimulated? A Randomised Placebo-Controlled Online Playfulness Intervention Study on Effects on Trait Playfulness, Well-being, and Depression," *Applied Psychology: Health and Well-Being* 13, no. 1 (2021): 129–51.

77 Hinds partnered with Mark Mortensen: Pamela Hinds and Mark Mortensen, "Understanding Conflict in Geographically Distributed Teams: The Moderating Effects of Shared Identity, Shared Context, and Spontaneous Communication," *Organization Science* 16, no. 3 (2005): 290–307.

77 "No matter how many friends you make": Alex Williams, "Why Is It Hard to Make Friends Over 30?," *New York Times,* July 13, 2012.

78 The philosopher Jason D'Cruz: Jason D'Cruz, "Volatile Reasons," *Australasian Journal of Philosophy* 91, no. 1 (2013).

80 Psychologists report that being gritty: Wen Jiang, Jiang Jiang, Xiaopeng Du, Dian Gu, Ying Sun, and Yue Zhang, "Striving and Happiness:

Between- and Within-Person-Level Associations Among Grit, Needs Satisfaction and Subjective Well-Being," *Journal of Positive Psychology* 15, no. 4 (2020): 543–55.

80 kind: Keiko Otake, Satoshi Shimai, Junko Tanaka-Matsumi, Kanako Otsui, and Barbara Fredrickson, "Happy People Become Happier Through Kindness: A Counting Kindness Intervention," *Journal of Happiness Studies* 7, no. 3 (2006): 361–75.

80 sociable: Victoria Reyes-García, Ricardo Godoy, Vincent Vadez, Isabel Ruíz-Mallén, et al., "The Pay-Offs to Sociability: Do Solitary and Social Leisure Relate to Happiness?," *Human Nature* 20 (2009): 431–46.

80 mindful: Cristián Coo and Marisa Salanova, "Mindfulness Can Make You Happy-and-Productive: A Mindfulness Controlled Trial and Its Effects on Happiness, Work Engagement and Performance," *Journal of Happiness Studies* 19, no. 6 (2018): 1691–711.

Chapter 8: The Beauty of DIY

81 get things done: Ayelet Fishbach, *Get It Done: Surprising Lessons from the Science of Motivation* (New York: Little, Brown Spark, 2022).

82 The copy I bought: Alan B. Krueger, "Introduction," in Adam Smith, *The Wealth of Nations* (1776; reprint, New York: Bantam Classic, 2003).

82 I even named the first book I wrote: Shigehiro Oishi, *The Psychological Wealth of Nations: Do Happy People Make a Happy Society?* (Malden, Mass.: Wiley-Blackwell, 2012).

83 "the typical scientist during my graduate years": Jerome Kagan, *The Three Cultures: Natural Sciences, Social Sciences, and the Humanities in the 21st Century* (New York: Cambridge University Press, 2009), vii–viii.

84 Marx famously speculated: Karl Marx, *Capital: A Critique of Political Economy,* vol. 1: *The Process of Capitalist Production,* ed. Frederick Engels, trans. Samuel Moore and Edward Aveling (Chicago: Charles H. Kerr, 1906).

84 In his presidential address: Kai Erikson, "On Work and Alienation," *American Sociological Review* 51, no. 1 (1986): 1–8.

85 Kohn found some evidence: Melvin Kohn, "Occupational Structure and Alienation," *American Journal of Sociology* 82, no. 1 (1976): 111–30.

88 The more answers someone waited for: Caroline Marvin and Daphna Shohamy, "Curiosity and Reward: Valence Predicts Choice and Information Prediction Errors Enhance Learning," *Journal of Experimental*

Psychology: General 145, no. 3 (2016): 266–72, https://doi.org/10.1037 /xge0000140.

89 Whillans and colleagues found: Ashley Whillans, Elizabeth Dunn, Paul Smeets, Rene Bekkers, and Michael Norton, "Buying Time Promotes Happiness," *Proceedings of the National Academy of Sciences* 114, no. 32 (2017): 8523–27.

Chapter 9: Do Aesthetic Experiences Count?

92 "I was always going to the bookcase": Virginia Woolf, *The Waves* (1931; reprint, Hertfordshire, UK: Wordsworth Classics, 2000), 141.

92 "I've read more than 4,000 books": "Meet Man Who Has Read Over 4,000 Books in His Library," *Reporters at Large,* January 29, 2023.

93 "These afternoons were crammed": Marcel Proust, *In Search of Lost Time,* vol 1: *Swann's Way,* trans. C. K. Scott Moncrieff and Terence Kilmartin, revised by D. J. Enright (1913; translation, New York: Modern Library, 2003), 116–17.

94 "Lord Darlington wasn't a bad man": Kazuo Ishiguro, *The Remains of the Day* (New York: Vintage, 1990), 243.

95 melding of attention, imagery, and feeling: Melanie Green and Timothy Brock, "The Role of Transportation in the Persuasiveness of Public Narratives," *Journal of Personality and Social Psychology* 79, no. 5 (2000): 701–21, https://doi.org/10.1037/0022-3514.79.5.701.

97 "those that are directed . . . social communication": Immanuel Kant, *Critique of Judgment,* trans. J. H. Bernard (1790, translated 1914; reprint, Mineola, N.Y.: Dover, 2005), 111.

97 Rollins, the legendary jazz saxophonist: Sonny Rollins, "Art Never Dies," *New York Times,* May 18, 2020.

97 David Brooks echoes: David Brooks, "The Power of Art in a Political Age," *New York Times,* March 2, 2023.

98 Heidegger's "Das Gerede": Martin Heidegger, *Being and Time,* trans. John Macquarrie and Edward Robinson (1927, translated 1962; reprint, New York: Harper Perennial, 2008), 212, 216.

98 Social media is endless chatter: Jonathan Haidt, *The Anxious Generation* (New York: Penguin, 2024).

98 "A painting is not about an experience": Rothko cited in Maleficent Twemlow, "A Painting as an Experience," Metropolitan Museum of Art, March 18, 2013.

99 complex ones are typically perceived: D. E. Berlyne, *Aesthetics and Psychobiology* (New York: Appleton, 1971).

99 Berlyne manipulated two factors: D. E. Berlyne and Sylvia Peckham, "The Semantic Differential and Other Measures of Reaction to Visual Complexity," *Canadian Journal of Psychology* 20, no. 2 (1966): 125–35.

99 Silvia conducted an intriguing experiment: Samuel Turner Jr. and Paul Silvia, "Must Interesting Things Be Pleasant? A Test of Competing Appraisal Structures," *Emotion* 6, no. 4 (2006): 670–74.

100 Silvia explored the role of comprehension: Paul Silvia, "What Is Interesting? Exploring the Appraisal Structure of Interest," *Emotion* 5, no. 1 (2005): 89–102.

100 we asked over 5,000 people about their reading: Nicholas Buttrick, Erin Westgate, and Shigehiro Oishi, "Reading Literary Fiction Is Associated with a More Complex Worldview," *Personality and Social Psychology Bulletin* 49, no. 9 (2022): 1408–20, https://doi.org/10.1177/01461672221106059.

101 we found empirical support: Lionel Trilling, *The Liberal Imagination: Essays on Literature and Society* (New York: Viking, 1950).

103 participants who saw the figure-ground drawings: Summarized in Shigehiro Oishi and Erin Westgate, "A Psychologically Rich Life: Beyond Happiness and Meaning," *Psychological Review* 129, no. 4 (2022): 790–811, https://doi.org/10.1037/rev0000317.

104 "games which bring with them no further interest": Kant, *Critique of Judgment,* 111.

104 watching sports could be construed: Stephen Mumford, *Watching Sport: Aesthetics, Ethics and Emotion* (Abingdon, UK: Routledge, 2012).

106 Proust talks about the role of art: Marcel Proust, *In Search of Lost Time,* vol. 6: *Time Regained,* trans. Andreas Mayor and Terence Kilmartin, revised by D. J. Enright (1927, translated 1981; reprint, New York: Modern Library, 2003), 299.

106 Ebert watched over 10,000 movies: Roger Ebert, "Reflections After 25 Years at the Movies," RogerEbert.com, April 8, 2016 (originally published 1992).

Chapter 10: The Point of Exploration

108 "And the purpose of life": Eleanor Roosevelt, *You Learn by Living* (New York: Harper, 1960).

108 Pascal would have called "diversions": Blaise Pascal, *Pensées and Other Writings,* trans. Honor Levi (1670; translation, Oxford: Oxford University Press, 1995).

108 English zoologist John Richard Krebs: John Krebs, Alejandro Kacelnik, and Peter Taylor, "Test of Optimal Sampling by Foraging Great Tits," *Nature* 275 (1978): 27–31.

109 we asked 585 UVA students what kind: Yingxue Liu, Youngjae Cha, and Shigehiro Oishi, "Exploring the Unknown: Identity Exploration Predicts Preference for a Psychologically Rich Life," Data Blitz presentation at the Society for Personality and Social Psychology meeting, Atlanta, Georgia, 2023.

110 psychologists Peter Todd and Geoffrey Miller: Peter Todd and Geoffrey Miller, "From Pride and Prejudice to Persuasion: Satisficing in Mate Search," in *Simple Heuristics That Make Us Smart,* eds. Gerd Gigerenzer, Peter Todd, and the ABC Research Group (New York: Oxford University Press, 1999), 287–308.

111 only 30 percent of college students followed: Walter Herbranson, Hunter Pluckebaum, Jaidyanne Podsobinski, and Zachary Hartzell, "Don't Let the Pigeon Chair the Search Committee: Pigeons (*Columba livia*) Match Humans' (*Homo sapiens*) Suboptimal Approach to the Secretary Problem," *Journal of Comparative Psychology* 136, no. 1 (2022): 3–19, https://doi.org/10.1037/com0000304.

112 people make suboptimal choices: Bruno Frey and Reiner Eichenberger, "Marriage Paradoxes," *Rationality and Society* 8, no. 2 (1996): 187–206.

112 Psychologists Samantha Cohen and Peter Todd: Samantha Cohen and Peter Todd, "Relationship Foraging: Does Time Spent Searching Predict Relationship Length?," *Evolutionary Behavioral Sciences* 12, no. 3 (2018): 139–51, https://doi.org/10.1037/ebs0000131.

114 Bossard, a sociologist at the University of Pennsylvania: James H. S. Bossard, "Residential Propinquity as a Factor in Marriage Selection," *American Journal of Sociology* 38, no. 2 (1932): 219–24.

114 Philadelphia was ethnically and racially segregated: Ken Finkel, "Roots of Segregation in Philadelphia, 1920–1930," *PhillyHistory Blog,* February 22, 2016. Tim Wilson shared this post with me.

115 Haandrikman and her colleagues: Karen Haandrikman, Carel Harmsen, Leo van Wissen, and Inge Hutter, "Geography Matters: Patterns of Spatial Homogamy in the Netherlands," *Population, Space and Place* 14, no. 5 (2008): 387–405.

116 In the late 1940s, social psychologists: Leon Festinger, Stanley Schachter, and Kurt Back, *Social Pressures in Informal Groups: A Study of Human Factors in Housing* (New York: Harper, 1950).

117 zeroed in on the familiarity effect: Robert B. Zajonc, "Attitudinal Effects of Mere Exposure," *Journal of Personality and Social Psychology* 9, no. 2, pt. 2 (1968): 1–27, https://doi.org/10.1037/h0025848.

118 field experiment in a real college classroom: Richard Moreland and Scott Beach, "Exposure Effects in the Classroom: The Development of Affinity Among Students," *Journal of Experimental Social Psychology* 28, no. 3 (1992): 255–76.

119 perceived similarity leads to attraction: Donn Byrne, *The Attraction Paradigm* (New York: Academic Press, 1971); R. Matthew Montoya and Robert Horton, "A Meta-Analytic Investigation of the Process Underlying the Similarity-Attraction Effect," *Journal of Social and Personal Relationships* 30, no. 1 (2012): 64–94.

120 use residential mobility data from the U.S.: Shigehiro Oishi, Felicity Miao, Minkyung Koo, Jason Kisling, and Kate Ratliff, "Residential Mobility Breeds Familiarity-Seeking," *Journal of Personality and Social Psychology* 102, no. 1 (2012): 149–62, https://doi.org/10.1037/a0024949.

123 Thaler discovered a related phenomenon: Daniel Kahneman, Jack Knetsch, and Richard Thaler, "Experimental Tests of the Endowment Effect and the Coase Theorem," *Journal of Political Economy* 98, no. 6 (1990): 1325–48.

124 consumers were asked to plan a snack: Itamar Simonson, "The Effect of Purchase Quantity and Timing on Variety-Seeking Behavior," *Journal of Marketing Research* 27, no. 2 (1990): 150–62.

124 related to a larger human tendency: Daniel Kahneman and Amos Tversky, "Prospect Theory: An Analysis of Decision Under Risk," *Econometrica* 47, no. 2 (1979): 263–91.

125 Loss aversion makes us conservative: Deborah Kermer, Erin Driver-Linn, Timothy Wilson, and Daniel Gilbert, "Loss Aversion Is an Affective Forecasting Error," *Psychological Science* 17, no. 8 (2006): 649–53.

125 tested how much people enjoy talking to strangers: Nicholas Epley and Juliana Schroeder, "Mistakenly Seeking Solitude," *Journal of Experimental Psychology: General* 143, no. 5 (2014): 1980–99.

127 evidence showing that multicultural experiences: Angela Ka-yee Leung, William Maddux, Adam Galinsky, and Chi-yue Chiu, "Multicultural Experience Enhances Creativity," *American Psychologist* 63, no. 3 (2008): 169–81.

127 attach a candle to a wall: A solution to the Duncker candle problem is as follows: First, take the tacks out of the box. Second, attach the empty box to the wall using a tack. Third, put the candle on the box and light the candle with a match!

127 A smile is a good example: Magdalena Rychlowska, Yuri Miyamoto, David Matsumoto, Ursula Hess, et al., "Heterogeneity of Long-History Migration Explains Cultural Differences in Reports of Emotional Expressivity and the Functions of Smiles," *Proceedings of the National Academy of Sciences* 112, no. 19 (2015): e2429–e2436.

128 benefits of multicultural experiences: William Maddux, Jackson Lu, Salvatore Affinito, and Adam Galinsky, "Multicultural Experiences: A Systematic Review and New Theoretical Framework," *Academy of Management Annals* 15, no. 2 (2021): 345–76.

128 undesirable outcomes correlated with multicultural experience: Salvatore Affinito, Giselle Antoine, Kurt Gray, and William Maddux, "Negative Multicultural Experiences Can Increase Intergroup Bias," *Journal of Experimental Social Psychology* 109 (2023): 104498.

128 those with more cross-cultural experiences cheated more: Jackson Lu, Jordi Quoidbach, Francesca Gino, Alek Chakroff, William Maddux, and Adam Galinsky, "The Dark Side of Going Abroad: How Broad Foreign Experiences Increase Immoral Behavior," *Journal of Personality and Social Psychology* 112, no. 1 (2017): 1–16, https://doi.org/10.1037/pspa0000068.

129 "if you're not busy being born": Walter Isaacson, *Steve Jobs* (New York: Simon & Schuster, 2011), 570. Jobs's Bob Dylan paraphrase comes from the song "It's Alright, Ma (I'm Only Bleeding)" (1965).

Chapter 11: Turn Adversity into a Psychologically Rich Experience

130 "For a typically healthy person": Friedrich Nietzsche, "Why I Am So Wise," in *On the Genealogy of Morals and Ecce Homo,* trans. Walter Kaufmann and R. J. Hollingdale (1887 and 1908 [1888]; reprint, New York: Vintage, 1989), 224.

130 earthquakes as a sort of catharsis: Friedrich Nietzsche, *Thus Spoke Zarathustra: A Book for All and None,* trans. Walter Kaufmann (1883–1892, translated 1954; reprint, New York: Penguin, 1978), 211.

131 "Why I Am So Wise," "Why I Am So Clever," and "Why I Write Such Good Books": Nietzsche, *On the Genealogy of Morals and Ecce Homo.*

131 "it permitted, it *commanded* me": Nietzsche, "Human, All Too Human," in *On the Genealogy of Morals and Ecce Homo,* 287.

131 "Looking from the perspective": Nietzsche, "Why I Am So Wise," in *On the Genealogy of Morals and Ecce Homo,* 223.

132 in one widely cited 1974 paper: Amos Tversky and Daniel Kahneman, "Judgment Under Uncertainty: Heuristics and Biases," *Science* 185, no. 4157 (1974): 1124–31.

132 an extraordinary personal story: Daniel Kahneman, "Daniel Kahneman: Biographical" (2002), Nobel Prize website.

133 Kahneman didn't characterize his life as meaningful: Amir Mandel, "Why Nobel Prize Winner Daniel Kahneman Gave Up on Happiness," *Haaretz,* October 7, 2018.

134 "It changed my perspective for life": Thomas Gaffney, "After Hurricane Sandy Wreaked Havoc, a Changed Perspective," *New York Times,* November 30, 2013.

134 Bridges and his son Jordan: Courtney Gisriel, "Survivor Stories: Family Reflects on How Hurricane Katrina Brought Them Closer Together," *Today,* NBC, September 27, 2018.

135 compassion: *Visions of Compassion,* edited by Richard J. Davidson and Anne Harrington (New York: Oxford University Press, 2002). Jennifer L. Goetz, Dacher Keltner, and Emiliana Simon-Thomas, "Compassion: An Evolutionary Analysis and Empirical Review," *Psychological Bulletin* 136, no. 3 (2010): 351–74. Christopher Peterson and Martin E. P. Seligman, *Character Strengths and Virtues: A Handbook and Classification* (New York: Oxford University Press, 2004).

135 To investigate, I spent my sabbatical year: Shigehiro Oishi, Reo Kimura, Haruo Hayashi, Shigeo Tatsuki, Keiko Tamura, Keiko Ishii, and Jane Tucker, "Psychological Adaptation to the Great Hanshin-Awazi Earthquake of 1995: 16 Years Later Victims Still Report Lower Levels of Subjective Well-Being," *Journal of Research in Personality* 55 (2015): 84–90.

136 Solnit documents numerous examples: Rebecca Solnit, *A Paradise Built in Hell: The Extraordinary Communities That Arise in Disaster* (New York: Penguin, 2009). Quotes on 16.

137 best, most direct evidence for this: Yiyuan Li, Hong Li, Jean Decety, and Kang Lee, "Experiencing a Natural Disaster Alters Children's Altruistic Giving," *Psychological Science* 24, no. 9 (2013): 1686–95.

138 trends in job applications at the municipality level: Shigehiro Oishi,

Ayano Yagi, Asuka Komiya, Florian Kohlbacher, Takashi Kusumi, and Keiko Ishii, "Does a Major Earthquake Change Job Preferences and Human Values?," *European Journal of Personality* 31, no. 3 (2017): 258–65.

139 "a treasure amidst ruins": Sa'di, *The Gulistan of Sa'di,* story 39. https://classics.mit.edu/Sadi/guilistan.2.i.html.

139 study examined whether individuals who were exposed: Gianluca Grimalda, Nancy Buchan, Orgul Ozturk, Adriana Pinate, Giulia Urso, and Marilynn Brewer, "Exposure to COVID-19 Is Associated with Increased Altruism, Particularly at the Local Level," *Scientific Reports* 11 (2021): 18950.

139 Did an unusual experience of COVID-19: Micael Dahlen and Helge Thorbjørnsen, "An Infectious Silver Lining: Is There a Positive Relationship Between Recovering from a COVID Infection and Psychological Richness of Life?," *Frontiers in Psychology* 13 (2022): 785224.

140 at least 6,000 Koreans were killed: Sonia Ryang, "The Great Kanto Earthquake and the Massacre of Koreans in 1923: Notes on Japan's Modern National Sovereignty," *Anthropological Quarterly* 76, no. 4 (2003): 731–48.

140 Vigilantes were formed and they inflicted: Solnit, *Paradise Built in Hell,* 1.

141 Most people do move on: Ann Masten, "Ordinary Magic: Resilience Processes in Development," *American Psychologist* 56, no. 3 (2001): 227–38, https://doi.org/10.1037/0003-066X.56.3.227.

141 James commented on this painting: William James, *The Varieties of Religious Experience: A Study in Human Nature* (New York: Longmans, Green, 1902), 50.

Chapter 12: A Story We Tell

142 "How often do we tell our own life story?": Julian Barnes, *The Sense of an Ending* (New York: Knopf, 2011), 104.

143 Wilson discusses this exact process: Timothy Wilson, *Redirect: The Surprising New Science of Psychological Change* (New York: Little, Brown, 2011), 11.

143 parents of college students taking an intro: Anne Wilson and Michael Ross, "From Chump to Champ: People's Appraisals of Their Earlier and Present Selves," *Journal of Personality and Social Psychology* 80, no. 4 (2001): 572–84, https://doi.org/10.1037/0022-3514.80.4.572.

144 traits such as musical skills and math abilities: Justin Kruger, "Lake Wobegon Be Gone! The 'Below-Average Effect' and the Egocentric Nature of Comparative Ability Judgments," *Journal of Personality and Social Psychology* 77, no. 2 (1999): 221–32, https://doi.org/10.1037/0022 -3514.77.2.221.

146 an intriguing experiment to show how: Timothy Wilson and Patricia Linville, "Improving the Academic Performance of College Freshmen: Attribution Therapy Revisited," *Journal of Personality and Social Psychology* 42, no. 2 (1982): 367–76, https://doi.org/10.1037/0022 -3514.42.2.367.

147 experiment telling one group of tenth-grade students: Huang-Yao Hong and Xiaodong Lin-Siegler, "How Learning About Scientists' Struggles Influences Students' Interest and Learning in Physics," *Journal of Educational Psychology* 104, no. 2 (2012): 469–84, https://doi .org/10.1037/a0026224.

148 numerous intervention studies of this sort: Gregory Walton and Timothy Wilson, "Wise Interventions: Psychological Remedies for Social and Personal Problems," *Psychological Review* 125, no. 5 (2018): 617–55, https://doi.org/10.1037/rev0000115; Rory Lazowski and Chris Hulleman, "Motivation Interventions in Education: A Meta-Analytic Review," *Review of Educational Research* 86, no. 2 (2016): 602–40.

149 McAdams even wrote a book: Dan McAdams, *George W. Bush and the Redemptive Dream: A Psychological Portrait* (New York: Oxford University Press, 2011).

150 individuals who tell a redemptive story: Jen Guo, Miriam Klevan, and Dan McAdams, "Personality Traits, Ego Development, and the Redemptive Self," *Personality and Social Psychology Bulletin* 42, no. 11 (2016): 1551–63.

150 Individuals high in openness to experience: Dan McAdams, Nana Akua Anyidoho, Chelsea Brown, Yi Ting Huang, Bonnie Kaplan, and Mary Anne Machado, "Traits and Stories: Links Between Dispositional and Narrative Features of Personality," *Journal of Personality* 72, no. 4 (2004): 761–84.

150 Rogers and colleagues asked half: Benjamin Rogers, Herrison Chicas, John Michael Kelly, Emily Kubin, et al., "Seeing Your Life as a Hero's Journey Increases Meaning in Life," *Journal of Personality and Social Psychology* 125, no. 4 (2023): 752–78.

151 deep processing: Fergus Craik and Endel Tulving, "Depth of Processing and the Retention of Words in Episodic Memory," *Journal of*

Experimental Psychology: General 104, no. 3 (1975): 268–94, https://doi.org/10.1037/0096-3445.104.3.268.

151 rehearsal: Edward Awh, John Jonides, and Patricia Reuter-Lorenz, "Rehearsal in Spatial Working Memory," *Journal of Experimental Psychology: Human Perception and Performance* 24, no. 3 (1998): 780–90, https://doi.org/10.1037/0096-1523.24.3.780.

151 consolidation: James McGaugh, "Memory Consolidation and the Amygdala: A Systems Perspective," *Trends in Neurosciences* 25, no. 9 (2002): 456–61.

151 we need to pay attention to what is happening: Fergus Craik and Michael Watkins, "The Role of Rehearsal in Short-Term Memory," *Journal of Verbal Learning and Verbal Behavior* 12 (1973): 599–607.

151 sensation-seekers did poorly in short-term memory: Tim Bogg and Peter Finn, "A Self-Regulatory Model of Behavioral Disinhibition in Late Adolescence: Integrating Personality Traits, Externalizing Psychopathology, and Cognitive Capacity," *Journal of Personality* 78, no. 2 (2010): 441–70.

152 Retelling: Elizabeth Marsh, "Retelling Is Not the Same as Recalling: Implications for Memory," *Current Directions in Psychological Science* 16, no. 1 (2007): 16–20.

152 Sixo, a character in Toni Morrison's *Beloved:* Toni Morrison, *Beloved* (1987; reprint, New York: Vintage, 2004), 321.

153 "If you are lucky enough": Ernest Hemingway, *A Moveable Feast* (New York: Scribner's, 1964).

153 by writing you can organize your thoughts: James Pennebaker and Janel Seagal, "Forming a Story: The Health Benefits of Narrative," *Journal of Clinical Psychology* 55, no. 10 (1999): 1243–54.

153 the main character, Macon Dead III: Toni Morrison, *Song of Solomon* (1977; reprint, New York: Vintage, 2004).

Chapter 13: Two Remaining Questions: Too Much Richness?
Is It Possible to Find Richness in the Familiar?

154 "Too much mystery is merely an annoyance": Dean Koontz, *Odd Thomas* (New York: Bantam, 2003), 4.

155 analyzed the Midlife in the United States (MIDUS) data: Shigehiro Oishi and Ulrich Schimmack, "Residential Mobility, Well-Being, and Mortality," *Journal of Personality and Social Psychology* 98, no. 6 (2010): 980–94, https://doi.org/10.1037/a0019389.

155 *New York Times* reported on our paper: Pamela Paul, "Does Moving a Child Create Adult Baggage?," *New York Times,* July 9, 2010.

158 Morris praised the show: Wesley Morris, "Review: Taylor Mac's 24-Hour Concert Was One of the Great Experiences of My Life," *New York Times,* October 10, 2016.

159 Needham wrote in *The Guardian:* Alex Needham, "Taylor Mac Review: 24-Hour-Long Pop Show Is Everything," *The Guardian,* October 10, 2016.

160 Polley published a book: Sarah Polley, *Run Towards the Danger: Confrontations with a Body of Memory* (New York: Penguin Press, 2022).

160 *Either/Or* is all about the conflicts: Søren Kierkegaard, *Either/Or: A Fragment of Life,* trans. Alastair Hannay (1843, translated 1992; reprint, London: Penguin, 2004).

161 "for me this is a matter": Kierkegaard, *Either/Or,* 405.

162 Fincham and colleagues did a fascinating study: Frank Fincham, Nathaniel Lambert, and Steven Beach, "Faith and Unfaithfulness: Can Praying for Your Partner Reduce Infidelity?," *Journal of Personality and Social Psychology* 99, no. 4 (2010): 649–59, https://doi.org/10.1037/a0019628.

162 "The historical nature of marital love": Kierkegaard, *Either/Or,* 435.

163 "The whole of life is lived": Kierkegaard, *Either/Or,* 422.

163 "In music an even tempo": Kierkegaard, *Either/Or,* 455.

163 one of the most famous relationship experiments: Arthur Aron, Christina Norman, Elaine Aron, Colin McKenna, and Richard Heyman, "Couples' Shared Participation in Novel and Arousing Activities and Experienced Relationship Quality," *Journal of Personality and Social Psychology* 78, no. 2 (2000): 273–84, https://doi.org/10.1037/0022-3514.78.2.273.

164 found that 40 percent of those married: Daniel O'Leary, Bianca Acevedo, Arthur Aron, Leonie Huddy, and Debra Mashek, "Is Long-Term Love More Than a Rare Phenomenon? If So, What Are Its Correlates?," *Social Psychological and Personality Science* 3, no. 2 (2012): 241–49.

164 the researchers used a neuroimaging technique: Bianca Acevedo, Arthur Aron, Helen Fisher, and Lucy Brown, "Neural Correlates of Long-Term Intense Romantic Love," *Social Cognitive and Affective Neuroscience* 7, no. 2 (2012): 145–59.

165 Aron said he and his wife: Kira Newman, "How Love Researcher Art Aron Keeps His Own Relationship Strong," *Greater Good Magazine,* July 23, 2018.

169 nostalgia—sentimental longing for one's past—has a number: Constantine Sedikides and Tim Wildschut, "Finding Meaning in Nostalgia," *Review of General Psychology* 22, no. 1 (2018): 48–61.

169 Woolf has enthusiastic fans across generations: Jenny Offill, "A Lifetime of Lessons in *Mrs. Dalloway*," *The New Yorker,* December 29, 2020.

170 "The world has raised its whip": Virginia Woolf, *Mrs. Dalloway* (1925; reprint, London: Macmillan Collector's Library, 2017), 17.

170 "He had been a Socialist": Woolf, *Mrs. Dalloway,* 57.

170 "Richard has improved . . . extraordinary excitement?": Woolf, *Mrs. Dalloway,* 216.

Chapter 14: A Good Life Without Regrets

172 "I really like familiarity": Levy cited in Ellen Carpenter, "Eugene Levy Takes Viewers Around the World (Hesitantly) in *The Reluctant Traveler*," *Hemispheres,* February 17, 2023.

172 Toni Morrison's *Jazz,* Violet: Toni Morrison, *Jazz* (1992; reprint, New York: Vintage, 2004), 208.

173 James invented the self-esteem equation: William James, *The Principles of Psychology* (New York: Henry Holt, 1890), 1: 310.

174 two main tasks of humans are to work and to love: Erik H. Erikson, *Childhood and Society* (New York: W. W. Norton, 1950).

174 I analyzed Payscale's survey: "The Most and Least Interesting Jobs," Payscale, www.payscale.com/data-packages/most-and-least -meaningful-jobs.

176 *Two Psychologists Four Beers:* Yoel Inbar and Alexa Tullett, "The Good Life," *Two Psychologists Four Beers* (podcast), episode 71.

176 When we asked participants: Shigehiro Oishi, Hyewon Choi, Minkyung Koo, Iolanda Galinha, Keiko Ishii, Asuka Komiya, Maike Luhmann, Christie Scollon, Ji-eun Shin, Hwaryung Lee, Eunkook Suh, Joar Vittersø, Samantha Heintzelman, Kostadin Kushlev, Erin Westgate, Nicholas Buttrick, Jane Tucker, Charles Ebersole, Jordan Axt, Elizabeth Gilbert, Brandon Ng, Jaime Kurtz, and Lorraine Besser, "Happiness, Meaning, and Psychological Richness," *Affective Science* 1 (2020): 107–15, https://doi.org/10.1007/s42761-020-00011-z.

178 travels to Ukraine in search of Augustine: Jonathan Safran Foer, *Everything Is Illuminated* (Boston: Houghton Mifflin, 2002).

180 people tend to regret the things they could have done: Thomas Gilovich and Victoria Husted Medvec, "The Experience of Regret: What, When, and Why," *Psychological Review* 102, no. 2 (1995): 379–95, https://doi.org/10.1037/0033-295X.102.2.379.

180 poet Ada Calhoun recalls how her parents: Ada Calhoun, "The Poet Who Taught Me to Be in Love with the World," *New York Times Magazine,* January 11, 2023.

182 On days when people do something new: Shigehiro Oishi, Hyewon Choi, Ailin Liu, and Jaime Kurtz, "Experiences Associated with Psychological Richness," *European Journal of Personality* 35, no. 5 (2021): 754–70.

183 the poem "Ed": Louis Simpson, "Ed," *Collected Poems* (New York: Paragon House, 1990).

Appendices

221 Appendix 1: Psychologically Rich Life Questionnaire: Taken from Shigehiro Oishi, Hyewon Choi, Nicholas Buttrick, Samantha Heintzelman, Kostadin Kushlev, Erin Westgate, Jane Tucker, Charles Ebersole, Jordan Axt, Elizabeth Gilbert, Brandon Ng, and Lorraine Besser, "The Psychologically Rich Life Questionnaire," *Journal of Research in Personality* 81 (2019): 257–70.

225 Appendix 2: Note on correlations: The correlations on psychological richness come from Shigehiro Oishi and Erin Westgate, "A Psychologically Rich Life: Beyond Happiness and Meaning," *Psychological Review* 129, no. 4 (2022): 790–811; the correlations on happiness and meaning (purpose in life) come from Jeromy Anglim, Sharon Horwood, Luke Smillie, Rosario Marrero, and Joshua Wood, "Predicting Psychological and Subjective Well-Being from Personality: A Meta-Analysis," *Psychological Bulletin* 146, no. 4 (2020): 279–323.

PSYCHOLOGICALLY RICH LIFE QUESTIONNAIRE (PRLQ)

We define a psychologically rich life as a life characterized by variety, depth, and interest. A life could be psychologically rich if a person experiences a variety of interesting things or feels and appreciates a variety of deep emotions. These can be via firsthand experience or vicariously through novels, films, or sports on TV. Take the Psychologically Rich Life Questionnaire, and find out your psychological richness score!

Please indicate the degree to which you agree or disagree with each of the following statements, using the 1 to 7 point scale below. Put your responses (numbers) next to the questions.

1	2	3	4	5	6	7
Strongly Disagree	Disagree	Slightly Disagree	Neither Agree nor Disagree	Slightly Agree	Agree	Strongly Agree

____1. My life has been psychologically rich*

____2. My life has been experientially rich*

____3. My life has been emotionally rich*

____4. I have had a lot of interesting experiences*

____5. I have had a lot of novel experiences*

____6. My life has been full of unique, unusual experiences*

___7. My life consists of rich, intense moments*

___8. My life has been dramatic

___9. I experience a full range of emotions via firsthand experiences such as travel and attending concerts*

___10. I have a lot of personal stories to tell others*

___11. On my deathbed, I am likely to say, "I had an interesting life"*

___12. On my deathbed, I am likely to say, "I have seen and learned a lot"*

___13. My life would make a good novel or movie*

___14. My life has been monotonous (r)

___15. I often feel bored with my life (r)

___16. My life has been uneventful (r)

___17. I can't remember the last time I've done or experienced something new (r)

Notes: The twelve-item version is composed of the items with an asterisk (*); (r) indicates a reverse item.

How to score:

Step 1. Convert your responses to Items 14 to 17 (these are reverse items) as follows: 1 to 7; 2 to 6; 3 to 5; 4 to 4; 5 to 3; 6 to 2; 7 to 1.

Step 2. Add your responses from Items 1 to 13, and add Step 1 scores (reversed scores).

Step 3. Then divide the total scores by 17. What did you get?

Example: If your original responses to Items 1 to 13 were 6, 5, 5, 4, 6, 6, 7, 5, 4, 5, 5, 6, 7, and Items 14 to 17 were 2, 2, 3, 1 then: Step 1: your Items 14 to 17 reversed scores are 6, 6, 5, 7. Step 2. Add Items 1 to 13 (i.e., 6+5+5+4+6+6+7+5+4+5+5+6+7) = 71 and add reversed Items 14 to 17 from Step 1 (i.e., 6+6+5+7) = 24. Step 3: (71+24)/17 = 5.59. That's it. 5.59 is your score.

How to interpret your score:

Below are the data from 1,213 American adults (mean age = 38.21).

The mean (average) score was 4.58, and the range was 1.18 to 7.00. The percentile scores are as below. If your score was 3.41 or below, you scored among the lowest 10 percent of Americans. If your score was 4.35, then roughly 40 percent of Americans were below you and roughly 60 percent were above you. If your score was 5.75 or higher, then you were among the top 10 percent in psychological richness.

Descriptive Statistics

	Psychrich
N	1213
Mean	4.584
Std. Deviation	0.971
Minimum	1.176
Maximum	7.000
10th percentile	3.412
20th percentile	3.881
30th percentile	4.063
40th percentile	4.353
50th percentile	4.588
60th percentile	4.882
70th percentile	5.176
80th percentile	5.382
90th percentile	5.741

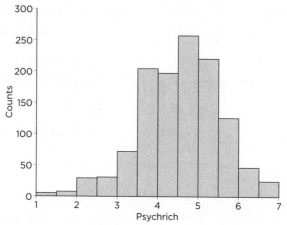

Distribution of Psychologically Rich Life Questionnaire
Scores (N = 1,213 Americans)

META-ANALYTIC CORRELATIONS BETWEEN A GOOD LIFE AND BIG FIVE PERSONALITY

	Richness	Happiness	Meaning
Openness	**.47**	.08	.21
Extraversion	.44	.32	.39
Neuroticism	−.18	**−.39**	−.45
Agreeableness	.27	.20	.28
Conscientiousness	.30	.27	**.50**

Note: The highest personality trait correlated with each dimension of a good life is noted in bold. The correlations on psychological richness come from Oishi and Westgate (2022), whereas the correlations on happiness and meaning (purpose in life) come from Anglim et al. (2020).

AN ALTERNATIVE
SUMMARY OF THE BOOK

Here is a parody of Kierkegaard's *Either/Or* that I've entitled *Neither/Nor*, in the form of imaginary correspondences between a son (A) and his father (B).

Dear Dad,

It is freaking cold in Northfield! It's October and already below freezing! Classes are OK. I thought I wrote a particularly strong essay on Plato's Cave. But Professor commented on my essay by saying, "These comments may seem harsh . . . I don't mean to say that you can't disagree with Plato, only that you should address his analysis in the course of making your case. Without that engagement, we're left with a stirring sermon but not so much argument and persuasion." Ouch! Not good. Probably I am going to get a B in that class—well, I hope at least a B. . . .

Baseball is going well, but I am so busy. My teammates are pretty amazing. One guy throws 95! Everyone can hit. I think I am a better defender than most, though. If only I could hit. Upperclassmen are all good students. Luke still hasn't gotten any B's yet! They all seem to know what they are doing. One of them is going to grad school at Karolinska Institute in Sweden. Two are going to law school. One is getting a CS degree, so not worried about job. I have no idea what I want to be. BTW, how come so many kids are so rich? One kid has a second house in Capri, Italy! They were talking about investment portfolio a few nights ago and which stocks were doing well. I have no idea. Should I be concerned?

Dear Son,

To say that Northfield is cold is as obvious as to say the earth is round. So, let's not say it. I lived in Minnesota myself for four years!

It is a wonderful state, but not blessed with warm weather. Most families at your school are richer than us. That's why we get financial aid! Most students there are super smart, too. But let's remember Mr. Johnson's story on move-in day. It is OK to be different! I told you about Sonja Lyubomirsky's research, right? Social comparison is bad for you. Avoid social comparisons, and remember Tim Wilson: Redirect!

More generally, it is easy to get into a happiness trap in college. Everyone else seems to be doing better than you. Everyone else seems to be having more fun than you. It is also easy to get into a meaning trap. Everyone else seems to know what they are doing. Everyone else seems to be making a difference in the world, while you are not. Neither happiness nor meaning is the only path to a good life. Well, first of all, life is long. You don't have to know exactly what you are doing at the age of 18. You might find something important at age 30, 40, or even 50, 60, or 70 and make a difference then.

Second, it is OK to fail here and there. One B would not kill you. Yes, I want you to get all A's, if possible. I am a Tiger Dad after all. But I admit (I told you already?) my first semester in college was a disaster; I got two C's and one D, I think. Of course, grades didn't matter in Japanese universities back then. After looking at my first-semester grades, my advisor Professor Nakano said, "君も低空飛行ですね。You, too, are flying pretty low," and laughed. The key word? "Too." I was not alone. Other advisees were struggling, too. I found hope in that word. He was a funny professor. I couldn't quite take off smoothly, but eventually found a jet stream. Be patient. Find the right wind. A "Chump to Champ!"

Dear Dad,

I can't believe my first year is almost over. I am not surprised I didn't play much, but still it was disappointing. That injury in February really hurt. . . . I need to register for the fall. What should I take? Intro to social psych should be easy? Some econ? Political science?

BTW, last Friday a few baseball friends and I went to a WWE wrestling match in Minneapolis. I thought it was a joke, but guess what? There were so many adoring fans, kids and their parents. Did you know that they do a huge anti-bullying campaign? We also went to this Vietnamese place nearby, and that was really good. Haven't had such a delicious pho all year!

Dear Son,

I can't believe your first year is almost over. Re: injury, that would help you see the world and yourself from a different perspective. Remember Nietzsche: "Looking from the perspective of the sick toward healthier concepts and values and, conversely, looking again from the fullness and self-assurance of a rich life down into the secret work of the instinct of decadence. . . . Now I know how, have the know-how, to reverse perspectives." It is not Kelly Clarkson; it is Nietzsche who first said what doesn't kill you makes you stronger. Ohtani came back from Tommy John surgery strong. Darvish did, too. A famous Japanese proverb: 七転八起. If you fall seven times, you get up eight times! That's the spirit, isn't it? I sent you Alison Gopnik's *Atlantic* article, too? A fascinating story of an intellectual exploration. Read it! Social psych should be easy for you. Nice to have one easy class, so that you can take some difficult ones!

I am so glad you guys found some time to have fun in the city. Those unplanned, spontaneous trips are the best!! Your perspective changed, too. That's great. I remember my grandpa and I went to a women's pro wrestling match when I was like 12? To this day, I don't know why he took me there or why he wanted to go. Indeed, I had totally forgotten about that until you mentioned WWE! My initial thought was, who would go there? Shocking to think that my grandpa was that kind of guy . . . He was pretty open-minded for his generation. I remember him bringing a homeless guy home and giving him some food and 500 yen (about $6). My dad was so mad that Grandpa brought a homeless guy home. Your great-grandfather was a really nice guy, also kind of playful. He loved sumo wrestling so much. I grew up watching sumo on TV, you know. I need to take you to sumo when we go to Japan next time.

Dear Dad,

I am in Copenhagen! It is beautiful and walkable. My roommates are very nice, though a bit messy. Classes are interesting and a lot easier than Carleton! I am so glad I finally learned how to ride a bicycle. Everyone bikes here. One class has a few field trips where we have to bike around the city.

Next weekend, I will go to Norway. A friend of mine from Carleton wants to go there, so I will follow her. Should be fun. BTW, I watched an old movie called *M* by Fritz Lang last weekend. Ebert recommended it. Have you watched? The main character "M" is really disturbed and disturbing. But, by the end, I kind of felt bad for him. Very strange and interesting!

I haven't played baseball at all here. Not sure how much I can play here. No baseball field nearby. I must figure this out. I also need to apply for an internship. . . . There are so many things to do. . . . "Must, must, must— detestable word." Virginia Woolf?

Dear Son,

I am so glad you are liking your study abroad so far. I told you my story at Bates. There was some ugly stuff happened there, too, but now all great stories. So glad we spent five dreadful summer days working on Dede's bike! Days 1 and 2 looked hopeless. You just could not stay on the bike for more than two seconds! Remember? I wish I had taught you how to bike when you were younger. . . .

Don't worry about baseball now. Absorb everything Denmark offers. Oh, I guess you do need to apply for an internship now, though, don't you? Good luck!

"Must, must, must—detestable word." Is it *Mrs. Dalloway*? No, no, that's from *The Waves*? Bernard? Tell me about it. I am that guy. You are too young to be Bernard. Be playful. Take a vacation from social and economic reality once in a while. Be open to be a fool now and then.

BTW, Lang's *M* is a masterpiece, my favorite, a dark, psychologically rich movie! You learn so much from novels and films. Fritz Lang knows how to tell a story. A story-editing genius.

Looking back at his time in Paris in his twenties, Ernest Hemingway said, "If you are lucky enough to have lived in Paris as a young man, then wherever you go for the rest of your life, it stays with you, for Paris is a moveable feast." Make Copenhagen your own moveable feast.

See you soon!

Love,

Dad

achievement and success, 14–15, 17, 27, 33
Adams-Pickett, Donna, 26–27
adversity, 130–41
aesthetic experiences, 92–107
    figure-ground drawing and, 102–4
    importance of, 106–7
    pleasantness and interestingness in, 99–100
Aesthetics and Psychobiology (Berlyne), 99
affective forecasting error, 14
af Klint, Hilma, 151–52, 171
agreeableness, 58, 64–68, 150, 225
Alice's Adventures in Wonderland (Carroll), 35, 182
Allport, Gordon W., 57–58
altruism, 41, 137–38
American Sociological Association, 84
Anglim, Jeromy, 64
Apple, 38
    iPhone, 15–16, 38, 128
Aristotle, 12
Aron, Art, 163–65, 171
Aron, Elaine, 165
art, 97–98, 106

comprehensibility of, 100
    paintings, 98–100
artistic activities, 50–51, 61, 62
aspirations, 173
athletes, 70–75, 79, 166
Atlantic, 36–37, 153
Augustine, St., 33
authoritarianism, 30
Axt, Jordan, 102
Aziz, Mohammed, 92–93

Back, Kurt, 116
Bar, Noma, 102–3
Barkley, Charles, 105
Barnes, Julian, 142
Beach Boys, 168
Beatles, 129, 168–69, 171
Being and Time (Heidegger), 98
Beloved (Morrison), 152
Berlyne, Daniel, 99
Bet-David, Patrick, 74
Biles, Simone, 70, 71, 79, 80, 166
Bittersweet (Cain), 51
books, reading, 92–94, 100–101, 106, 130
Bossard, James, 114
Bourdain, Anthony, 64

Bower, Ann, 38–39
Bowman, Bob, 70
Brave New World (Huxley), 18, 22
Bridges, Joe, 134
Bridges, Jordan, 134–35
Brooks, David, 97–98
Bryant, Kobe, 74
Buddhism, 36–37
Bullshit Jobs (Graeber), 25
Bush, George H. W., 143
Bush, George W., 143, 149
Buttrick, Nick, 100

Cain, Susan, 51
Calhoun, Ada, 180
Candide (Voltaire), 35
candle problem, 127
Capaldi, Lewis, 9
Carroll, Lewis, 35
Carver, Raymond, 45, 46
Centers for Disease Control
    (CDC), 13, 112
Cervantes, Miguel de, 35
Cha, Louis, 61, 62
Cha, Youngjae, 85–86
challenge, 52
childhood moves, 154–58
Chiu, Chi-yue, 127
Choi, Hyewon, 46, 102
cities, 119–20
Clark, Jim, 20–21
Clash, The, 1, 3, 154
Clinch, Nicholas, 54
Cohen, Samantha, 112
Colet, Louise, 24
college life, 109–10
comfort zone, 125, 160, 182
commuters, 125–26
concert, twenty-four-hour, 158–60

confidence, 63
conscientiousness, 29, 58, 64–68,
    75, 150, 225
Costa, Paul, 69
Cottee, Simon, 30–31
COVID-19 pandemic, 48, 77,
    139–40, 168–69
creativity, 126–29, 175
Critique of Judgment (Kant), 97
Csikszentmihalyi, Mihaly, 6

Dahlen, Micael, 139–40
Daily Progress, 54–56
dating, 110–13, 121–22, 126, 163–64
Davis, Miles, 171
D'Cruz, Jason, 78
Decety, Jean, 137
Deci, Ed, 7
deliberatio, 179
Denmark, 21
Desideri, Ippolito, 36–37
Diener, Ed, 6, 7, 12, 18
diversity, 52
division of labor, 83–86, 89
DIY projects, 81–91, 127, 130
Dolu, Charles François, 37
Don Quixote (Cervantes), 35
Duncker candle problem, 127
Dweck, Carol, 8
Dylan, Bob, 128–29, 169, 171

earthquakes, 130, 135–38, 140,
    148
Ebert, Roger, 106–7
Ecce Homo (Nietzsche), 73, 130
"Ed" (Simpson), 183
Einstein, Albert, 147–48
Either/Or (Kierkegaard), 34–35,
    160–64, 171

Neither/Nor parody of, 227–30
Ellison, Larry, 21
Emmons, Bob, 6
emotions, 107
  dilution of, 85
  negative, 16–19, 23, 47–48, 51, 52,
    64, 89, 91, 136
  positive, 47–48, 51, 64, 89
  psychological richness and,
    47–48, 51–52
  regulation and stability of, 18, 19,
    64–68
  time-saving services and, 89
endowment effect, 123–24
energy, 63
Enlightenment, 36–37
Epley, Nick, 125–26
Erikson, Erik, 70
Erikson, Kai, 84–85
eudaimonic approach, 6–7
Everything Is Illuminated (Safran
  Foer), 177–78
expeditus, 35, 81, 179
experiences
  accumulation of, 10, 95, 148, 181
  reflection on, 151
  exploration, 33–42, 43, 57, 65,
    108–29
  benefits of, 126–29
  exploitation and, 109–10, 112
  extraversion, 16, 28, 29, 58, 59,
    62–67, 69, 75, 150, 225

failure, 14, 16–17, 27, 31
familiarity, 172, 181
  mere exposure effect and,
    117–26
  richness in, 125, 160–63, 181
"fake it till you make it," 15–16

Festinger, Leon, 116
figure-ground drawing, 102–4
films, 94–97, 106, 108, 130
Fincham, Frank, 162
fixed mindset, 8
Flaubert, Gustave, 24
Forbes, 21
Ford, Henry, 82
Franklin, Aretha, 169, 171
freedom versus security, 180
Freud, Sigmund, 174
friendship, 77–78, 116–17, 178,
  182
Fujimoto, Takashi, 134, 137

Galileo Galilei, 147–48
Galinsky, Adam, 127
Gallup World Polls, 27–28
Gelb, David, 165
genetics, 7, 8
Gilbert, Dan, 7, 14, 19
goals, 66
Goldberg, Lew, 58
Goldfinch, The (Tartt), 3
good enough, 19–20
good life, 3–4, 8, 11, 23, 25, 30–32,
    56, 68, 172, 179
  personality traits and, 225
Gopnik, Alison, 36–37, 56–57, 67,
    71, 153
Graeber, David, 25
gratitude, 4, 162, 171
great tit (*Parus major*), 108–10
Greece, ancient, 130–31
growth mindset, 8
Guardian, 159

Haandrikman, Karen, 115
Hangover (Bar), 102–3

happiness, 3–5, 8–11, 12, 31–32,
  33–34, 42, 52, 64, 75, 80, 133, 141,
  155, 172, 173, 176, 178–79, 182
  aspirations and, 173
  college life and, 109–10
  core features and metaphors of,
    8–10
  criticisms of, 24–25
  day of, 45–47
  division of labor and, 85, 86
  eudaimonic approach to, 6–7
  extraversion and, 16, 64, 65
  hedonic approach to, 7
  meaning and, 7–8
  obituary studies and, 53–57
  of others, putting before our own,
    4–5, 25
  outsourcing and, 89, 90
  personality traits and, 63–65,
    67–68
  pressure to be happy, 12–19, 23, 31
  psychological richness versus, 8,
    10, 11
  relationships and, 15, 33
  research on, 4, 6, 7, 14–15, 17
  as selfishness, 25
  smiling and, 16
  specialization and, 87
  success and, 14–15, 17, 33
  trap of, 12–23, 27, 32
"Happiness" (Carver), 45, 46
Harvard Business Review, 24
hedonic approach, 7
Heidegger, Martin, 98
Heintzelman, Samantha, 27
Hemingway, Ernest, 152–53, 182
Herbranson, Walter, 111
Hesse, Hermann, *Narcissus and
  Goldmund,* 33–35, 56, 67, 179

heuristics, 132
  "take a dozen," 112–13, 181
Hinds, Pamela, 77
hiring, 111, 121–22, 126
Holleran, Madison, 13
Holshouser, Anna, 136
Home Alone, 95
Homer, 35
Hong, Huang-Yao, 147
houses, homes, 122–24, 127
  loss of, 134–36, 138
Houston Rockets, 104–5
Huckabee, Mike, 65–67
Hume, David, 36–37
hurricanes, 28, 130, 134–35, 140,
  148
Huxley, Aldous, *Brave New World,*
  18, 22
hygge, 21

illness, 130, 131, 136
immigrants, 50, 66, 67
Inbar, Yoel, 176
India, 37–38, 126
In Search of Lost Time (Proust), 93,
  106
Institute of International
  Education, 48
intellectual activities, 61, 62, 67
intelligence, 8
intercontinental ballistic missiles
  (ICBMs), 61
introversion, 16, 62–64, 67, 68, 155
iPhone, 15–16, 38, 128
Isaacson, Walter, 39
Ishiguro, Kazuo, 93–94

James, William, 9, 12, 82, 141, 173
Jazz (Morrison), 172–73

Jiro Dreams of Sushi (Gelb), 165–67
job candidates, 111, 121–22, 126
Jobs, Steve, 15–16, 24, 29, 37–39, 56,
    126, 128–29
Jordan, Michael, 72
Joyce, James, 35, 181

Kagan, Jerome, 83–85
Kahneman, Daniel, 7, 17–18,
    124–25, 131–33
Kant, Immanuel, 97, 104
Kennedy, John F., 29
Kenyatta, Kahaari, 12
Kenyon, Jane, 46
Kepler, Johannes, 110–11, 113
Kierkegaard, Søren, *Either/Or,*
    34–35, 160–64, 171
  Neither/Nor parody of, 227–30
King, Laura, 27
Kohn, Melvin, 85
Koontz, Dean, 154
Krebs, Richard, 108
Krueger, Alan, 82
Kubrick, Stanley, 69, 79
Kurosawa, Akira, 95
Kurtz, Jaime, 50
Kusama, Yayoi, 171

"Land of Happy, The"
    (Silverstein), 24
Larsen, Randy, 6
Leibniz Prize, 72–73
Leung, Angela Ka-yee, 126–28
Levy, Eugene, 172, 181
Lewis, Michael, 20
Liberal Imagination, The (Trilling),
    101
Life of Haifisch, The (MacLeod),
    100

Linda (taxi driver), 40–42, 53, 57
Lin-Siegler, Xiaodong, 147
Linville, Patricia, 146–48
living and studying abroad, 48–52,
    59, 60, 128, 130
Lorge, Irving, 117
loss aversion, 124–25
Love It or List It, 123, 124
Lucasfilm, 38
Lyubomirsky, Sonja, 7, 21

Mac, Taylor, 158–60
MacLeod, Scott, 100
Maddux, William, 126–27
Major League Baseball (MLB), 74,
    104
Malone, Karl, 105
marriage, 113–16, 119, 161–65, 171
  mate selection, 110–13, 121–22, 126
Marsh, Abigail, 41
Marx, Karl, 84–85
Masten, Ann, 141
Matrix, The, 96
maximizer mindset, 20, 21
McAdams, Dan, 149
McCrae, Robert, 69
meaning, 4, 7–11, 25–29, 31–32,
    33–34, 42, 45–47, 52, 66, 80, 133,
    172, 173, 178–79, 182
  college life and, 109–10
  core features and metaphors of,
    8–10
  division of labor and, 85, 86
  happiness and, 7–8
  misplaced, 30–31
  obituary studies and, 53–57
  personality traits and, 65–68
  and pressure to make a
    difference, 31

meaning *(continued)*
 psychological richness versus, 8,
   10, 11
 specialization and, 87
 trap of, 24–32
 work and, 25–26, 174–75
Melville, Herman, 35
memorableness, 52, 95
memory, 151–53, 163
mere exposure effect, 117–26
Midlife in the United States
   (MIDUS), 155
Miller, Geoffrey, 110, 112–13
Mister Rogers' Neighborhood, 63–64
Moby-Dick (Melville), 35
moral relativism, 128
Moreland, Richard, 118
Morgan, Alex, 72
Morley, Christopher, 43
Morris, Wesley, 158–60
Morrison, Toni, 5, 35, 152, 153,
   172–73
Mortensen, Mark, 77
Mossner, Ernest, 36
Moveable Feast, A (Hemingway),
   153, 182
moves, frequent, 154–58
movies, 94–97, 106, 108, 130
Mrs. Dalloway (Woolf), 169–71
multicultural experiences, 126–28
Mumford, Stephen, 104

Narcissus and Goldmund (Hesse),
   33–35, 56, 67, 179
National Basketball Association
   (NBA), 74, 104, 105
national parks, 39–40, 60, 63, 67,
   108
natural disasters, 130

 earthquakes, 130, 135–38, 140, 148
 hurricanes, 28, 130, 134–35, 140,
   148
 negative effects of, 18, 140
 prosocial behavior and, 136–39,
   142
nature, 75, 108
Nazi Germany, 93, 132–33
Needham, Alex, 159, 160
negative emotions, 16–19, 23,
   47–48, 51, 52, 64, 89, 91, 136
negative events, fear of, 181
Netherlands, 115–16, 119
Netscape, 20
neuroticism, 28, 29, 58, 64, 66, 68,
   75, 150, 225
Newton, Isaac, 147–48
New Yorker, 14, 169
New York Times, 12, 13, 77, 134, 155,
   158–59
 obituaries in, 53–57, 61
New York Times Magazine, 180
NeXT, 38
Nietzsche, Friedrich, 22–23, 73,
   130–31, 135, 181
Nobel Prize, 33, 72–73, 131–33
nostalgia, 169
novels, reading, 92–94, 100–101,
   106, 130
novelty, 52, 165, 171

Obama, Barack, 27
Obama, Michelle, 26, 27
obituaries, 53–57, 61
Odbert, Henry S., 57–58
Odyssey (Homer), 35
Offill, Jenny, 169–71
Ohtani, Shohei, 74
Oishi, Yoshi, 1–4, 21

Olajuwon, Hakeem, 104
Oliver, Mary, 46
Olympic Games, 70–71, 80
O'Neal, Shaquille, 74–75, 80
Ono, Jiro, 165–67, 171
On the Move (Sacks), 5
openness to experience, 58–62,
    64–68, 69, 75, 150, 225
optimism, 29
Orlando Magic, 105
Osaka, Naomi, 79
"Otherwise" (Kenyon), 46
outsourcing, 83, 88–91
ownership, psychology of, 123–24

paintings, 98–100
Paradise Built in Hell, A (Solnit),
    136–37
Parasite, 96–97
Pascal, Blaise, 108
Payscale, 174–75
PBS NewsHour, 26, 40
Pei, I. M., 56
Pennebaker, James, 153
personality traits
  good life and, 225
  happiness and, 63–65, 67–68
  meaningfulness and, 65–68
  narrative identity and, 149–50
  psychological richness and,
    57–63, 67–68, 69, 80
perspective change, 101–2, 107, 131,
    139, 142
Phelps, Hilary, 70
Phelps, Michael, 70, 71, 79, 166
Philadelphia, 114–16, 119
Phoenix Suns, 105
Picasso, Pablo, 171
pigeons, 111, 181

playfulness, 69–80, 167, 182
poetry, 45–46, 106
politics, 30, 48, 97–98
Polley, Sarah, 160
*Portrait of the Artist as a Young
    Man, A* (Joyce), 35
Principles of Psychology, The
    (James), 82, 173
productivity, 81–84, 86, 91
propinquity effect, 116
Proust, Marcel, 93, 106, 130
Proyer, René, 75
psychological immune system,
    19, 65
psychological resilience, 141
psychological richness, 5–8, 10–11,
    32, 39, 40, 42, 53–68, 80, 91, 172,
    173, 176, 178–79
  adversity and, 130–41
  aesthetic experiences and, 92–107
  building a portfolio of, 151–53
  college life and, 109–10
  core features and metaphors of,
    6, 8–10
  day of, 45–48
  devotion to career and, 165–67,
    171
  division of labor and, 85, 86
  emotions and, 47–48, 51–52
  familiarity and, 125, 160–63, 181
  figure-ground drawing and, 102–4
  focus group studies on, 43–45
  happiness and meaning versus,
    8, 10, 11
  ingredients of, 43–52
  lessons of, 179–83
  nostalgia and, 169
  obituary studies and, 53–57, 61
  outsourcing and, 89, 90

psychological richness *(continued)*
  personality traits and, 57–63,
    67–68, 69, 80
  perspective change and, 101–2,
    107, 131, 139, 142
  playfulness and, 75–76
  questionnaire on, 221–24
  specialization and, 87, 88
  sports and, 105, 106
  stories in, 10, 90, 91, 142–53,
    181–82
  studying abroad and, 48–52, 130
  too much, 154–60
  top ten list on, 180–83
purpose, 27–29

Ramo, Simon, 54, 61, 62
Rashomon, 95–96
reading books, 92–94, 100–101, 106,
  130
Redirect (Wilson), 143, 145, 148
Reese, James, 49
reflective judgment, 97
regrets, 4–5, 10, 11, 39, 180
relationships, 64–65, 67–68
  friendship, 77–78, 116–17, 178, 182
  happiness and, 15, 33
  work, 65
relationships, romantic, 174
  dating, 110–13, 121–22, 126, 163–64
  marriage, 113–16, 119, 161–65, 171
  novelty in, 165, 171
  physical distance and, 113–16
  prayer and, 162
  self-expansion theory of, 164–65
religion, 28–29
Reluctant Traveler, The, 172
Remains of the Day, The (Ishiguro),
  93–94

Reni, Guido, 141
resilience, 141
responsibilities, 70, 79, 182
risk, 160
Rogers, Benjamin, 150
Rogers, Fred, 63–64
Rollins, Sonny, 97, 98
Roosevelt, Eleanor, 108
Ross, Lee, 21
Ross, Michael, 143–45
Rothko, Mark, 98
Run Towards the Danger (Polley),
  160
Ryan, Brad, 39–40, 67
Ryan, Joy, 39–40, 53, 60, 63, 67
Ryan, Richard, 7
Ryff, Carol, 6–7, 155

Sacks, Oliver, 5, 8, 179
Safran Foer, Jonathan, 177–78
Saint Dahl, Henry, 55
Sartre, Jean-Paul, 5
satisficer mindset, 4, 19–23
Schachter, Stan, 116
Schimmack, Uli, 155
Schindler's List, 108
Schroeder, Juliana, 125–26
Schwartz, Barry, 19
Schwartz, Tony, 24
Science, 132
scientists, 72–73, 83–84
secretary problem, 111, 121–22, 126
security versus freedom, 180
self-assurance, 63
self-esteem, 29, 173
selfishness, 25
self-sacrifice, 4, 5
Seligman, Martin, 6, 133
sensation-seekers, 151

Sense of an Ending, The (Barnes), 142

Shining, The, 69, 79

Sidis, William James, 73

Silverstein, Shel, 24

Silvia, Paul, 99–100

Simpson, Louis, 183

smiling, 16, 127–28

Smith, Adam, 81, 82

social comparison, 20–21

social media, 13, 21, 98

Solnit, Rebecca, 136–37

Song of Solomon (Morrison), 153

specialization, 71–73, 79, 81–82, 84–88, 91, 180–81

spontaneity, 76–80, 179, 182

  friends and, 77–78, 182

sports

  athletes, 70–75, 79, 166

  watching, 98, 104–7

stability, 3, 33, 65

  emotional, 64–68

Stanford University, 24

staying versus going, 1, 3, 4, 11, 35, 154, 180, 182

Steger, Michael, 28–29

Steinberg, Saul, 14

Steves, Rick, 64

Stockton, John, 105

Stoics, 24

stores, 119–21

stories, 10, 90, 91, 142–53, 181–82

  editing, 143–48, 153

  narratives in, 149–50

Straits Times, 56, 61

strangers, 25, 120, 125–26

studying and living abroad, 48–52, 59, 60, 128, 130

success and achievement, 14–15, 17, 27, 33, 173–74

suicide, 13, 29

Sula (Morrison), 5, 35

sushi, 165–67, 171

Swann's Way (Proust), 93

"take a dozen" heuristic, 112–13, 181

Tarantino, Quentin, 15

Tartt, Donna, 3, 25

terrorism, 30–31, 67

Thaler, Richard, 123

There Will Be Blood, 152

37 percent rule, 111–13

Thorbjørnsen, Helge, 139–40

Thorndike, Edward, 117

Thunberg, Greta, 65–67

Thus Spoke Zarathustra (Nietzsche), 22–23

Time Regained (Proust), 106

Todd, Peter, 110, 112–13

Tolstoy, Leo, 9

Tomjanovich, Rudy, 105

Tow Siang Hwa, 56

Toy Story, 38

Treatise of Human Nature, A (Hume), 36

Trilling, Lionel, 101

Tullett, Alexa, 176

Turner, Samuel, Jr., 99

Tversky, Amos, 124–25, 131–33

Two Psychologists Four Beers, 176

University of Pennsylvania, 12, 13

University of Virginia (UVA), 20, 21, 40, 43, 44, 87, 100, 109, 110, 121, 163, 176

Up All Night, 78

Utah Jazz, 105
UVA Today, 157

vacations, 75, 175–79
Varieties of Religious Experience, The (James), 9
variety, 124
volatile reason, 78
Voltaire, 35

Walker, Kara, 171
War and Peace (Tolstoy), 9
Watching Sport (Mumford), 104
Waves, The (Woolf), 92
Wealth of Nations, The (Smith), 81, 82
Western Enlightenment, 36–37
Westgate, Erin, 100
Whillans, Ashley, 89
"Wild Geese" (Oliver), 46
Williams, Alex, 77–78
Wilson, Anne, 143–45
Wilson, Tim, 19, 146–48
  Redirect, 143, 145, 148
Wittgenstein, Ludwig, 133
Woolf, Virginia, 92, 148, 169–71

word frequency research, 117–18
work, 7, 47, 173–75
  alienation and, 84–85
  creativity in, 175
  devotion to career, 165–67, 171
  division of labor and, 83–86, 89
  DIY projects, 81–91, 127, 130
  meaning in, 25–26, 174–75
  outsourcing of, 83, 88–91
  productivity and, 81–84, 86, 91
  prosocial, 138
  relationships in, 65
  satisfaction in, 174–75
  specialization in, 81, 82, 84–88, 91, 180–81
  success in, 173–74
  teams in, 77, 86, 87
World War II, 93–94, 133, 153
wrestling matches, 44–45, 52, 59, 108

Yesterday, 169
You Learn by Living (Roosevelt), 108

Zajonc, Bob, 117–19, 121

Shigehiro (Shige, pronounced *Shee-gay*) Oishi is the Marshall Field IV Professor of Psychology at the University of Chicago. He is considered one of the foremost authorities on happiness, meaning, and culture and has been awarded major prizes in his field of psychology. He is the author of an academic book, *The Psychological Wealth of Nations,* and his research has been featured in major media outlets, including *The New York Times, The Washington Post, The Wall Street Journal,* and the *Financial Times.*